KU-494-352

Contents

Preface to the Third Edition

It is over four years since the last edition of this work appeared on
the bookshelves. During that time the county courts have been
busy considering the practical application of the assured shorthold
tenancy and assured tenancy régimes. The higher courts have also
been called upon to determine important issues of principle. In this
edition, the text has been updated with the inclusion of a myriad of
county court cases, cases from the Court of Appeal, changes
introduced by statutory instrument and the relevant parts of the
Civil Procedure Rules and Practice Directions. Judge James Fox-
Andrews has now taken a general consultancy role but, as always,
his general scrutiny has been invaluable.

The law is stated as it stood on September 1 2001.

Del W. Williams

Table of abbreviations

AC: Appeal Cases
All ER: All England Reports
CA: Court of Appeal
Ch: Chancery (Law Reports)
CL: Current Law
CLY: Current Law Year Book
EG: Estates Gazette
EGCS: Estates Gazette Case Summaries
EGD: Estates Gazette Digest
EGLR: Estates Gazette Law Reports
HL: House of Lords
HLR: Housing Law Reports
KB: King's Bench (Law Reports)
LA: Legal Action
P&CR: Planning & Compensation Reports
PLSCS: Property Law Service Case Summaries
QB: Queen's Bench (Law Reports)
RVR: Rating and Valuation Reports
TLR: Times Law Reports
WLR: Weekly Law Reports

Table of statutes

In this book the statutes list below which are frequently referred to are given the following short titles:

Landlord and Tenant Act 1954 – 1954 Act
Rent (Agriculture) Act 1976 – 1976 Act
Rent Act 1977 – 1977 Act
Housing Act 1980 – 1980 Act
Housing Act 1985 – 1985 Act
Housing and Planning Act 1896 – 1986 Act
Housing Act 1988 – 1988 Act
Housing Act 1996 – 1996 Act

Other statutes

Agricultural Holdings Act 1986

Capital Gains Tax 1979
Charities Act 1993
Companies Act 1985
County Courts Act 1984

Family Law Act 1996
Finance Act 1982
Finance Act 1988

General Rate Act 1967

Housing Associations Act 1985
Housing (Consequential Provisions) Act 1985
Human Rights Act 1998

Immigration and Asylum Act 1999
Income and Corporation Taxes Act 1988

Increase of Rent and Mortgage Interest (Restrictions) Act 1920

Landlord and Tenant Act 1927
Landlord and Tenant Act 1985
Landlord and Tenant Act 1987
Law of Property Act 1925
Leasehold Reform Act 1967
Leasehold Reform, Housing and Urban Development Act 1993
Local Government Act 1963
Local Government Act 1985
Local Government, Planning & Land Act 1980

New Towns Act 1981

Rent Act 1974
Rent (Amendment) Act 1985

Social Security Act 1975

Table of cases

Historical background and the future

1.1 Introduction to historical background

A major objective of the Conservative Government in its third term of office was to increase the rented accommodation market. It had been contended that the effect of the Rent Acts over many years, particularly since the Second World War, had been to decrease the availability of rented accommodation in the private sector. Compared with many parts of the Western World the private rented sector formed a small part of the total housing stock.

The tinkering that took place before 1980 did little to encourage investors to provide rented accommodation. One Government's measures were almost invariably reversed by the next, creating uncertainty and disillusionment among those who might otherwise have been prepared to provide additional rented accommodation.

1.2 Housing Act 1980

By the Housing Act 1980 (hereinafter referred to as the 1980 Act) a new class of tenancy was created – the assured tenancy (a tenancy of a newly erected building) – which was subject to substantially the same rules as business tenancies under Part II of the Landlord and Tenant Act 1954 (hereinafter referred to as the 1954 Act). This new tenancy got off to a very hesitant start. By April 1986 there were only 600 such tenancies, mainly in the Yorkshire and Humberside areas.

In 1986 the provisions relating to assured tenancies were extended by the Housing and Planning Act 1986 (hereinafter referred to as the 1986 Act) to include dwellings where 'qualifying works' had been carried out. Only an approved body could be a landlord of an assured tenancy under the 1980 Act. The approval required was that of the Secretary of State. By this means control was exercised over the identity of the landlord. In the early days a substantial number of landlords were either charities or housing associations. The most recent figure of approved bodies was about 420. Provision was made for the situation where the landlord ceased to be an approved body.

1.3 Housing and Planning Act 1986

Under the 1980 Act an assured tenancy could only be created in respect of a dwelling which was, or formed part of, a building which was erected and on which construction work first began on or after August 8 1980 when the Act came into force. Further, before the tenant first occupied the dwelling-house under the tenancy, no part of it could have been occupied by any person as his residence except under an assured tenancy.

Under the 1986 Act buildings already erected could be the subject of an assured tenancy so long as qualifying works had first been carried out. Qualifying works meant works, involving expenditure attributable to the dwelling-house of not less than the prescribed amount, which were carried out within the period of two years preceding the grant of the first relevant tenancy at a time when the premises constituting the dwelling-house at the date of such grant either were not a dwelling-house or no part of them was occupied by a person as his residence. Qualifying works could be carried out before or after the date on which the 1986 Act came into force.

Provision was made for apportionment of costs where appropriate. Immediately before the coming into force of the 1988 Act the prescribed amount was £7,000 in Greater London and £5,000 elsewhere. The dwelling-house had to be fit for human habitation at the date of the grant of the first assured tenancy. Provisions were made, for an approved landlord to obtain a certification of fitness. There were two further conditions in respect of an assured tenancy granted after qualifying works had been carried out:

(1) the dwelling-house must not have been occupied by any person as his residence except under an assured tenancy;
(2) the first assured tenancy must not have been granted to a person whether alone or jointly with others who occupied or was entitled to occupy the dwelling-house as either:

  (a) a protected or statutory tenant within the meaning of the Rent Act 1977 (hereinafter called the 1977 Act);
  (b) a secured tenant within the meaning of Part IV of the Housing Act 1985 (hereinafter called the 1985 Act); or
  (c) a protected occupier or statutory tenant within the meaning of the Rent (Agriculture) Act 1976 (hereinafter called the 1976 Act).

Tenancies of newly erected or improved buildings could not be assured tenancies if, for example, they were granted in consideration of a premium or at a low rent. Provisions were made to tailor Part II of the 1954 Act to assured tenancies. Notices were specified for various matters.

From the landlord's point of view the significant advantage of an assured tenancy was that he could charge a market rent. The first rent was one he could freely negotiate with his tenant. The tenancy could contain rent review provisions. If a fresh tenancy was granted by the court then pursuant to section 34 of the 1954 Act the rent would be an open market one subject only to minor limitations.

After the passing of the 1986 Act the pace of the creation of assured tenancies increased a little. The Department of the Environment reported in October 1987 on a monitoring exercise it carried out on the scheme as at the April 1 1987. At that time 3,674 assured tenancies were identified. The figures of a similar exercise as at April 1 1988 were about 8,000.

However, in the overall context of housing this was a small amount. There were a number of reasons why the creation of assured tenancies proceeded at such a slow rate. The requirement that the landlord should be an approved body undoubtedly proved restrictive. Although the business tenancy provisions of Part II of the 1954 Act were tailored for assured tenancies they were likely in practice to prove an ill-fitting suit. Grounds for possession of a business tenancy in some respects were significantly different from those which were suitable for residential tenancies. Although as far as the authors know the provisions for the payment of compensation by a landlord to a residential tenant on the coming to an end of his tenancy in certain circumstances were never put to the test, they did not appear immediately relevant.

1.4 Housing Act 1988

The Housing Act 1988 created a new form of assured tenancy which was not the subject of the strict qualifying conditions of the former type of assured tenancy under the Housing Act 1980. In addition, a new form of tenancy called an assured shorthold tenancy was also created. These two forms of tenancy are extensively discussed in this book. The Act applies to tenancies coming into effect on or after January 15 1989.

1.5 Business Expansion Scheme

An additional fillip for rented accommodation was provided in the Finance Act 1988 by the extension until December 31 1993 of the

Business Expansion Scheme to the provision of assured tenancies. There is little doubt that the decision to extend the Business Expansion Scheme up to December 1993 to include companies specialising in the letting of residential property on the new assured tenancy basis had a substantial effect and altered significantly the duration of many tenancies granted under that Scheme. Two-thirds of the assured tenancies under the 1980 and 1986 Acts up to April 1 1987 were for 21 years or more.

For landlords who look only for a rental income there are considerable benefits in granting long leases with appropriate rent review provisions. The initial rent will be a market one. Rent review provisions are likely to be index-linked or index-linked plus a percentage. Rent reviews determined by arbitrators which are appropriate for lettings of commercial properties under business tenancies where very substantial rents may be determined may not be the preferred means of determining an open market rent.

So long as tenants comply with their obligations such landlords would view it as commercially sensible that the tenant should remain paying the market rent. There would be little reason to prevent assignment. So long as the landlord retains the right to vet the proposed assignee it is economically more favourable to a landlord that the existing tenant finds a new occupier at his expense rather than that of the landlord. Only if the landlord were looking for vacant possession with a view to profitable sale would the position be different.

1.6 Housing Act 1996

Under the Housing Act 1988 the assured tenancy was the standard form of tenancy, with the assured shorthold tenancy being created only by complying with section 20(1) of that Act. The Housing Act 1996 has reversed that position with the effect that on or after February 28 1997 any new assured tenancy will automatically be an assured shorthold tenancy unless it falls within the categories in Schedule 2A to the 1988 Act. It is to be noted that under the Housing Act 1996 (Commencement No 7 and Savings) Order 1997 SI 1997 No 225 certain savings are made as follows:

(1) The insertion of section 8A in the Housing Act 1988 and the amendment to section 8 of and Schedule 2 to that Act (repossession: assured tenancies) shall have no effect in a case where:

(a) a notice under section 8 of that Act (notice of proceedings for possession) has been served before the commencement date; or

(b) the court has dispensed with the requirement of such a notice and the proceedings for possession were started before February 28 1997.

(2) The amendments to section 21(1) and (4) of the Housing Act 1988 (recovery of possession on expiry or termination of assured shorthold tenancy) shall have no effect in a case where a landlord has served a notice under section 8 of that Act (notice of proceedings for possession) before the February 28 1997.

1.6.1 *Assured tenancies post-1996 Act*

Section 19A provides that an assured tenancy which:

(a) is entered into on or after the day on which section 96 of the 1996 Act comes into force (otherwise than pursuant to a contract made before that day); or

(b) comes into being by virtue of section 5 of the coming to an end of an assured tenancy (namely, a statutory periodic tenancy);

is an assured shorthold tenancy unless it falls within any paragraph in Schedule 2A.

The exemptions contained in Schedule 2A are as follows:

(i) *Tenancies excluded by notice*: paras 1, 2

An assured tenancy in respect of which a notice is served before the assured tenancy is entered into by the person who is to be the landlord under the assured tenancy on the person who is to be the tenant under that tenancy. The notice must state that the assured tenancy to which it relates is not to be an assured shorthold tenancy; para 1(1), (2) of Schedule 2A. Further, an assured tenancy in respect of which a notice is served after the assured tenancy has been entered into and is served by the landlord under the assured tenancy on the tenant under that tenancy stating that the assured tenancy to which it relates is no longer an assured shorthold tenancy.

(ii) *Tenancies containing an exclusionary provision*: para 3

An assured tenancy which contains a provision to the effect that the tenancy is not an assured shorthold tenancy.

(iii) *Assured tenancy by succession under section 39*: para 4

An assured tenancy by succession arising under section 39 of the 1988 Act other than one to which section 39(7) applies. The statutory succession rules were changed by the 1988 Act the main effect of which was that where a tenant holding a regulated tenancy under the Rent Act 1977 died and was succeeded by a member of the family (other than a spouse) he acquires an assured tenancy under the 1988 Act. Para 4 of Schedule 2A provides that in such circumstances the successor will acquire an assured tenancy save where section 39(7) applies. Section 39(7) provides that if immediately before the death of the predecessor, the landlord might have recovered possession of the dwelling-house under Case 19 in Schedule 15 to the Rent Act 1977, the assured periodic tenancy to which the successor becomes entitled shall be an assured shorthold tenancy (whether or not in the case of a tenancy to which the provision applies, it fulfils the conditions in sect 20(1) above).

(iv) *Former secure tenancies*: para 5
An assured tenancy which became an assured tenancy on ceasing to be a secure tenancy.

(v) *Security of tenure at end of long residential tenancy*: para 6
The provisions providing for a tenant to be afforded the protection of a statutory tenancy at the end of a long lease under the Landlord and Tenant 1954 Part 1 were amended by Schedule 10 to the Local Government and Housing Act 1989. The effect of that amendment was that where a long lease came to an end after January 15 1999 the tenant was entitled to an assured tenancy. Para 6 of Schedule 2A provides that that position remains the same.

(vi) *Replacement tenancy*: para 7
The provisions contained in para 7 of Schedule 2A apply where a landlord grants a new tenancy to a tenant who is already an assured tenant. Para 7 provides that an assured tenancy will arise where a tenancy is:

(a) granted to a person (alone or jointly with others) who, immediately before the tenancy was granted, was the tenant (or, in the case of joint tenants, one of the tenants) under an assured tenancy other than a shorthold tenancy ('the old tenancy');
(b) is granted (alone or jointly with others) by a person who was at that time the landlord (or one of the joint landlords) under the old tenancy, and
(c) is not one in respect of which a specified notice has been served.

An assured shorthold tenancy arises where such a prescribed notice is served before the assured tenancy is entered into and is served by the person who is to be the tenant under the assured tenancy on the person who is to be the landlord under that tenancy (or, in the case of joint landlords, or at least one of the persons who are to be joint landlords) and states that the assured tenancy to which it relates is to be a shorthold tenancy.

(vii) *Statutory periodic tenancy:* para 8

An assured tenancy which comes into being by virtue of section 5 of the 1988 Act on the coming to an end of an assured tenancy which is not an assured shorthold tenancy. The effect of these provisions are that the statutory periodic tenancy which arises on the expiry of the contractual assured tenancy will be an assured tenancy.

(viii) *Assured agricultural occupancies*: para 9

1.6.2 Assured shorthold tenancies post-1996 Act

Introduction

The 1996 Act has introduced changes to the assured shorthold regime by:

(a) removing the requirement of a pre-tenancy notice;
(b) removing the requirement of a fixed-term of less than six months;
(c) removing the bar on the power of a landlord to determine the tenancy at any time earlier than six months from the beginning of the tenancy.

1.6.2.1 Security of tenure and other matters

An assured shorthold tenant has the protection of section 21(5) which provides that where an order for possession is made in relation to a section 19A tenancy the order cannot take effect earlier than

(a) in the case of a tenancy which is not a replacement tenancy, six months after the beginning of the tenancy, and
(b) in the case of a replacement tenancy, six months after the beginning of the original tenancy.

For the purposes of these provisions an 'original tenancy' is where the replacement tenancy came into being on the coming to an end of a tenancy which was not a replacement tenancy, to the immediately preceding tenancy, and where there have been successive replacement tenancies, to the tenancy immediately preceding the first in the succession of replacement tenancies. A 'replacement tenancy' is a tenancy which comes into being on the coming to an end of an assured shorthold tenancy and under which, on its coming into being, the landlord and the tenant are the same as under the earlier tenancy as at its coming to an end and the premises let are the same, or substantially the same, as those let under the earlier tenancy as at that time.

Section 21 of the 1988 Act provides for the landlord to be able to recover possession on the expiry or termination of an assured shorthold tenancy. The 1996 Act has provided that the section 21 notice must be in writing and this applies to both pre- and post-1996 Act assured shorthold tenancies.

1.6.2.2 *Grounds for possession*

The grounds for possession contained in the 1988 Act have been retained save that a new ground has been introduced and amendments made to Ground 8.

Ground 8 in Schedule 2 of the 1988 Act provides for a mandatory order for possession where there are rent arrears. The length of the arrears required for this ground has been reduced by the 1996 Act as follows:

(a) where rent is payable weekly or fortnightly from 13 to eight weeks unpaid;
(b) where rent is payable monthly from three to two months.

A new ground has been introduced. Ground 17 provides that the landlord may be able to recover possession where the grant of the tenancy was induced by a false statement by the tenant or a person acting at the tenant's instigation.

Ground 14 allowing the landlord to seek possession where the tenant or any person residing in the dwelling-house has been guilty of conduct amounting to a nuisance or annoyance has been substituted by a new Ground 14. The new provisions have been expanded to include misconduct by a tenant's visitor. Further, the illegal conduct has been expanded to encompass any arrestable offence committed in, or in the locality of, the dwelling-house.

1.6.2.3 *Terms of the assured shorthold tenancy*

Section 20A provides a duty on the landlord to provide the tenant with a statement as to the terms of the tenancy. A tenant holding under an assured shorthold tenancy to which section 19A applies, may serve a notice in writing on the landlord requiring him to provide him with a written statement of any term of the tenancy as specified below, namely:

(a)   the date on which the tenancy began or came into being;
(b)   the rent payable and the dates on which it is payable;
(c)   the detailed provisions of any rent review;
(d)   in the case of a fixed-term tenancy, the length of the fixed term.

The landlord cannot be required to give a written statement where such a statement has previously been given to the tenant and the terms have not been varied since that statement.

The statement provided is not to be regarded as conclusive evidence of what was agreed by the parties to the tenancy in question.

Where a landlord fails, without reasonable excuse, to provide a written statement within 28 days of receipt of a request for the same he is liable on conviction to a fine.

1.6.2.4 Rent and the Rent Assessment Committee

Section 22 of the 1988 Act allows an assured shorthold tenant to refer the matter of the rent to the rent assessment committee on the ground that it is excessive, namely that it is significantly higher than the rents payable under assured or assured shorthold tenancies of similar dwellinghouses in the locality.

Where the tenancy is granted under section 19A, section 22(2)(a) provides that the application must be made before six months has elapsed since the beginning of the tenancy or, in the case of a replacement tenancy, since the beginning of the original tenancy.

Chapter 2

Phasing out of the Rent Act and other transitional provisions

2.1 General introduction

2.1.1 The 1988 Act, in sections 34 to 39 inclusive, contains provisions for the phasing out of the Rent Act 1977, together with other transitional provisions. These are important provisions which have been amended by the Local Government and Housing Act 1989 but remain largely unaffected by the Housing Act 1996.

2.1.2 The main contents of sections 34 to 39 may be summarised as follows:

(a) New protected tenancies under the Rent Act 1977 are restricted to special cases; section 34.
(b) New agricultural occupancies under the Rent (Agriculture) Act 1976 are restricted to special cases; section 35.
(c) A housing association tenancy cannot be granted save in exceptional circumstances; section 35.
(d) Only in limited circumstances is it possible to create a secure tenancy; section 35.
(e) New restricted contracts are limited to transitional cases; section 36.
(f) No further assured tenancies under the Housing Act 1980 can be created; section 37.
(g) Where an existing tenancy is transferred from the public to the private sector the tenancy is not capable of being a protected tenancy, protected occupancy, or a housing association tenancy or a secure tenancy save in a limited respect; section 38.
(h) The rules on statutory succession are amended; section 39.

2.1.3 It is important to note that protected, secure, housing association and agricultural occupancies entered into before, or pursuant to a contract made before, January 15 1989 are entirely unaffected by the Housing Act 1988. Unless and until some event occurs such as the death of the tenant or a public body ceasing to have the interest of the landlord the tenant will continue to enjoy the same protection as he did prior to January 15 1989.

2.2 New protected tenancies and agricultural occupancies: section 34

2.2.1 Under section 34 new protected tenancies under the Rent Act 1977 or agricultural occupancies under the Rent (Agriculture) Act 1976 are restricted to special cases. A tenancy entered into on or after January 15 1989 cannot be a protected tenancy unless:

(a) it was entered into pursuant to a contract made before January 15 1989; or

(b) it is granted to a person (alone or jointly with others) who, immediately before the tenancy was granted, was a protected or statutory tenant and was so granted by the person who at that time was the landlord (or one of the joint landlords) under the protected or statutory tenancy; or

(c) it is granted to a person (alone or jointly with others) in the following circumstances:

   (i) prior to the grant of the tenancy, an order for possession of the dwelling-house was made against him (alone or jointly with others) on the ground that suitable alternative accommodation was available to him under the Rent Act 1977 or Rent (Agriculture) Act 1976; and

   (ii) the tenancy is of the premises which constitute the suitable alternative accommodation as to which the court was so satisfied; and

   (iii) in the proceedings for possession the court considered that, in the circumstances, the grant of an assured tenancy would not afford the required security and, accordingly, directed that the tenancy would be a protected tenancy; or

(d) it is a tenancy under which the interest of the landlord was at the time the tenancy was granted held by a New Town corporation but which was transferred to the private sector after November 15 1990 and the tenancy is granted before or pursuant to a contract made before November 15 1990.

In *Goringe* v *Twinsectra* [1994] CLY 2723 T had resided in the premises in question with H since 1960. H became a statutory tenant and T succeeded to the statutory tenancy of the premises on H's death in 1977. In 1989 T agreed with the landlord to move to other premises belonging to the landlord. In 1992 T was informed that the landlord had disposed of his interest and the new landlord contended that T was an assured tenant. The Recorder in Staines County Court held that T retained the protection of the Rent Act 1977 by virtue of the operation of section 34(1)(b) of the 1988 Act. The new tenancy did not have to be of the same, or substantially the same, premises.

In *Giddy* v *Murray* (1995) Legal Action March p12 the defendant was a Rent Act protected tenant and in 1990 he moved to larger premises on the ground floor of the same house. The landlord claimed that the new letting was an assured tenancy. District Judge Armon Jones in Clerkenwell County Court held that by virtue of section 34(1)(b) the tenant was protected by the Rent Act 1977. It is to be noted that a similar conclusion was reached in *Kotecha* v *Rimington* (1991) Legal Action March p15 (Leicester County Court) and *Singh* v *Dalby* (1992) Legal Action September p22 (Newcastle-upon-Tyne County Court).

The operation of section 34 was considered by the Court of Appeal in *Laimond Properties Ltd* v *Al-Shakarchi* [1998] EGCS 21 where it was held that pursuant to section 34(1)(c) the court was entitled to hold that the tenancy of the alternative accommodation was an assured tenancy so that in such a case section 34(1)(b) was not applicable. The provisions of section 34(1)(b) were limited to the position where the tenant has security of tenure under the Rent Act 1977 and accepts the offer of a new tenancy. Para (b) is not restricted to new tenancies of the same premises and in the context of a possession action founded upon alternative accommodation para (b) is displaced by para (c) whereby protected status is preserved only if the court considers that the grant of an assured tenancy will not afford the required security. In *Arogol Co Ltd* v *Rajah* [2001] 29 EG 119 (CS) the Court of Appeal held that, in interpreting the provisions, it is the identity of the landlord and tenant that matters and not the identity of the premises. There is nothing in section 34(1)(b) to suggest that the premises should be the same.

It is to be noted that in this context the terms 'protected tenant' and 'statutory tenant' do not include a tenant under a protected shorthold tenancy or a protected or statutory tenant which was let under a protected shorthold tenancy which has ended and in respect of which either there has been no grant of a further tenancy or any grant of a further tenancy has been made to the person who immediately before the grant, was in possession of the dwelling-house as a protected or statutory tenant. A 'protected shorthold tenancy' includes a tenancy which, in proceedings for possession under Case 19 in Schedule 15 to the 1977 Act, is treated as a protected shorthold tenancy.

Where the circumstances considered above do not exist, with the result that the tenancy is not a protected one, then if the tenancy is an assured one section 34(3) provides that it shall be an assured shorthold tenancy whether or not it fulfils the conditions in section 20(1) of the 1988 Act unless, before the tenancy is entered into, the landlord serves notice on the tenant that it is not to be a shorthold tenancy.

2.2.3 The Rent (Agriculture) Act 1976 provides security of tenure for agricultural workers who had previously been licensees in respect of the tied cottages which they occupied or who had been tenants under a tenancy with a rent of less than two thirds of the rateable value. Under section 34(4)(a) or (b) of the 1988 Act a licence or tenancy which is entered into on or after January 15 1989 cannot be a relevant licence or relevant tenancy for the purposes of the 1976 Act unless it is entered into in pursuance of a contract made before January 15 1989 or it is granted to a person (alone or jointly with others) who, immediately before the licence or tenancy was granted, was a protected occupier or statutory tenant under the 1976 Act and is so granted by the person who at that time was the licensor or landlord under the protected occupancy or statutory tenancy in question.

A relevant licence is a licence of a separate dwelling-house with exclusion occupation and which, if it were a tenancy, would have been protected by the Rent Act but for the fact that the right to occupy was at a low rent or at no rent. A relevant tenancy is a tenancy of a dwelling-house let as a separate dwelling which would be protected by the Rent Act but for the same fact.

2.3 Removal of special regimes for housing association tenancies

2.3.1 Section 35 contains provisions restricting new housing association tenancies to special cases. A tenancy which is entered into on or after January 15 1989 cannot be a housing association tenancy unless:

(a)   it is entered into in pursuance of a contract made before January 15 1989; or

(b)   it is granted to a person, alone or jointly with others, who, immediately before the tenancy was granted, was a tenant under a housing association tenancy and is so granted by the person who at that time was the landlord under that housing association tenancy; or

(c) it is granted to a person, alone or jointly with others, in the following circumstances:

(i) prior to the grant of the tenancy, an order for possession of a dwelling-house was made against him, alone or jointly with others, on the court being satisfied on the grounds set out in Part II of Schedule 2 to the 1985 Act (grounds on which a court may order possession if suitable alternative accommodation is available) or Part III (grounds on which a court may order possession if it considers it reasonable and suitable alternative accommodation is available); and

(ii) the tenancy is of the premises which constitute the suitable alternative accommodation as to which the court was so satisfied; and

(iii) in the proceedings for possession the court directed that the tenancy would be a housing association tenancy; or

(d) it is a tenancy under which the interest of the landlord was at the time the tenancy was granted held by a New Town corporation and which was transferred to the private sector after November 15 1990 and the tenancy is granted before or pursuant to a contract made before November 15 1990; section 35(1),(2).

2.3.2 Special provisions are made in respect of the grant of a tenancy whether on or after January 15 1989 by a registered housing association, within the meaning of the Housing Associations Act 1985 of a defective dwelling to a former owner-occupier under section 554 of that Act, pursuant to an obligation (see now new section 554(2A) introduced by para 61 of Schedule 17 to the 1988 Act). It is to be assumed for the purposes only of section 86(2)(b) of the 1977 Act (tenancy would be a protected tenancy but for sections 15 or 16 – landlord's interest belonging to a housing association or a housing co-operative) that the tenancy was granted before January 15 1989.

2.4 Restriction on grant of secure tenancies

2.4.1 A tenancy or licence which is entered into after January 15 1989 cannot be a secure tenancy unless:

(a) the interest of the landlord belongs to a local authority, a new town corporation, or an urban development corporation, all within the meaning of section 80 of the 1985 Act, [or a housing action trust established under Part III of this Act]; or

(b)   the interest of the landlord belongs to a housing co-operative within the meaning of section 27B of the 1985 Act (agreements between local housing authorities and housing co-operatives) and the tenancy or licence is of a dwelling-house comprised in the housing co-operative agreement falling within that section; or

(c)   it is entered into in pursuance of a contract made before January 15 1989; or

(d)   it is granted to a person (alone or jointly with others), who immediately before it was entered into, was a secure tenant and is so granted by the body which at that time was the landlord or licensor under the secure tenancy; or

(e)   it is granted to a person (alone or jointly with others) in the following circumstances:

(i)   prior to the grant to the tenancy or licence, an order for possession of a dwelling-house was made against him (either alone or jointly with others) on the court being satisfied on the grounds set out in Part II of Schedule 2 to the 1985 Act (grounds on which the court may order possession if suitable alternative accommodation is available) or Part III (grounds on which a court may order possession if it considers it reasonable and suitable alternative accommodation is available); and

(ii)   the tenancy or licence is of the premises which constitute the suitable accommodation as to which the court was so satisfied; and

(iii)   in the proceedings for possession the court considered that, in the circumstances, the grant of an assured tenancy would not afford the required security and, accordingly, directed that the tenancy or licence should be a secure tenancy; or

(f)   if it is granted pursuant to an obligation under section 554(2A) of the Housing Associations Act 1985 (as introduced by para 61 of Schedule 17 to the 1988 Act).

2.4.2 Provision is made for the position where while a protected or statutory tenancy is continuing, the interest of the landlord comes to be held by a housing association, a housing trust, or the Housing Corporation or the Secretary of State as a result of the exercise of a specified function. In such circumstances other provisions in the Act are to be disregarded and the tenancy will become a housing association tenancy or a secure tenancy as the case may be; section 35(5).

2.5 New restricted contracts limited to transitional cases

2.5.1 Section 36(1) provides that a tenancy or other contract entered into after January 15 1989 cannot be a restricted contract for the purposes of the 1977 Act unless it is entered into in pursuance of a contract made before January 15 1989. Provision is made for the situation where a restricted contract was entered into before or pursuant to a contract made before January 15 1989 but was varied thereafter. However, that provision is subject to a number of qualifications. A variation affecting the amount of rent does not include a reference to a reduction or increase of rent by a rent tribunal under section 78 of the 1977 Act. Further, it does not include a reference to a variation which is made by the parties and has the effect of making the rent expressed to be payable under the contract the same as the rent for the dwelling which is entered in the register under section 79 of the 1977 Act.

2.6 Transfer of 1980 Act assured tenancies to assured tenancies under the 1988 Act

2.6.1 Assured tenancies under the Housing Act 1980 can be labelled 'Mark 1' assured tenancies for the purpose of the following discussion. Provisions as to 'Mark 1' assured tenancies are contained in sections 1(3), (4) and 37 of the 1988 Act. Under the provisions of section 1(3) of the 1988 Act a tenancy under which a dwelling-house was let as a separate dwelling and which immediately before the commencement of the 1988 Act was an assured tenancy under the 1980 Act becomes an assured tenancy under the 1988 Act. In the case of these converted 'old style' assured tenancies only the exclusions relating to Crown tenancies and local authority and public tenancies in paras 11 and 12 of Schedule 1 to the 1988 Act apply and none of the other exclusions in that Schedule. Thereafter sections 56 to 58 and Schedule 5 to the 1980 Act cease to apply to such a converted tenancy.

Section 37(1) provides that a tenancy entered into on or after January 15 1989 cannot be an assured tenancy for the purposes of the 1980 Act. The following is a suggested analysis of the various possibilities concerning the transfer of 'Mark 1' assured tenancies to the new scheme of the 1988 Act:

(a) A tenancy which immediately before January 15 1989 was an assured tenancy under the 1980 Act becomes an assured tenancy under the 1988 Act; section 1(3)(a)(b). In such a case

Part I of Schedule 1 has effect as if it consisted only of paragraphs 11 (Crown tenancies) and 12 (local authority tenancies).

(b) A tenancy entered into on or after the commencement of the 1988 Act cannot be an assured tenancy for the purposes of the 1980 Act; section 37(1).

(c) Where a tenant under the 1980 Act made an application to the court, under section 24 of the 1954 Act, for the grant of a new tenancy before January 15 1989 and the application was continuing on January 15 1989, such a tenancy is not converted into an assured tenancy under the 1988 Act; section 37(2).

(d) If, in the circumstances outlined in (c) (above), the court makes an order under section 29 of the 1954 Act that tenancy is an assured tenancy under the 1988 Act; section 37(3).

(e) Where a contract was entered into for the grant of an assured tenancy under the 1980 Act before January 15 1989, but at that date the tenancy had not been granted, the contract is deemed to be a contract for the grant of an assured tenancy within the 1988 Act; section 37(4)(a),(b).

It is to be noted that in the case of (d) and (e) (above) Part I of Schedule 1 to the 1988 Act (which defines those tenancies which cannot be assured tenancies) has effect as if the only excluded tenancies were those contained in paragraphs 11 and 12 (Crown tenancies and local authority tenancies etc. respectively).

2.7 Transfer of existing tenancies from public to private sector

2.7.1 Section 38 makes provision for the position where the interest of a landlord under a tenancy is held by a public body at a time when it belongs to:

(a) a local authority, a new town corporation or an urban development corporation; or

(b) a housing action trust; or

(c) the Development Board for Rural Wales; or

(d) Her Majesty in right of the Crown or to a government department or is held in trust for Her Majesty for the purpose of a government department.

In general, section 38 provides that upon the transfer of an existing tenancy from the public sector to the private sector such a tenancy will become an assured tenancy under the 1988 Act.

2.7.2 Where a tenancy is entered into before, or pursuant to a contract made before, January 15 1989 then if on January 15, or if it is later, at the time it is entered into, the interest of the landlord is a public body or the tenancy is a housing association tenancy and either the interest of the landlord ceases to be held by a public body or the tenancy ceases to be a housing association tenancy then certain consequences ensue. From that time the tenancy is not capable of being a protected tenancy, a protected occupancy or a housing association tenancy.

The tenancy is not capable of being a secure tenancy unless (and only at a time when) the interest of the landlord is (or is again) held by a public body. The provisions of paragraph 1 of Part I of Schedule 1 to the 1988 Act which provide that a tenancy which is entered into before, or pursuant to a contract made before, January 15 1989 cannot be an assured tenancy are of no effect. Whether or not in such circumstances the tenancy becomes or remains an assured tenancy depends on whether the qualifying conditions are satisfied. Provision is also made for a housing association tenancy which ceases to be of that nature.

The provisions already noted regarding tenancies where the interest of the landlord is held by a public body and housing association tenancies apply equally to tenancies where the interest of the landlord is held by a new town corporation, save that instead of January 15 1989 the relevant date is November 15 1990 or such earlier or later date as the Secretary of State may specify by statutory instrument. Where the interest passes to a registered housing association the tenancy continues to be a secure tenancy and capable of being a housing association tenancy; section 38 (4A). Section 38(4B) of the 1988 Act contains saving provisions dealing with the case where the Secretary of State makes a disposal under Part III of the Housing Associations Act 1985 and the interest of the landlord under the secure tenancy passes to a registered social landlord. In such a case the tenancy continues to be a secure tenancy.

Chapter 3

Assured Tenancies: pre- and post-Housing Act 1996

3.1 Introduction to pre-Housing Act 1996 assured tenancies

3.1.1 Under the Housing Act 1988 the assured tenancy was the standard form of tenancy with the assured shorthold tenancy being created only by complying with section 20(1) of the 1988 Act. The Housing Act 1996 has reversed that position with the effect that, under section 19A of the 1988 Act, as from February 28 1997 any new assured tenancy will automatically be an assured shorthold tenancy unless it falls within the categories in Schedule 2A of the 1988 Act.

3.1.2 The qualifying conditions for pre-Housing Act 1966 assured tenancies can be analysed as follows:

(i)   a 'tenancy'
(ii)   'a dwelling-house is let as a separate dwelling'
(iii)   occupation as only or principal home
(iv)   rateable value limits
(v)   exclusion from assured tenancies

3.2 Qualifying conditions for pre-Housing Act 1996 assured tenancies

3.2.1 A 'tenancy'

There must be a tenancy under which a dwelling-house is let as a separate dwelling so that a licence agreement cannot amount to an assured tenancy. The test to be applied in such a case is as enunciated in *Street* v *Mountford* [1985] 1 EGLR 128, namely that for a tenancy to arise there must be exclusive possession for a term at a rent so that if the occupier is not a lodger he must be a tenant.

In *A G Securities* v *Vaughan* [1988] 2 EGLR 78 the House of Lords held that in the circumstances the overlap of periods of occupation did not create a single term by an amalgam of the individual periods and there was no single sum of money payable for use and occupation. The four unities required for a joint tenancy were not present and the reality was that there were four separate licences. Reference can usefully be made to *Aslan* v *Murphy (No 1)* [1989] 2 EGLR 57 and *Antoniades* v *Villiers* [1988] 2 EGLR 78. In *Antoniades* the House of Lords held that the two agreements were inter-dependent and it would be unreal to regard them as separate independent licences.

In *Bruton* v *London and Quadrant Housing Trust* [1999] 2 EGLR 59 the Trust entered into an agreement with B under which a 'weekly licence' of a flat was granted to him and both parties intended that the effect of the agreement would be to constitute a licence. The block of flats in question was owned by a local authority who had granted a licence to the charitable trust to provide short-term accommodation. The House of Lords held that the agreement conferred on B a right to exclusive possession and as B occupied the flat for a term in return for periodic payments the agreement created a tenancy in accordance with the decision in *Street* v *Mountford*. There were no special circumstances which required an alternative conclusion as (i) the character of the landlord as a charitable institution was irrelevant; (ii) the resultant breach of the licence granted to the Trust by the local authority was irrelevant and (iii) disposals by way of weekly tenancies were not *ultra vires* the local authority nor the Trust. In *Mehta* v *Royal Bank of Scotland plc* The Times January 25 1999 the court held that in determining whether a tenancy existed the 'hallmark' principles in *Street* v *Mountford* were not decisive in circumstances where other factors of equal importance to and in addition to those 'hallmarks' were in existence. In *Stirling* v *Leadenhall Residential 2 Ltd* [2001] EWCA Civ 1011 the Court of Appeal held that after an assured tenancy had come to an end as a result of a possession order the continued presence of the tenant with the payment of an amount equivalent to the rent amounted to a tolerated trespass and not a new tenancy.

3.2.2 'Dwelling-house let as a separate dwelling'

It is a question of fact whether premises are a house or not and in *Langford Property Co Ltd* v *Goldrich* [1949] 1 KB 511 a house was held to include a flat. The question of whether a dwelling-house is let as a separate dwelling was considered in *British Land Co Ltd* v *Herbert Silver (Menswear) Ltd* [1958] 1 QB 530 in the context of the Rent Act provisions where Upjohn J was of the opinion that on the issue whether the premises are let as a separate dwelling you must look to the bargain made between the parties and see for what purpose the parties intended the premises would be used. If that does not provide an answer, you look to all the surrounding circumstances and see what must have been in the contemplation of the parties; if that yields no solution, you must look to the nature of the premises and the actual user at the relevant time.

In this context it is necessary to consider whether the dwelling-house is let as a separate dwelling because the tenancy can be an assured tenancy if the dwelling-house is occupied by a tenant or joint tenants (section 1(1)(a)). In *Uratemp Ventures Ltd* v *Collins* [2001] 43 EG 186 (CS) the House of Lords held that the presence or absence of cooking facilities in the part of the house occupied by the tenant was not relevant. In *Chelsea Yacht and Boat Club Ltd* v *Pope* [2000] 2 EGLR 23 the Court of Appeal held that a houseboat could fall within the definition of dwelling-house in the 1988 Act if it was so annexed to the land as to make it part of the land but a houseboat on a river was neither part of the land nor of the same genus as real property and the 1988 Act did not apply. There are particular provisions in section 3(1) of the 1988 Act where the tenant is sharing accommodation with persons other than the landlord. Where a tenant has exclusive occupation of any accommodation (the separate accommodation) and the terms of his tenancy include the use of other accommodation in common with another person(s) (not being or including the landlord), and the sharing of such accommodation is the only reason for the tenancy's exclusion from being an assured tenancy, the separate accommodation is deemed to be held on an assured tenancy.

There are special provisions applicable to shared accommodation which are contained in section 10. Under these provisions, in any case falling within the circumstances envisaged in section 3, no order shall be made for possession of any of the shared accommodation while the tenant is in possession of the separate accommodation (whether on the application of the immediate landlord, of the tenant or any person under whom that landlord derives title) unless a like order has been made (or is made at the same time) in respect of the separate accommodation. The landlord may apply to the court to make such order as it thinks just, namely:

(a)   terminating the right of the tenant to use the whole or any part of the shared accommodation other than living accommodation; or

(b)   modifying his right to use the whole or any part of the shared
      accommodation, whether by varying the persons or
      increasing the number of persons entitled to the use of that
      accommodation or otherwise.

However, no order can be made under section 10 so as to effect any
termination or modification of the rights of the tenant which, apart
from section 3(3), could not be effected by or under the terms of the
tenancy.

The position where the dwelling-house is let together with other
land is dealt with in section 2(1)(a)–(b) so that if the main purpose
of the letting is the provision of a home for the tenant (or where
there are joint tenants at least one of them) the 'other land' is treated
as part of the dwelling-house. Where the main purpose is not the
provision of a home the dwelling is not treated as let as a separate
dwelling. There is a further saving provision in section 4(1)
whereby if a tenant of a dwelling-house has sublet part, but not the
whole, of the dwelling-house then as against the landlord or any
superior landlord no part of the dwelling-house is to be treated as
excluded from being a dwelling-house let on an assured tenancy by
reason only that the terms of the subletting include the use of
accommodation in common with other persons.

The tenant, or each of the joint tenants, must be an individual so
that an assured tenancy cannot be held by a company. It is clear that
this provision in the 1988 Act emanates from the long-standing rule
under the Rent Acts enunciated in *Skinner* v *Geary* [1931] 2 KB 546
that the 'protection which the Acts afford is to the tenant in his own
home. It is a personal thing.'

3.2.3 Occupation as only or principal home

It is clear from section 1(1)(b) that the qualifying conditions will not
be met unless the dwelling-house is occupied as his only or
principal home. The question of whether the test of 'occupation' is
satisfied is one of fact but it is submitted that a non-occupying
tenant cannot satisfy the test and cannot, therefore, hold an assured
tenancy. If the assured tenancy is held by joint tenants only one of
the tenants is required to occupy to satisfy the condition in section
1(1)(b). In *Ujima Housing Association* v *Ansah* [1998] 30 HLR 831 U let
a flat to A under an assured tenancy and A sublet the flat under an
assured shorthold tenancy. The Court of Appeal held that the
question of whether A remained in occupation of the flat as his

principal residence was to be decided objectively. A was benefiting financially from the subletting, was not in physical occupation nor entitled to occupation at the end of U's notice to quit and had not left any personal possessions in the property. It is useful to consider the decision in *Brown* v *Brash* [1948] 2 KB 247 where it was held that in the context of the Rent Acts the question of occupation was one of fact and degree and the question of absence from occupation could be approached as follows:

(1)   The onus is on the tenant to rebut the presumption that his possession has ceased.

(2)   To rebut it he must, at all events, establish a *de facto* intention on his part to return after his absence.

(3)   But neither in principle nor on the authorities can this be enough. To suppose that he can absent himself for five or 10 years or more and retain possession and his protected status simply by proving an inward intention to return after so protracted an absence would be to frustrate the spirit and policy of the Act.

(4)   Notwithstanding an absence so protracted the authorities suggest that its effect may be averted if he couples and clothes his inward intention with some formal, outward, and visible sign of it, i.e. installs in the premises some caretaker or representative, be it a relative or not, with the status of a licensee and with the function of preserving the premises for his own ultimate homecoming. There will then, at all events, be someone to profit by the housing accommodation involved which will not stand empty. It may be that the same result can be secured by leaving on the premises a deliberate symbol of continued occupation such as furniture. Apart from authority, in principle possession in fact (for it is with possession in fact and not with possession in law that we are here concerned) requires not merely '*animus possidendi*' but '*corpus possessionis*', namely some visible state of affairs in which *animus possidendi* finds expression.

(5)   If the caretaker (to use that term for short) or the furniture be removed from the premises otherwise than quite temporarily, we are of opinion that the protection, artificially prolonged by their presence, ceases, whether the tenant wills or desires such removal or not.

In considering the question whether a particular tenant can satisfy the test of 'his only or principal home' under section 1(1)(b) regard should be had to the question of whether a person can qualify as an assured tenant if he is also occupying another dwelling-house in addition to the one held under an assured tenancy. On a similar issue under the 1977 Act the tests to be applied were outlined in *Hampstead Way Investments Ltd* v *Lewis-Weare* [1985] 1 EGLR 120:

(i)   A person may have two dwelling-houses, each of which he occupies as his home, so that, if either of them is let to him, his tenancy of it is protected by the 1977 Act.

(ii) Where a tenant is a tenant of two different parts of the same house under different lettings by the same landlord and carries on some of his living activities in one part of the house and the rest of them in the other part, neither tenancy would normally be protected. If, however, the true view of the facts is that there was, in substance, a single combined or composite letting of the two parts of the house as a whole, then the tenancies of both parts together will, or anyhow may, be protected.

(iii) Where a person owns one dwelling-house which he occupies as his home for most of the time, and is at the same time the tenant of another dwelling-house which he occupies rarely or for limited purposes it is a question of fact and degree whether he occupied the latter dwelling-house as his second home.

3.2.4 *Rateable value limits*

There are different rules for determining whether a tenancy satisfies the 'rateable value' tests for an assured tenancy. A tenancy cannot be an assured tenancy in the following circumstances:

(i)   In the case of a tenancy which was entered into before April 1 1990 (or on or after that date in pursuance of a contract made before that date) the dwelling-house had a rateable value on March 31 1990 exceeding £750 (£1,500 in Greater London).

(ii) In the case of a tenancy which is entered into on or after April 1 1990 (otherwise than where the dwelling-house had a rateable value on March 31 1990 in pursuance of a contract made before April 1 1990) and under which the rent payable for the time being is payable at a rate exceeding £25,000 a year. It is to be noted that in this context 'rent' does not include any sum payable by the tenant as is expressed (in whatever terms) to be payable in respect of rates, council tax, services, management, repairs, maintenance or insurance unless it could not have been regarded by the parties to the tenancy as a sum so payable.

There are provisions in Part II of Schedule I to the 1988 Act for ascertaining the rateable value of the dwelling-house. In the case of the dwelling-house which is a hereditament for which a rateable value is then shown on the valuation list it is that rateable value. However, if the dwelling-house forms part only of such a hereditament or consists of or forms part of more than one such hereditament, its rateable value shall be taken to be such value as is found by a proper apportionment or aggregation of the rateable value or values so shown. Any question arising as to the proper apportionment or aggregation of any value or values is to be determined by the county court; para 15(2) of Schedule 1 to the 1988 Act.

3.2.5 Exclusions from assured tenancies

The following tenancies cannot be assured tenancies under section 1(1)(c) of and Schedule 1 to the 1988 Act:

(i) Tenancies entered into before the commencement of the 1988 Act

A tenancy entered into before, or pursuant to a contract made before, January 15 1989, except, of course, most assured tenancies under the 1980 Act. In addition, certain existing tenancies may become assured tenancies under section 38 where there is a transfer of the landlord's interest from the public to the private sector or where a housing association tenancy ceases to be one.

(ii) Tenancies of dwelling-houses with high rateable values

A tenancy:

(a)   which is entered into, on or after April 1 1990 (otherwise than, where the dwelling-house had a rateable value on March 31 1990, in pursuance of a contract made before April 1 1990); and
(b)   under which the rent payable for the time being is payable at a rate exceeding £25,000 a year.

Further, a tenancy:

(a)   which was entered into before April 1 1990, or on or after that date in pursuance of a contract made before that date; and
(b)   under which the dwelling-house had a rateable value on March 31 1990 which, if it is in Greater London, exceeded £1,500 and, if it is elsewhere, exceeded £750.

In this context 'rent' does not include any sum payable by the tenant as is expressed (in whatever terms) to be payable in respect of rates, council tax, services, management, repairs, maintenance or insurance, unless it could not have been regarded by the parties to the tenancy as a sum so payable. In *Bankway Properties Ltd* v *Dunsford* [2001] EGCS 53 a clause which provided that as from (a certain date) the rent was to be £25,000 p.a. was held to be unenforceable as an unlawful contracting out of the security of tenure provisions of the 1988 Act, or, alternatively, it was repugnant to the statutory purpose of the 1988 Act and was to be ignored.

(iii) *Tenancies at low rent*

A tenancy under which for the time being no rent is payable; para 3 of Schedule 1. Further, a tenancy:

(a)   which is entered into on or after April 1 1990 (otherwise than where the dwelling-house had a rateable value on March 31 1990, in pursuance of a contract made before April 1 1990); and

(b)   under which the rent payable for the time being is payable at a rate of, if the dwelling-house is in Greater London, £1,000 or less a year and, if it is elsewhere, £250 or less a year.

A tenancy:

(a)   which was entered into before April 1 1990 or, where the dwelling-house had a rateable value on March 31 1990, on or after April 1, 1990 in pursuance of a contract made before that date; and

(b)   under which the rent payable for the time being is less than two-thirds of the rateable value of the dwelling-house on March 31 1990.

In this context rent does not include any sum payable by the tenant as is expressed (in whatever terms) to be payable in respect of rates, council tax, services, management, repairs, maintenance or insurance unless it could not have been regarded by the parties to the tenancy as a sum so payable.

(iv) *Business tenancies under the 1954 Act*

A tenancy to which Part II of the Landlord and Tenant Act 1954 Pt II applies.

(v) Licensed premises

A tenancy under which the dwelling-house consists of or comprises premises licensed for the sale of intoxicating liquors for consumption on the premises.

(vi) Tenancies of agricultural land

A tenancy under which the dwelling-house:
(a)   is comprised in an agricultural holding; and
(b)   is occupied by the person responsible for the control (whether as tenant or as servant or agent of the tenant) of the farming of the holding.

A tenancy under which the dwelling-house:
(a)   is comprised in the holding held under a farm business tenancy; and
(b)   is occupied by the person responsible for the control (whether as tenant or as servant or agent of the tenant) of the management of the holding.

In this paragraph 'agricultural holding' means any agricultural holding within the meaning of the Agricultural Holdings Act 1986 held under a tenancy in relation to which that Act applies, and 'farm business tenancy' and 'holding', in relation to such a tenancy, have the same meaning as in the Agricultural Tenancies Act 1995.

(vii) Tenancies of agricultural holdings

A tenancy under which the dwelling-house:
(a)   is comprised in an agricultural holding within the meaning of the Agricultural Holdings Act 1986; and
(b)   is occupied by the person responsible for the control (whether as tenant or as servant or agent of the tenant) of the farming of the holding.

(viii) Lettings to students

A tenancy which is granted to a person who is pursuing, or intends to pursue a course of study provided by a specified educational institution and is so granted either by that institution or by another specified institution or body of persons. This is intended to cover the situation where the institution owns the premises.

(ix) Holiday lettings

A tenancy the purpose of which is to confer on the tenant the right to occupy the dwelling-house for a holiday.

(x) Resident landlords

A tenancy in respect of which the following conditions are fulfilled cannot be an assured tenancy where it is let by a resident landlord:

(a) that the dwelling-house forms part only of a building and, except in a case where the dwelling-house also forms part of a flat, the building is not a purpose-built block of flats; and

(b) that the tenancy was granted by an individual who, at the time when the tenancy was granted, occupied as his only or principal home another dwelling-house which,

   (i)   in the case mentioned in paragraph (a) above, also forms part of the flat; or

   (ii) in any other case, also forms part of the building;

(c) that, subject to Part III of Schedule 1, at all times since the tenancy was granted the interest of the landlord under the tenancy has belonged to an individual who, at the time he owned that interest, occupied as his only or principal home another dwelling-house which,

   (i)   in the case mentioned in paragraph (a) above, also formed part of the flat; or

   (ii) in any other case, also formed part of the building; and

(d) that the tenancy is not one which is excluded from this sub-paragraph by sub-paragraph (3) below.

Sub-paragraph (3) of paragraph 10 of Schedule 1 provides

(3) A tenancy (in this sub-paragraph referred to as 'the new tenancy') is excluded from sub-paragraph (1) above if –

   (a) it is granted to a person (alone, or jointly with others) who, immediately before it was granted, was a tenant under an assured tenancy (in this sub-paragraph referred to as 'the former tenancy') of the same dwelling-house or of another dwelling-house which forms part of the building in question; and

   (b) the landlord under the new tenancy and under the former tenancy is the same person or, if either of those tenancies is or was granted by two or more persons jointly, the same person is the landlord or one of the landlords under each tenancy.

(xi) Crown tenancies

A tenancy under which the interest of the landlord belongs to the Crown or to a government department or is held in trust for the Crown for the purposes of a government department cannot be an assured tenancy. But the exclusion does not apply where the interest belongs to the Crown and is under the management of the Crown Estates Commissioners or is held by the Secretary of State under Part III of the Housing Associations Act 1985.

(xii) Local authority tenancies

A tenancy under which the interest of the landlord belongs to one of the following cannot be an assured tenancy:

(a) a local authority, namely:
   (i) the council of a county, county borough, district or London borough;
   (ii) the Common Council of the City of London;
   (iii) the Council of the Isles of Scilly;
   (iv) the Broads Authority;
   (v) a National Park Authority;
   (vi) the Inner London Education Authority; and
   (vii) a joint authority, within the meaning of the Local Government Act 1985;
   (viii) a police authority under the Police Act 1996;
(b) the Commission for the New Towns;
(c) an urban development corporation established by an order under section 135 of the Local Government, Planning and Land Act 1980;
(d) a development corporation, within the meaning of the New Towns Act 1981;
(e) the London Fire and Emergency Planning Authority;
(f) an authority established under section 10 of the Local Government Act 1985 (waste disposal authorities);
(g) a residuary body, within the meaning of the Local Government Act 1985; or
(h) The Residuary Body for Wales;
(i) a fully mutual housing association, within the meaning of Part I of the Housing Associations Act 1985; or
(j) a housing action trust established under Part III of the 1988 Act.

(xiii) Transitional cases

The following existing tenancies cannot be assured tenancies:

(a) a protected tenancy, within the meaning of the 1977 Act;
(b) a housing association tenancy, within the meaning of Part VI of the 1977 Act;
(c) a secure tenancy;
(d) where a person is a protected occupier of a dwelling-house, within the meaning of the 1976 Act, the relevant tenancy, within the meaning of that Act, by virtue of which he occupies the dwelling-house.

(xiv) Arrangements by a local authority

If a local authority, acting in pursuance of its duty under sections 63, 65(3) or 68(1) of the 1985 Act, makes arrangements with another person to provide accommodation, a tenancy granted by that other person in pursuance of the arrangements to a person specified by the local authority cannot be an assured tenancy before the expiry of the period of 12 months beginning with the date on which the tenant received notice under section 64(1) or 68(3) of the 1985 Act unless (before the expiry of that period) the tenant is notified by the landlord that the tenancy is to be regarded as an assured tenancy; section 1(5),(6).

(xv) Accommodation for asylum-seekers

A tenancy granted by a private landlord under arrangements for the provision of support for asylum-seekers or dependants of asylum-seekers under Part VI of the Immigration and Asylum Act 1998.

3.3 Assured tenancies: post-Housing Act 1996

3.3.1 Introduction

Under the Housing Act 1988 the assured tenancy was the standard form of tenancy with the assured shorthold tenancy being created only by complying with section 20(1) of the 1988 Act. The Housing Act 1996 has reversed that position with the effect that, under section 19A of the 1988 Act, as from February 28 1997 any new assured tenancy will automatically be an assured shorthold tenancy unless it falls within the categories in Schedule 2A of the 1988 Act.

3.3.2 *Assured tenancies under non-shorthold rule*

Section 96 and Schedule 7 of the 1996 Act inserts Schedule 2A into the 1988 Act, the effect of which is that unless the tenancy falls within one of the exemptions in Schedule 2A it cannot be an assured tenancy. The exemptions are as follows.

(i)   *Tenancies excluded by notice*: paras 1, 2

An assured tenancy in respect of which a notice is served before the assured tenancy is entered into by the person who is to be the landlord under the assured tenancy on the person who is to be the tenant under that tenancy. The notice must state that the assured tenancy to which it relates is not to be an assured shorthold tenancy; para 1(1), (2) of Schedule 2A. Further, an assured tenancy in respect of which a notice is served after the assured tenancy has been entered into and is served by the landlord under the assured tenancy on the tenant under that tenancy stating that the assured tenancy to which it relates is no longer an assured shorthold tenancy.

(ii) *Tenancies containing an exclusionary provision*: para 3

An assured tenancy which contains a provision to the effect that the tenancy is not an assured shorthold tenancy.

(iii) *Assured tenancy by succession under section 39*: para 4

An assured tenancy by succession arising under section 39 of the 1988 Act other than one to which section 39(7) applies. The statutory succession rules were changed by the 1988 Act, the main effect of which was that where a tenant holding a regulated tenancy under the Rent Act 1977 died and was succeeded by a member of the family (other than a spouse) he acquired an assured tenancy under the 1988 Act. Para 4 of Schedule 2A provides that in such circumstances the successor will acquire an assured tenancy save where section 39(7) applies. Section 39(7) provides that if immediately before the death of the predecessor, the landlord might have recovered possession of the dwelling-house under Case 19 in Schedule 15 to the Rent Act 1977, the assured periodic tenancy to which the successor becomes entitled shall be an assured shorthold tenancy (whether or not in the case of a tenancy to which the provision applies it fulfils the conditions in section 20(1)).

(iv) *Former secure tenancies*: para 5

An assured tenancy which became an assured tenancy on ceasing to be a secure tenancy.

(v)   *Security of tenure at end of long residential tenancy*: para 6
      The provisions providing for a tenant to be afforded the
      protection of a statutory tenancy at the end of a long lease
      under the Landlord and Tenant Act 1954 Part I were amended
      by Schedule 10 to the Local Government and Housing Act
      1989. The effect of that amendment was that where a long
      lease came to an end after January 15 1999 the tenant was
      entitled to an assured tenancy. Para 6 of Schedule 2A provides
      that that position remains the same.

(vi) *Replacement tenancy*: para 7
      The provisions contained in para 7 of Schedule 2A apply
      where a landlord grants a new tenancy to a tenant who is
      already an assured tenant. Para 7 provides that an assured
      tenancy will arise where a tenancy:

      (a)   is granted to a person (alone or jointly with others) who,
            immediately before the tenancy was granted, was the tenant (or,
            in the case of joint tenants, one of the tenants) under an assured
            tenancy other than a shorthold tenancy ('the old tenancy');
      (b)   is granted (alone or jointly with others) by a person who was at
            that time the landlord (or one of the joint landlords) under the
            old tenancy; and
      (c)   is not one in respect of which a specified notice has been served.

      An assured shorthold tenancy arises where such a prescribed
      notice is served before the assured tenancy is entered into and
      is served by the person who is to be the tenant under the
      assured tenancy on the person who is to be the landlord under
      that tenancy (or, in the case of joint landlords, on at least one
      of the persons who are to be joint landlords) and states that the
      assured tenancy to which it relates is to be a shorthold tenancy.

(vii) *Statutory periodic tenancy*: para 8
      An assured tenancy which comes into being by virtue of
      section 5 of the 1988 Act on the coming to an end of an assured
      tenancy which is not an assured shorthold tenancy. The effect
      of these provisions is that the statutory periodic tenancy
      which arises on the expiry of the contractual assured tenancy
      will be an assured tenancy.

(viii)*Assured agricultural occupancies*: para 9
      Para 9 of Schedule 2A to the 1988 Act provides:

      (1)   An assured tenancy –
            (a)   in the case of which the agricultural worker condition is,
                  by virtue of any provision of Schedule 3 to this Act, for the

time being fulfilled with respect to the dwelling-house subject to the tenancy; and

    (b)   which does not fall within sub-paragraph (2) or (4) below.

(2)   An assured tenancy falls within this sub-paragraph if –

    (a)   before it entered into, a notice –

        (i)   in such form as may be prescribed, and

        (ii)   stating that the tenancy is to be a shorthold tenancy,

    is served by the person who is to be the landlord under the tenancy on the person who is to be the tenant under it, and

    (b)   it is not an excepted tenancy.

(3)   For the purposes of sub-paragraph (2)(b) above, an assured tenancy is an excepted tenancy if –

    (a)   the person to whom it is granted or, as the case may be, at least one of the persons to whom it is granted was, immediately before it is granted, a tenant or licensee under an assured agricultural occupancy; and

    (b)   the person by whom it is granted or, as the case may be, at least one of the persons by whom it is granted was, immediately before it is granted, a landlord or licensor under the assured agricultural occupancy referred to in paragraph (a) above.

(4)   An assured tenancy falls within this sub-paragraph if it comes into being by virtue of section 5 above on the coming to an end of a tenancy falling within sub-paragraph (2) above.

The effect of the above provisions is that any new assured agricultural occupancies will not be an assured shorthold unless a notice is served on the tenant before the tenancy is granted but these provisions cannot be used where the parties to the new tenancy are the same as the existing tenancy.

3.3.3 Qualifying conditions for post-Housing Act 1996 assured tenancies

It is to be noted that the other qualifying conditions for post-Housing Act 1996 assured tenancies are as discussed in paras 3.2.1 to 3.2.4.

Chapter 4

Terms of an assured tenancy

4.1 Security of tenure for an assured tenancy

4.1.1 Introduction

It is an important provision of the 1988 Act that a tenant of an assured tenancy has security of tenure unless and until a court orders otherwise. Such a tenant may, of course, by his voluntary act bring the tenancy to an end, for example by surrender. Even if a fixed term tenancy contains powers for a landlord to determine the tenancy in certain circumstances and the landlord exercises that power an order of the court is still required before the landlord is entitled to possession. In summary, a fixed term assured tenancy cannot be brought to an end by the landlord unless he obtains an order of the court or he exercised a contractual power to determine the tenancy, but this does not include a power of entry or forfeiture under section 45(4). In *Artesian Residential Investments Ltd* v *Beck* [1999] 2 EGLR 30 the Court of Appeal held that sections 5 and 45(4) expressly provide that forfeiture is not available to bring an assured tenancy to an end and under section 5(1) an order for possession *ipso facto* brings the assured tenancy to an end.

4.1.2 Statutory periodic tenancy

On a fixed term tenancy coming to an end by effluxion of time the tenant is entitled to remain in possession under a statutory periodic tenancy. Such a tenancy comes into being immediately after the ending of the fixed term and it is deemed to have been granted by the person who was the landlord under the fixed tenancy immediately before it came to an end. In *Laine* v *Cadwallader* [2001] L&TR 8 the Court of Appeal held that the tenants were under an obligation to serve a notice to quit to determine the assured periodic tenancy which had arisen pursuant to section 5(2) of the 1988 Act as the landlords appeared to have regarded the dropping off of the keys as an informal notice to quit or offer to terminate which had not been accepted. The premises comprised in this

statutory periodic tenancy are the same as those in the fixed term
tenancy. The periods of a statutory periodic tenancy are the same as
those for which rent was last payable under the fixed term tenancy.
Save in the respects indicated below the statutory periodic tenancy
is one under which the other terms are the same as those of the
fixed term tenancy immediately before it came to an end, except
that any term which makes provision for determination by the
landlord or the tenant shall not have effect while the tenancy
remains an assured tenancy. All the terms set out in this last
paragraph are called 'the implied terms'.

4.1.3 Changing the terms of the tenancy

If either party wishes the terms of the statutory periodic tenancy to
be different from those contained in the fixed term tenancy, then
not later than the first anniversary of the day on which the fixed
term tenancy came to an end either party may serve on the other a
notice in the prescribed form proposing terms of the statutory
periodic tenancy different from the implied terms and if the
landlord or the tenant considers it appropriate, proposing an
adjustment of the amount of rent to take account of the proposed
terms. The rent adjustment in these circumstances is of a quite
different nature from the increase of rent which may take place
under section 13. If either party on whom such a notice is served is
content with the proposed new terms and, where applicable, the
proposed adjustment consequent thereon he need do nothing. On
the date proposed in the notice, which must be a date not earlier
than three months from the date the notice is served, the terms
proposed in the notice become terms of the tenancy in substitution
for any of the implied terms dealing with the same subject-matter
and the amount of the proposed rent adjustment (if any) are varied.

4.1.4 Role of rent assessment committee

If, however, the party on whom the notice is served is not content
with the proposal he must then make an application in the
prescribed form referring the notice to a rent assessment committee.
That prescribed form is to be found in Appendix D. Upon such
reference the committee is required to consider the terms proposed
in the notice and to determine whether those terms or some other
proposed terms (dealing with the same subject-matter as the
proposed terms) are such as, in its opinion, might reasonably be

found in an assured periodic tenancy of the dwelling-house concerned, being a tenancy:

(a)   which begins on the coming to an end of the fixed term tenancy; and

(b)   which is granted by a willing landlord on terms which, except in so far as they relate to the subject matter of the proposed terms, are those of the statutory periodic tenancy at the time of the committee's consideration.

It matters not that the notice under its consideration is silent as to a proposed adjustment of rent because the committee which determines any terms different from the implied terms is required, if it considers it appropriate, to specify such an adjustment to take account of the term so determined. In making an adjustment whether a notice requests such an adjustment or not, the committee has to disregard any effect on the terms or the amount of the rent attributable to the granting of a tenancy to a sitting tenant.

In the event of a reference to the committee by a landlord or a tenant, the date of the coming into effect of terms determined by it is, unless the landlord and tenant otherwise agree, the date directed by the committee. But in the case of an adjustment of rent, in the absence of agreement between the landlord and the tenant, the committee cannot direct a date earlier than the date specified in the notice. The parties may by written notice to the committee terminate the reference either because they no longer want a determination or because the tenancy has come to an end.

4.1.5 Circumstances in which a statutory periodic tenancy does not arise

A statutory periodic tenancy does not arise if, on the coming to an end of the fixed term tenancy, the tenant is entitled, by virtue of the grant of another tenancy, to possession of the same or substantially the same dwelling-house as was let to him under the fixed term tenancy. It has been noted that 'Crown tenancies' and 'local authority tenancies etc.' cannot be assured tenancies. Provision is made in sections 5 and 6 with the result that such statutory periodic tenancies likewise cannot be assured tenancies. If at any time on or before the date on which a fixed term tenancy or a periodic tenancy is entered into or at any time during the currency of the fixed term tenancy the person who is to be or is the tenant under that tenancy:

(a)   enters into an obligation to do any act which apart from the
      Act would cause the tenancy to come to an end at a time when
      it is an assured tenancy; or
(b)   executes, signs or gives any surrender, notice to quit or other
      document which apart from the Act would have the effect of
      bringing the tenancy to an end at a time when it is an assured
      tenancy, the obligation referred to is not enforceable or, as the
      case may be, the surrender, notice to quit or other such
      document has no effect.

These provisions are markedly different in wording from the
provisions in section 38 of the 1954 Act (restrictions on agreements
excluding provisions of Part II) but their effect will be substantially
the same. Any device which purports to have the effect of depriving
a tenant of his security of tenure is likely to be held of no effect. The
decision in *Allnatt London Properties Ltd* v *Newton* [1981] 1 EGLR 49
(the Vice-Chancellor) affirmed by the Court of Appeal [1983] 1
EGLR 73 may be applicable. In that case, Sir Robert Megarry held
that a covenant in a lease stipulating that if a tenant desired to
assign or underlet the demised premises he had to offer to
surrender his lease to the landlord in consideration of a payment by
the landlord of the net premium (if any) of the lease for the
unexpired residue of the lease did not in itself offend against section
38(1) because it did not purport to preclude the tenant from making
an application or request under Part II; however, an agreement
entered into for a surrender of the lease did offend and was void.

It should be noted that a statutory periodic tenancy does not
come into being on the termination of an assured contractual
periodic tenancy. In *Laine* v *Cadwallader* [2001] L&TR 8 the Court of
Appeal held that the tenants were under an obligation to serve a
notice to quit to determine the assured periodic tenancy which had
arisen pursuant to section 5(2) of the 1988: in the circumstances the
landlords appeared to have regarded the dropping off of the keys
as an informal notice to quit or offer to terminate. A notice to quit
served by the landlord is not effective but a tenant may serve such
a notice and on its expiry he ceases to have an assured tenancy or
indeed any tenancy so that section 7 does not apply. If the tenant
does not quit on due date the landlord has an immediate right to
possession which he may enforce in the courts.

During the continuance of an assured fixed term tenancy or a
contractual periodic tenancy (whether created *ab initio* or coming
into force on the ending of a fixed term tenancy by virtue of its

express provisions) the provisions of section 6 (fixing of terms of statutory periodic tenancy) cannot be invoked. A landlord may seek to increase the rent during the continuance of a contractual periodic tenancy which contains no rent review provisions, but he cannot do so in respect of a fixed term tenancy lacking such provisions.

4.2 Rent and other terms of an assured tenancy

4.2.1 Rent under periodic assured tenancies

At the date of the initial letting and, subject to sections 13–16 of the 1988 Act, during the continuance of the tenancy, the rent under the tenancy is the amount agreed between the parties, but there are provisions in section 13 of the Act for seeking an increase in rent under an assured periodic tenancy. These provisions, which enable a landlord under an assured tenancy to serve a notice on the assured tenant proposing a new rent, apply to (i) a statutory periodic tenancy and (ii) any other assured periodic tenancy which does not have a provision under which the rent for a particular period will or may be greater than the rent for an earlier period, namely a provision for reviewing the rent.

4.2.2 Provisions under the 1988 Act for increasing the rent

In the case of a statutory periodic tenancy or any other periodic tenancy which does not have a provision for reviewing the rent the landlord may serve on the tenant a notice proposing a new rent to take effect at the beginning of a new period of the tenancy specified in the notice. However, the new period must not begin earlier than:

(a) the minimum period after the date of the service of the notice which is:
   (i)   six months in the case of a yearly tenancy;
   (ii) one month in the case of a periodic tenancy of less than one month;
   (iii) a period equal to the period of the tenancy in any other case; and
(b) the first anniversary of the date on which the first period of the tenancy began (except in the case of a statutory periodic tenancy); and
(c) if the rent under the tenancy had previously been increased, by a notice under section 13(2) or a determination under

section 14, the first anniversary of the date on which the increased rent took effect.

There is a prescribed form for the landlord's notice under section 13(2) of the 1988 Act which is to be found at Appendix D. Where a notice has been served under section 13(2) the new rent takes effect as specified in that notice unless before the beginning of the new period either (i) the tenant refers the notice to a rent assessment committee or (ii) the landlord and tenant agree on a variation of the rent which is different from that proposed in the notice or agree that the rent should not be varied. In *Tadema Holdings Ltd* v *Ferguson* [1999] EGCS 138 the Court of Appeal held that a section 13(2) notice which used the predecessor to the prescribed form in the Assured Tenancies and Agricultural Occupancies (Forms) Regulations 1997 was 'substantially to the same effect' and the tenant was not misled by the fact that the increased rent was stated as an annual figure. In *Woodford* v *Halesworth* (1997) Legal Action March p13 the landlord served a section 13(2) notice seeking to increase the rent and the county court held that a section 13 notice is invalid if it specifies dates which are not the commencement of a new period of tenancy.

4.2.3 *Determination of rent by a rent assessment committee*

If a tenant under an assured tenancy has received a notice proposing a new rent which satisfies section 13(2) of the 1988 Act an assured tenant may refer the notice to a rent assessment committee. The rent assessment committee is to determine the rent at which it considers that the dwelling-house concerned might reasonably be expected to let in the open market by a willing landlord under an assured tenancy; section 14(1). There is no definition of the term 'willing landlord' in the 1988 Act but it has been considered in the context of rent review. In *F R Evans (Leeds) Ltd* v *English Electric Co Ltd* [1978] 1 EGLR 93 Donaldson J (as he then was) held that the term 'willing lessor' was an abstraction, a hypothetical person with a right to grant a lease of the premises who wants to let the premises at an appropriate rent but who is not afflicted by personal difficulties such as a cash flow crisis. In *Dennis & Robinson Ltd* v *Kiossos Establishment* [1987] 1 EGLR 133 (a case involving rent review) the Court of Appeal was of the opinion that a requirement to determine an open market rent necessarily imports the assumption of a willing lessee and a willing lessor. However, it is a matter for the valuer (using his experience and judgment) to determine the strength of the market and there is no assumption as to the state of the market. The assured tenancy to be considered is one which satisfies the following qualifications (section 14(2)):

(a) which is a periodic tenancy having the same periods as those of the tenancy to which the notice relates;
(b) which begins at the beginning of the new period specified in the notice;
(c) the terms of which (other than those relating to the amount of the rent) are the same as those of the tenancy to which the notice relates; and
(d) in respect of which the same notices, if any, have been given under any of Grounds 1 to 5 of Part I, Schedule 2 to this Act, as have been given (or have effect as if given) in relation to the tenancy to which the notice relates.

4.2.4 Relevant factors for the committee

In the context of the provisions of section 14 the word 'rent' does not include any service charge within the meaning of section 18 of the Landlord and Tenant Act 1985, but includes any sums payable by the tenant to the landlord on account of the use of furniture or for any of the matters referred to in section 18(1)(a) of the 1985 Act whether or not payable separately. In *R v London Rent Assessment Panel ex parte Cadogan Estates Ltd* [1997] 2 EGLR 134 Kay J held that a rent assessment committee is required to determine a market rent even where this would be in excess of £25,000 and thus taking the tenancy outside the protection afforded by the 1988 Act. In making a determination under section 14 in any case where the landlord (or a superior landlord) is liable to pay council tax in respect of a hereditament of which the dwelling-house forms part, the rent assessment committee shall have regard to the amount of council tax which, as at the date of service of the section 13(2) notice, was set by the billing authority (i) for the financial year in which that notice was served and (ii) for the category of dwellings within which that hereditament fell on that date. However, any discount or other reduction affecting the amount of council tax payable is to be disregarded; section 14 (3A) of the 1988 Act. It is to be noted that sections 14A and 14B were inserted into the 1988 Act to take account of the introduction of council tax. Section 14A deals with the case of an interim increase before April 1 1994 of rent under an assured periodic tenancy in certain cases where the landlord is liable for council tax. Section 14B provides for the role of a rent assessment committee in such an interim determination.

In making a determination for the purposes of section 14, the rent assessment committee must disregard the following:

(a) any effect on the rent attributable to the granting of a tenancy to a sitting tenant;

(b) any increase in the value of the dwelling-house attributable to a relevant improvement carried out by a person who at the time it was carried out was the tenant, if the improvement–

   (i) was carried out otherwise than in pursuance of an obligation to his immediate landlord, or

   (ii) was carried out pursuant to an obligation to his immediate landlord being an obligation which did not relate to the specific improvement concerned but arose by reference to consent given to the carrying out of that improvement; and

(c) any reduction in the value of the dwelling-house attributable to a failure by the tenant to comply with any terms of the tenancy.

A 'relevant improvement' for the purposes of section 14(2)(b) of the 1988 Act is one which either was carried out during the tenancy to which the notice being referred to the rent assessment committee relates or which satisfies the following conditions, namely that:

(a) it was carried out not more than 21 years before the date of service of the notice; and

(b) at all times during the period beginning when the improvement was carried out and ending on the date of service of the notice, the dwelling-house has been let under an assured tenancy; and

(c) on the coming to an end of an assured tenancy at any time during that period, the tenant (or, in the case of joint tenants, at least one of them) did not quit.

The provisions contained in section 14(2),(3) of the 1988 Act are somewhat complex and contain elements of the disregards applicable under section 34 of the 1954 Act. There is no definition of 'improvement' in the 1988 Act, but in interpreting the phrase under the Landlord and Tenant Act 1927 it has been held that whether works to the demised premises constitute an improvement should be considered from the tenant's viewpoint: *Lambert* v *F W Woolworth & Co Ltd (No 2)* [1938] Ch 883. Further, demolition and reconstruction can amount to an improvement: *National Electric Theatres Ltd* v *Hudgell* (1939) 133 EG 273.

If a notice to increase the rent under section 13(2) has been referred to the rent assessment committee the rent determined by the committee is the rent under the tenancy with effect from the beginning of the new period specified in the notice or such later date as the committee may direct (not being later than the date the rent is determined) if it appears to the committee that the date of the new period specified in the notice would cause undue hardship to the tenant. It is open to the landlord and tenant to agree when the rent under the tenancy will take effect; section 14(7) of the 1988 Act. In addition, the landlord and tenant may give notice to the rent assessment committee that they no longer require the determination of the rent and there are similar provisions where the tenancy has come to an end; section 14(8) of the 1988 Act.

4.2.5 Varying the terms of assured periodic tenancies

It is possible for the landlord and tenant under an assured tenancy to vary by agreement any term of the tenancy including a term relating to rent; section 13(5) of the 1988 Act. It thus appears that the parties can agree on the inclusion of a clause allowing the revision of rent but the most appropriate form of rent review provision for inclusion in an assured tenancy is an important aspect. It may be that the provision for the revision of rent in such a tenancy would be more appropriately linked with an index such as the Retail Price Index or other similar indexation scale. In other cases, a more conventional form of rent review clause may be more appropriate where the assured periodic tenancy is of a longer term e.g. determination by arbitration or expert.

4.2.6 Rent under fixed term assured tenancies

The provisions of section 13(2) of the 1988 Act do not apply in the case of fixed term assured tenancies so that rent review provisions should be included in such tenancies. Where the fixed term is of a fairly short length it may be that the provision as to rent review would be most appropriately satisfied by being linked to an index. In the case of a longer fixed term assured tenancy a more conventional form of rent review clause may be more appropriate. In such a case regard should be had to the following factors:

(a) stipulations as to time in the service of notices;
(b) interval of rent review;
(c) formula and machinery for determining the new rent;
(d) provisions in event of disagreement.

(A) Service of notices

It is frequently the case that the rent review procedure is activated by the service of a 'trigger' notice which commences the rent review process. In most cases, the notice will be served by the landlord on the tenant and the main problem that has arisen in this area is whether a failure to keep strictly to the timetable set in the rent review clause will result in the landlord losing his rights to a reviewed rent. In *United Scientific Holdings Ltd* v *Burnley Borough Council* [1977] 2 EGLR 61, the House of Lords laid down the general rule that time was not of the essence in the service of notices in a rent review process, but stated that there could be exceptions to this general rule. It is possible to make time of the essence by stating expressly in the lease that it should be so, but time can also be made of the essence where there is an inter-relationship between the rent review clause and some other clause in the lease. Such was the case in *Al Saloom* v *Shirley James Travel Service Ltd* [1981] 2 EGLR 96 where an underlease contained both a break clause and a rent review clause and the last date on which the landlord could serve the rent review notice was the same as that on which the tenant could give notice exercising his option to determine the underlease. In these circumstances, it was held that the presence of the break clause had the effect of making time of the essence. Where the lease provides for a period between service of the rent review notice and the exercise of the break clause, so as to allow the tenant to determine whether he wishes to continue in occupation, the service of the rent review notice will be of the essence. In *United Scientific (supra)* it was suggested that extreme delay in the service of a trigger notice may have a prejudicial effect on the landlord's case. The question of what constitutes unreasonable delay has arisen on several occasions. In *H West & Son Ltd* v *Brech* [1982] 1 EGLR 113 a delay of 18 months was not sufficient to affect the landlord's rights (see also *Accuba* v *Allied Shoe Repairs* [1975] 1 WLR 1559 where also 18 months delay was insufficient and contrast with *Telegraph Properties (Securities) Ltd* v *Courtaulds Ltd* [1981] 1 EGLR 104 where a six-year delay was fatal to the landlord's action). In *Amherst* v *James Walker (Goldsmith & Silversmith) Ltd* [1983] 2 EGLR 108 Oliver, LJ commented:

> But I know of no ground for saying that mere delay, however lengthy, destroys the contractual right. It may put the other party in a position, where, by taking the proper steps, he may become entitled to treat himself as discharged from his obligation: but that does not occur automatically and from the mere passage of time ...

In *United Scientific* (*supra*) the House of Lords recognised that a contra-indication may make time of the essence for the service of a rent review trigger-notice. What amounts to a contra-indication is the subject of dispute. In *Henry Smith's Charity Trustees* v *AWADA Trading and Promotion Services Ltd* [1984] 1 EGLR 116 the clause contained an elaborate time schedule and provided that the rent stated by the landlord be deemed to be the rent if the tenant's counter-notice was not served in time. The Court of Appeal held that where the parties had not only set out a timetable but had provided what was to happen in the absence of strict compliance with that timetable the general rule was rebutted. The Court of Appeal reached a different conclusion in the interpretation of a 'deeming' provision in *Mecca Leisure Ltd* v *Renown Investments (Holdings) Ltd* [1984] 2 EGLR 137. In *Greenhaven Securities Ltd* v *Compton* [1985] 2 EGLR 117 the rent review clause provided that if the parties had not, within a 15-month time-limit, agreed on an arbitrator or made an application for the appointment of an arbitrator the new rent should be a sum equal to the old rent. Goulding J distinguished the decision in *Mecca* and held that the default provision constituted a contra-indication. The opposite view was taken in *Taylor Woodrow Property Co Ltd* v *Lonrho Textiles Ltd* [1985] 2 EGLR 120 where the court noted that in *Henry Smith*'s the deeming provisions were two-way whilst in *Mecca* they were one-way. In *Taylor Woodrow* the deeming provision was one-way so that time was not of the essence in the service of the counter-notice. In *Starmark Enterprises Ltd* v *CPL Distribution Ltd* [2001] 32 EG 89 (C.S) the Court of Appeal held that *Mecca* was wrongly decided and that the *ratio* of *AWADA* was that provisions for a default rent, like the deeming provisions in the instant case, were a decisive, or virtually decisive, contra-indication displacing the presumption that time is not of the essence.

(B) *Interval of rent review*

It is clearly important for the interval of rent review to be expressly stated so that, for example, on a 21-year lease the rent review clause may become operative in the 7th and 14th years. Where it is not so, the rent review clause runs the risk of being inoperable. In *Brown* v *Gould* [1972] Ch 53 the option for a new lease was for a term of 21 years 'at a rent to be fixed, having regard to the market value of the premises at the time of exercising the option'. The court held that if no machinery was stated for working out the formula, the court would determine the matter itself. A liberal approach to the construction of an option to purchase was adopted in *Sudbrook Trading Estate Ltd* v *Eggleton* [1983] 1 EGLR 47.

(C) Formula and machinery

The formula and machinery have, of necessity, a direct relationship with the interval of rent review. Valuers are faced with enough problems on rent review without the clause adding to those problems by failing to define the rental on review. Such was the case in *Beer* v *Bowden* [1981] 1 All ER 1070 where the clause provided only that the rent should be the fair market rent for the premises. In the particular circumstances of the case the Court of Appeal stated that the rent should be the fair market rent for the premises. See also *Thomas Bates & Sons Ltd* v *Wyndham's (Lingerie) Ltd* [1981] 1 EGLR 91 where a term was implied that the rent was to be that which is 'reasonable as between the parties'. By way of contrast, in *King* v *King* [1980] 2 EGLR 36 the court refused to look at the defective rent review clause from a reasonableness viewpoint.

Some novel provisions on rent are being considered by draughtsmen seeking to increase the landlord's benefit as in *Bovis Group Pension Fund Ltd* v *GC Flooring & Furnishing Ltd* [1983] 1 EGLR 129 where the clause provided for the new rent to be assessed by reference to the rent that could be obtained if the premises were let for office purposes and the court stated that it was to be assumed that the building had planning permission for office use notwithstanding that no such permission had, in fact, been granted. Similarly, in *Pugh* v *Smiths Industries Ltd* [1982] 2 EGLR 120 it was held that the rent review should be on a literal construction of the lease where the formula provided that the presence of the review clause should be disregarded in calculating the new rent (see also *Lister Locks Ltd* v *TEI Pension Trust Ltd* [1982] 2 EGLR 124). The converse situation applied in *GREA Real Property Investments Ltd* v *Williams* [1979] 1 EGLR 121 where it was decided that the effect of improvements on a rent review of premises in shell-form only had to be disregarded. If no such improvements disregard clause is present, the tenant will have to pay increased rent on his own improvements (contrast with the situation on a lease renewed under section 34 of the 1954 Act). If a strict user clause is present in the lease, this may also have a dampening effect on the new rental level as in *Plinth Property Investments Ltd* v *Mott, Hay & Anderson* [1979] 1 EGLR 17. See also *Law Land Company Ltd* v

Consumers' Association Ltd [1980] 2 EGLR 109. The factors contained in the hypothetical lease for the purpose of the determination of the revised rent may pose problems for the valuer. In *National Westminster Bank plc* v *Arthur Young McClelland Moores & Co* [1985] 2 EGLR 13 the court held that in that particular lease the fair market rent had to be ascertained on the assumption that there was no rent revision clause contained in the hypothetical terms which the arbitrator had to apply. A similar conclusion was reached (at first instance) in *Equity & Law Life Assurance Society plc* v *Bodfield Ltd* [1986] 2 EGLR 144. Different conclusions from these two cases were reached in *Datastream International Ltd* v *Oakeep Ltd* [1986] 1 EGLR 98 and *MFI Properties Ltd* v *BICC Group Pension Trust Ltd* [1986] 1 EGLR 115. In *British Gas Corporation* v *Universities Superannuation Scheme Ltd* [1986] 1 EGLR 120 Browne-Wilkinson V–C said that the correct approach in these circumstances was as follows:

(a) words in a rent exclusion provision which require all provisions as to rent to be disregarded produced a result so manifestly contrary to commercial common sense that they cannot be given literal effect;

(b) other clear words which require the rent review provision (as opposed to all provisions as to rent) to be disregarded must be given effect to, however wayward the result; and

(c) subject to (b), in the absence of special circumstances it is proper to give effect to the underlying commercial purpose of a rent review clause and to construe the words so as to give effect to that purpose by requiring future rent reviews to be taken into account in fixing the open market rental under the hypothetical letting.

These were stressed as being only 'guidelines' by the Court of Appeal in the *Equity & Law Life* case [1987] 1 EGLR 124.

(D) Disagreement

A well drafted rent review clause should always provide for a procedure in the event of disagreement between the landlord and tenant on the new rent level. It should be made clear whether reference to an arbitrator or independent expert is desired.

Chapter 5

Assured shorthold tenancies: pre- and post-Housing Act 1996

5.1 Qualifying conditions for pre-Housing Act 1996 assured shorthold tenancies

5.1.1 Introduction

The 1988 Act introduced a new form of tenancy entitled an assured shorthold tenancy which was a variant of an assured tenancy under the 1988 Act. The assured shorthold tenancy provides the landlord with a facility for repossessing the demised premises at the end of the term. The tenancy also allows the tenant to refer the question of the rent payable under the assured shorthold tenancy to a rent assessment committee if the tenant considers that the rent payable is significantly in excess of the rents payable under either assured tenancies or assured shorthold tenancies under the 1988 Act. A assured tenancy which is not one to which section 19A applies, is an assured shorthold tenancy if the following conditions are met:

(a) it is a fixed term tenancy granted for a term certain of not less than six months;

(b) there is no power for the landlord to determine the tenancy at any time earlier than six months from the beginning of the tenancy; and

(c) a notice in respect of it is served as follows:

    (i) is in such form as may be prescribed;

    (ii) is served before the assured tenancy is entered into;

    (iii) is served by the person who is to be the landlord under the assured tenancy on the person who is to be the tenant under that tenancy; and

    (iv) states that the assured tenancy to which it relates is to be a shorthold tenancy.

Notices prescribed in respect of assured shorthold tenancies are found in Appendix D.

There is a saving provision in section 20(4) of the 1988 Act to the effect that on the coming to an end of an assured shorthold tenancy, if a new assured tenancy of the same or substantially the same premises comes into being under which the landlord and tenant are the same as at the coming to an end of the earlier tenancy, the new tenancy is deemed to be an assured shorthold tenancy whether or not it fulfils the conditions in (a) and (b) above.

In *Lower Street Properties Ltd* v *Jones* [1996] EGCS 37 by an agreement dated March 28 1989 P was granted an assured shorthold tenancy of residential premises for a six-month term. Following certain correspondence P's request to remain in possession until March 26 1990 was allowed. A new three-month agreement was then entered into in April 1990 and a purported notice under section 20(2) of the Housing Act 1988 was served on P. On July 23 1990 another purported notice under section 20(2) was served on P and the parties entered into a six-month tenancy purporting to be an assured shorthold tenancy. A notice under section 21(1) was served on P in November 1990 enabling the landlord to recover possession at the end of the term but in fact no steps were taken and P was allowed to remain in possession and died in February 1992. On his death P's tenancy was vested in the defendant pursuant to section 18 of the Act. In June 1994 the plaintiff landlord served a notice under section 21(4) seeking possession at the end of the period of the tenancy which would end after the expiry of two months after the notice. Proceedings were commenced just before the notice expired.

The Court of Appeal held, *inter alia*, that on the expiration of the first tenancy in late 1989, P became an assured shorthold tenant for the second time and the process was repeated thereafter at intervals until his death. Sometimes he had a fixed term, sometimes a periodic term. Although the two attempts to create assured shorthold tenancies in April and July 1990 were ineffective, the term was only three months in April and a defective notice was served in July, the tenancies were none the less assured shorthold tenancies by reason of section 20(4).

It is to be noted that section 20(3), (4) does not apply where the new tenancy is one to which section 19A applies. The assured shorthold tenancy must satisfy the basic requirements of an assured tenancy, namely, there must be a letting of a separate dwelling-house to an individual occupying such a dwelling-house as his only or principal home. In *Mundy* v *Hook* [1997] EGCS 119 the Court of Appeal held that the parties, although not *ad idem* as to the inclusion of a garage in the agreement, had concluded an oral agreement which satisfied the requirements of section 20 of the 1988 Act.

5.1.2 *Tenancies which cannot be assured shorthold tenancies*

A tenancy cannot be an assured shorthold tenancy where immediately before the new tenancy was granted the person to whom it was granted was a tenant under an assured tenancy which was not a shorthold tenancy and was granted by the landlord under the assured tenancy; section 20(3)(a),(b) of the 1988 Act. A further exclusion is contained in section 20(5) of the 1988 Act whereby the saving provision in section 20(4) (explained above) does not apply if, before the new assured tenancy is entered into, the landlord served notice on the tenant that the new tenancy was not to be a shorthold tenancy. The same exclusion applies where instead of the notice being served before the new assured tenancy is entered into it is served before a statutory periodic tenancy takes effect in possession. It is to be noted that section 20(3),(4) does not apply where the new tenancy is one to which section 19A applies. The assured shorthold tenancy must satisfy the basic requirements of an assured tenancy, namely, there must be a letting of a separate dwelling-house to an individual occupying such a dwelling-house as his only or principal home. It has been noted that an assured shorthold tenancy must be a fixed term tenancy granted for a term certain of not less than six months. In *Goodman* v *Evely* [2001] PLSCS 17 the defendants were tenants under a tenancy agreement which stated that it was for a 'term certain of one year from November 1 1995 and (if the landlord shall not have previously served notice on the tenant of intention to take proceedings for recovery of possession of the property at the expiry of such term) thereafter from month to month'. After the expiry of the fixed term the defendants continued in occupation on a monthly basis. The landlord claimed that the tenancy was an assured shorthold tenancy and sought possession. The county court judge held that it was an assured tenancy but the landlord appealed and an order for possession was made. The second defendant appealed contending that the tenancy agreement could not be an assured shorthold tenancy under section 20 of the 1988 Act as it did not amount to a fixed term tenancy within the meaning in section 45(1) of the 1988 Act. The Court of Appeal held that the tenancy was not excluded by section 45(1) as it was not simply a periodic tenancy: it was a fixed term tenancy and remained an assured shorthold tenancy within section 20 of the 1988 Act.

5.1.3 *Rent under an assured shorthold tenancy*

The rent assessment committee has two functions in the case of an assured shorthold tenancy, namely: (a) the determination of the rent following a notice served by the landlord proposing an increase in rent; and (b) the determination of the rent where the tenant considers that the rent payable under the tenancy is significantly higher than the rents payable under assured or assured shorthold tenancies of similar dwelling-houses in the locality.

If a tenant under a statutory periodic tenancy arising at the end of an assured shorthold tenancy (or a derivative tenancy under section 20(4)) has received a notice proposing a new rent which satisfies section 13(2) of the 1988 Act he may refer the notice to a rent assessment committee. The rent assessment committee is to determine the rent at which it considers the dwelling-house concerned might reasonably be expected to let in the open market by a willing landlord under an assured shorthold tenancy; section 14(9). In *Tadema Holdings Ltd* v *Ferguson* [1999] EGCS 138 the appellant-tenant had lived in a flat for 54 years and which his parents had originally occupied in 1945. In 1965 the landlord's predecessor in title granted a three-year lease, expressed to commence on June 24 1965, to the tenant's father at a rent of £225 pa payable by monthly instalments. On the death of the father in 1981 the appellant's mother became the statutory tenant and, at the time of her death in January 1997, the registered rent was £200 per month. In January 1997 the landlord's agent acknowledged that the appellant occupied the flat under an assured tenancy by succession and informing him that it was intended to increase the rent to £800 per month. In June 1997 the landlord served a section 13(2) notice purporting to increase the rent to £9,600 pa but the form used had been superseded by the Assured Tenancies and Agricultural Occupancies (Forms) Regulations 1997. In June 1998 the landlord obtained an unopposed order for possession but in the course of the eviction it became clear that the tenant was suffering from a mental disorder and the order was set aside. The landlord commenced a second action seeking possession on grounds 8 and 11. The Court of Appeal held that the old form used was 'substantially to the same effect'. The tenant was not misled by the fact that the increased rent was stated as an annual figure as this was consistent with the 1965 agreement there being no suggestion that the basis of payment was to be changed. The course of dealings showed that rent was payable on the 20th of each month so that even though the increase should have been expressed to take affect on the 24th of each month, the notice was not defective. The incapacity of the tenant had no bearing on the validity of the notices. In *Woodford* v *Halesworth* (1997) Legal Action March p13 the landlord served a notice under section 13(2) seeking to increase the rent and the county court judge held that a section 13 notice is invalid if it specifies dates which are not the commencement of a new period of tenancy.

5.1.4 *Reference of excessive rent to rent assessment committee*

Under the 1988 Act, if a tenant under an assured shorthold tenancy considers that the rent payable under the tenancy is significantly higher than the rents payable under assured tenancies or assured shorthold tenancies of similar dwelling-houses in the locality, he may make an application to the rent assessment committee for the determination of the rent which, in the committee's opinion, the landlord might reasonably be expected to obtain under the assured shorthold tenancy; section 22(1) of the 1988 Act. The prescribed form is in Appendix D. There appear to be several problem areas in the interpretation of these provisions, in particular (i) there is no definition of the term 'significantly higher' although it may be that this would be substantial; (ii) the 'locality' is not defined but some guidance may be obtained from the authorities on the interpretation of section 70 of the 1977 Act.

If the rent assessment committee makes a determination under section 22 of the 1988 Act its determination takes effect from such date as it may direct but this date cannot be earlier than the date of the application. In addition, if at any time on or after the determination takes effect the rent which would be payable under the tenancy exceeds the rent so determined the excess is irrecoverable from the tenant; section 22(4)(b) of the 1988 Act. There is a limit placed upon the date of service of a notice to increase the rent under section 13(2) as no such notice may be served in respect of the assured shorthold tenancy of the dwelling-house in question until after the first anniversary of the date on which the determination by the rent assessment committee under section 22 takes place. Under section 22(3)(a),(b) the rent assessment committee cannot make a determination unless there is a sufficient number of similar dwelling-houses in the locality let on assured tenancies or assured shorthold tenancies and the rent payable under the assured shorthold tenancy in question is significantly higher than the rent which the landlord might reasonably be expected to be able to obtain under the tenancy having regard to the level of rents payable under the tenancies.

5.1.5 Restrictions on the right to refer to the rent assessment committee

It is not possible to refer the matter of the excessive rent to a rent assessment committee in every case. No application may be made under section 22 if:

(a) the rent payable under the tenancy is a rent previously determined under section 22; or

(b) the tenancy is one to which section 19A of the 1988 Act applies and more than six months have elapsed since the beginning of the tenancy or, in the case of a replacement tenancy, since the beginning of the original tenancy; or

(c) the tenancy is an assured shorthold tenancy falling within section 20(4).

The saving provision in section 20(4) of the 1988 Act is also applicable in this context because it provides that on the coming to an end of an assured shorthold tenancy, if a new assured tenancy of the same or substantially the same premises comes into being under which the landlord and tenant are the same as at the coming to an end of the earlier tenancy, the new tenancy is deemed to be an assured shorthold tenancy whether or not it fulfils the conditions in (a) and (b) above. In such a case no application may be made for a determination.

Where an assured tenancy ceases to be an assured shorthold tenancy by virtue of falling within paragraph 2 of Schedule 2A and at the time when it so ceases to be an assured shorthold tenancy there is pending before a rent assessment committee an application in relation to it under section 22, the fact that it so ceases to be an assured shorthold tenancy shall, in relation to that application, be disregarded for the purposes of this section; section 22(5A).

5.1.6 *Recovery of possession on expiry or termination*

A landlord under an assured shorthold tenancy can recover possession either under the provisions of sections 5–12 of, and Schedule 2 to, the 1988 Act or under the provisions of section 21. The application of sections 5–12 of and Schedule 2 to the 1988 Act are dealt with in detail in Chapter 7. Under section 21 on or after the coming to an end of a fixed term assured shorthold tenancy a court must make an order for possession if it is satisfied (section 21(1)(a),(b)):

(a) that the assured shorthold tenancy has come to an end and no further assured tenancy (whether shorthold or not) is for the time being in existence, other than an assured shorthold periodic tenancy (whether statutory or not), and

(b) the landlord or, in the case of joint landlords, at least one of them has given to the tenant not less than two months' notice in writing stating that he requires possession of the dwelling-house.

The notice referred to in section 21(1)(b) may be given before or on the day on which the tenancy comes to an end and notwithstanding that on the coming to an end of the fixed term tenancy a statutory periodic tenancy arises. If the court makes an order for possession of a dwelling-house under section 21 of the 1988 Act any statutory periodic tenancy which has arisen on the coming to an end of the assured shorthold tenancy ends on the day on which the order takes effect. Further, section 21(4)(a),(b) provides:

Without prejudice to any such right as is referred to in subsection (1) above, a court shall make an order for possession of a dwelling-house let on an assured shorthold tenancy which is a periodic tenancy if the court is satisfied –

(a) that the landlord or, in the case of joint landlords, at least one of them has given to the tenant a notice [in writing] stating that, after a date specified in the notice, being the last day of a period of the tenancy and not earlier than two months after the date the notice was given, possession of the dwelling-house is required by virtue of this section; and

(b) that the date specified in the notice under paragraph (a) above is not earlier than the earliest day on which, apart from section 5(1) above, the tenancy could be brought to an end by a notice to quit given by the landlord on the same date as the notice under paragraph (a) above.

The inter-relationship between section 21(4) and the Human Rights Act 1998 was considered in *Poplar Housing & Regeneration*

Community Association Ltd v *Donoghue* [2001] PLSCS 104 where the
claimant Association was formed by the local authority for the
purpose of transferring the local authority's housing stock to it. The
claimant was initially a tenant of the local authority but was
subsequently declared to be intentionally homeless and the demised
property was transferred to the Association who served a notice
under section 21(4) of the 1988 Act and commenced proceedings.
The defendant claimed that to make an order would contravene
Articles 6 and 8 of the European Convention on Human Rights in
Schedule 1 of the Human Rights Act 1988. The trial judge held that
to read section 21(4) as being incompatible with the Human Rights
Act 1988 would enable people who were intentionally homeless to
jump the housing queue and impede the human rights of others.
The Court of Appeal held that the Housing Association was
performing a public function in terminating the tenancy and
seeking possession so that Article 8(1) applied. Section 21(4) did not
offend Article 8 as the purpose of section 21(4) fell within Article
8(2). Although this was a borderline case, the provision of
accommodation and seeking possession by the claimant Association
meant that its role was so close to that of the local authority that it
was performing a public function. Section 21(4) was not in conflict
with Article 8 nor Article 6 as the issue was whether the restricted
powers of the court were legitimate and proportionate.

5.1.7 Inter-relationship between section 21(1)(b) and 21(4)

The proper interpretation of section 21(1)(b) and 21(4) has been
considered by the courts on numerous occasions with, it is
submitted, sometimes conflicting decisions. In *Ujima Housing
Association* v *Richardson* [1996] 2 CL 159, D was an assured
shorthold tenant and remained in possession as a statutory
periodic tenant following the expiry of the six months' term certain
provided for in the tenancy agreement. The landlord sought
possession but the notice of termination served on D was headed
'section 21(4)(a) Notice'. Such notice satisfied the requirements of
section 21(1)(b) of the 1988 Act because it gave D not less than two
months' notice that the landlord required possession. However, it
did not comply with the requirements of section 21(4) of the 1988
Act because the last day of the period set out in the notice did not
expire on the last day of a period of the tenancy. Judge Graham in
Shoreditch County Court held that a notice complying with either
section 21(4)(a) or 21(1)(b) would suffice to terminate D's statutory

periodic tenancy after the expiry of the fixed term. The heading of the notice in this case did not render it invalid as it provided D with 'not less than two months' notice' pursuant to section 21(1)(b) and no form is prescribed for a notice under either section. In *Rose* v *Anastasiou* (1996) Legal Action March p12 the defendant was an assured shorthold tenant and on August 25 1995 the landlord served a section 21 notice on the defendant stating October 25 1995 as the day on which possession was required. Tiber J in Edmonton County Court held that the section 21 notice was defective as it failed to give two months' clear notice. The inter-relationship of a break clause and section 21(1)(b) was considered by the Court of Appeal in *Aylward* v *Fawaz* [1996] EGCS 199 where A granted the appellant a tenancy of a flat for one year commencing on July 1 1995 which was determinable by either party after the end of the first six months on the giving of one month's notice. As the tenancy was an assured shorthold tenancy section 21(1)(b) applied so that the notice could not be less than two months. On February 13 1996 A purported to determine the tenancy by written notice expressed to expire after April 14 1996 as follows 'I give you notice that I require possession of the [flat]'. The Court of Appeal held, *inter alia*, that the notice was clear and unambiguous and indicated in terms that possession of the premises was required. The fact that it was framed in the terms of section 21(1)(b) did not detract from the clarity required.

In *Wakefield-Wylde* v *Fraser* (1998) Legal Action July p11 the landlord served an undated section 20 notice on the prospective joint tenants. The county court judge held that the notice was valid and there was no question of the tenants having been misled. As one tenant had telephoned the landlord with four weeks' notice to quit she had waived the necessity of the landlord having to serve a section 21 notice. In the circumstances the service of a section 21 notice on the other tenant was valid. In *Transeuropean Carriage Co* v *Abou-Hamdan* (1998) Legal Action July p12 the assured shorthold tenancy expired on March 1 1995 and on October 3 1997 the landlord served a notice under section 21(1)(b) stating that possession would be required after January 5 1998. The county court judge held that section 21(1), (2) and (3) apply to notices given on or before a fixed term tenancy comes to an end but section 21(4) applies to assured shorthold tenancies which are periodic tenancies. In *Turpitt* v *Elizabeth* (1998) Legal Action August p21 E was an assured shorthold tenant and on February 28 1997 entered into a further assured shorthold tenancy for a 12-month term commencing on March 2 1997. After E signed the agreement the landlord served a notice under section 21(1)(b) that possession would be required on the last day of the tenancy. The county court judge held that as the tenancy did not commence until March 3 1997 there was no relationship between the landlord and tenant when the section 21(1)(b) notice was served and the claim for possession was dismissed. The decision in *Ujima Housing Association* v *Richardson* [1996] 2 CL 159 was not followed in *Chignell Investments Ltd* v *Deghdak* [1999] Legal Action June p23 where D held a flat under a six-month assured shorthold tenancy and it was accepted by both parties that a 'week' in the context of the agreement began on a Wednesday. D remained in possession as a statutory periodic tenant and the landlord served a notice under section 21(4)(a) expiring on a Friday. The county court judge held that section 21(1) deals with a notice served before the end of a fixed term and section 21(4) applies where the original term has expired so that the notice was invalid. The decision in *Chignell* was not followed in *Brich Island Properties Ltd* v *Whyatt* (Unreported) September 29 1999 where the county court judge held that the distinction to be drawn between section 21(1)(b) and 21(4) related to the distinction between fixed and periodic terms; there was no logic in making a distinction between cases on the basis of a few days' difference in the service of the notices. In *Smith* v *Wilson* (1999) Legal Action November p28 the landlord served a protected shorthold tenancy notice on the tenant referring to his intention to grant the tenant a fixed term tenancy of one year from June 1 1990 to May 21 1991. The tenant moved into the premises on July 28 1990 and the written agreement referred to a fixed term of one year commencing on September 1st 1990. The county court judge held, *inter alia*, that the error of date on the notice, and the use of a protected shorthold tenancy form, amounted to serious errors such that the notice was not 'substantially to the like effect' so that the tenant was an assured tenant. In *F* v *Pazuki* [2000] 11 CL 137 the claimant served a notice under section 21(1) but did not comply with section 21(4). The county court judge held that a section 21(1) notice cannot be served after the expiry of a fixed term as it is limited to cases where the notice is served before the fixed term has expired. Section 21(4) dealt with cases where the fixed term had come to an end and an assured shorthold period tenancy had arisen.

Finally, under section 21(4)(a),(b) there are provisions for dealing with the case of a periodic assured shorthold tenancy. In such a case the court must make an order for possession if it is satisfied that the landlord has given to the tenant a notice in writing stating that, after a date specified in the notice (which must not be earlier than the earliest day on which the tenancy could be brought to an end by a notice to quit given by the landlord on the same day as that notice), which is to be (i) the last day of the period of the tenancy and (ii) not earlier than two months after the date the notice was given, possession of the dwelling-house is required.

One of the issues considered by the Court of Appeal in *Lower Street Properties Ltd* v *Jones* [1996] EGCS 37 was whether a section 21(4) notice seeking possession must specify the date on which possession is required. The Court of Appeal held, *inter alia*, that a notice under section 21(4) which provides that it will expire at the end of the period of the tenancy after the expiry of two months from the service of the notice is a valid notice without specifying a particular date. Further, proceedings for possession could not be commenced before the expiration of the section 21(4) notice. In *Gracechurch International SA* v *Tribhovan* (Unreported) 14 April 2000 the Court of Appeal, having dismissed the landlord's action for possession on the ground that the landlord's section 21(4) notice was invalid, held, further, that the county court judge need go no further than decide only such issues as are necessary to dispense with the action.

5.1.8 *Effect of re-entry provisions*

Section 20 of the 1988 Act reads

> (1) ... an assured shorthold tenancy is an assured tenancy ... (b) in respect of which there is no power for the landlord to determine the tenancy at any time earlier than six months from the beginning of the tenancy'.

The absence in section 20(1)(b) of the words 'except in pursuance of a provision for re-entry for forfeiture for non-payment of rent or breach of any other obligation of the tenancy' might have given rise to problems but for the provisions of section 45(4). Section 45(4) provides:

> For the avoidance of doubt, it is hereby expressly declared that any reference in this Part of this Act (however expressed) to a power for a landlord to determine a tenancy does not include a reference to a power of re-entry or forfeiture for any breach of any term or condition of the tenancy.

5.2 Assured shorthold tenancies post-Housing Act 1996

5.2.1 Introduction

The Housing Act 1996 introduced significant changes to the provisions of the Housing Act 1988. Under the 1988 Act the assured tenancy was the main form of tenancy with the assured shorthold tenancy only being created by complying with the provisions of section 20(1). The 1996 Act has reversed this position by inserting section 19A into the 1988 Act to the effect that after the commencement of the relevant provisions in the 1996 Act, any new assured tenancy will automatically be an assured shorthold tenancy unless it falls within the categories in Schedule 2A to the 1988 Act. Section 19A provides that an assured tenancy which:

(a) is entered into on or after the day on which section 96 of the 1996 Act comes into force (otherwise than pursuant to a contract made before that day); or

(b) comes into being by virtue of section 5 on the coming to an end of an assured tenancy (namely, a statutory periodic tenancy)

is an assured shorthold tenancy unless it falls within any paragraph in Schedule 2A.

The circumstances contained in Schedule 2A have been discussed in Chapter 3.

The 1996 Act has introduced changes to the assured shorthold regime by:

(a) removing the requirement of a pre-tenancy notice;

(b) removing the requirement of a fixed-term of less than six months;

(c) removing the bar on the power of a landlord to determine the tenancy at any time earlier than six months from the beginning of the tenancy.

5.2.2 Security of tenure and other matters

An assured shorthold tenant has the protection of section 21(5) which provides that where an order for possession is made in relation to a section 19A tenancy the order cannot take effect earlier than:

(a) in the case of a tenancy which is not a replacement tenancy, six months after the beginning of the tenancy; and

(b) in the case of a replacement tenancy, six months after the beginning of the original tenancy.

For the purposes of these provisions an *'original tenancy'* is where the replacement tenancy came into being on the coming to an end of a tenancy which was not a replacement tenancy, to the immediately preceding tenancy, and where there have been successive replacement tenancies, to the tenancy immediately preceding the first in the succession of replacement tenancies. A *'replacement tenancy'* is a tenancy which comes into being on the coming to an end of an assured shorthold tenancy and under which the landlord and the tenant are the same as under the earlier tenancy as at its coming to an end and the premises let are the same or substantially the same as those let under the earlier tenancy as at that time.

Section 21 of the 1988 Act provides for the landlord to be able to recover possession on the expiry or termination of an assured shorthold tenancy. As already noted the 1996 Act has provided that the section 21 notice must be in writing and applies to both pre- and post-1996 Act assured shorthold tenancies.

5.2.3 *Terms of the assured shorthold tenancy*

The Housing Act 1996 has inserted section 20A into the 1988 Act. Section 20A places a duty on the landlord to provide the tenant with a statement as to the terms of the tenancy. A tenant holding under an assured shorthold tenancy to which section 19A applies may serve a notice in writing on the landlord requiring the landlord to provide him with a written statement of any term of the tenancy as specified below, which is not evidenced in writing:

(a)   the date on which the tenancy began, if it is a statutory periodic tenancy or a tenancy to which section 39(7) applies, the date on which the tenancy came into being;

(b)   the rent payable under the tenancy and the dates on which it is payable;

(c)   any term providing for a review of the rent payable under the tenancy; and

(d)   in the case of a fixed-term tenancy, the length of the fixed term.

The landlord cannot be required to give a written statement where such a statement has previously been given to the tenant and the terms have not been varied since that statement. The statement provided is not to be regarded as conclusive evidence of what was agreed by the parties to the tenancy in question. Where a landlord fails, without reasonable excuse, to provide a written statement within 28 days of receipt of a request for the same he is liable on conviction to a fine not exceeding level 4 on the standard scale. Where a term of a statutory periodic tenancy is one which has effect by virtue of section 5(3)(e) or a term of a tenancy to which section 39(7) applies is one which has effect by virtue of section 39(6)(e), section 20A(1) has effect in relation to it as if para (b) related to the term of the tenancy from which it derives.

Chapter 6

Notices and the Housing Act 1988

6.1 Notices of proceedings for possession

6.1.1 Introduction to section 8

Section 8 deals with notices which a landlord must serve if he wishes to recover possession. The notice served by the landlord or in the case of joint landlords by at least one of them must inform the tenant that:

(a)   he intends to begin proceedings for possession of the dwelling-house on one or more of the grounds specified in the notice (which of course must be a ground in Part I or II of Schedule 2);
(b)   the proceedings will not begin earlier than a date specified in the notice, in accordance with section 8(4) and 8(4A); and
(c)   those proceedings will not begin later than 12 months from the date of service of the notice.

If a notice under section 8 specified Ground 14 (whether with or without other grounds) the date specified in the notice shall not be earlier than the date of the service of the notice; section 8(4).

Under section 8(4A) an additional limitation arises when one of the grounds for possession (whether with or without other grounds or with any ground other than Ground 14) is Ground 1, 2, 5, 6, 7, 9 or 16 in Schedule 2. In such a case the date specified in the section 8 notice shall not be earlier than two months from the date of service of the notice.

A further limitation arises in the case of a periodic tenancy. The date specified cannot be earlier than the earliest date on which the tenancy could be brought to an end by a notice to quit given by the landlord on the same date as the date of the service of the notice. In any other case the date specified in the notice shall not be earlier than the expiry of the period of two weeks from the date of the service of the notice; section 8(4B).

In advance of the expiry of a fixed term tenancy by effluxion of time and the coming into being of a statutory periodic tenancy, a notice may be served so long as the date specified is after the

65

coming to an end of the fixed term, unless of course the landlord having power to do so has exercised his power to determine the tenancy at an earlier date. The notice is also effective if the ground or grounds specified relate/s to events which occurred during a fixed term tenancy notwithstanding that the tenancy has become a statutory periodic tenancy; section 8(6).

In *Marath* v *McGillivray* [1996] EGCS 22 the landlords lived abroad and the appellant was the tenant of a basement flat on an assured shorthold tenancy. The landlords obtained an order for possession. The Court of Appeal held, *inter alia*, that section 8 was satisfied if it was clear to the tenant by the notice that the landlord was alleging that more than three months' rent arrears were due at the date of the notice and that there was some method whereby the tenant could ascertain what was alleged to be due. The court shall not make an order for possession on any of the grounds in Schedule 2 unless that ground and particulars of it are specified in the notice, but the grounds specified in such a notice may be altered or added to with leave of the court; section 8(2).

In *Mountain* v *Hastings* [1993] 2 EGLR 53 the Court of Appeal considered whether a notice seeking possession under section 8 was in the prescribed form by reason of failing to provide the full text of each ground for possession relied upon. The Court of Appeal held, *inter alia*, that the section 8 notice was defective in that it did not specify Ground 8. The ground in Schedule 2 may validly be 'specified in the notice' in words different from those in which the ground is set out in the schedule, provided that the words used set out fully the substance of the ground. The notice did not specify the ground by the words 'at least three months rent is unpaid.'

In *Kelsey* v *King* (1995) HLR 270, the county court judge held that the section 8 notice was defective as it failed to give adequate details of the allegations of nuisance but held, further, that it would be just and equitable to dispense with the notice having regard, *inter alia*, to the late stage in the proceedings at which any point on the deficiency of the notice was taken. The Court of Appeal refused to interfere with the county court judge's exercise of discretion. In *McShane* v *Williams Sutton Trust* [1977] 1 L&T Review D67 the Court of Appeal held that a judge at first instance must not rule on dispensation from section 8 without the tenant being in court. In the circumstances the decision to dispense with the service of the section 8 notice was wrong.

Power is given to the court to dispense with the requirements of the notice when it is just and equitable to do so. It would seem likely that very compelling circumstances would have to exist before a court would be justified in dispensing with the need for a notice.

6.1.2 *Additional notice requirements for ground of domestic violence*

Section 8A was inserted by the Housing Act 1996 and provides that where the ground specified in a notice under section 8 (whether with or without other grounds) is Ground 14A in Schedule 2 and the partner who has left the dwelling-house as mentioned in that ground is not a tenant of the dwelling-house, the court shall not entertain proceedings for possession of the dwelling-house unless:

(a) the landlord or, in the case of joint landlords, at least one of them has served on the partner who has left a copy of the notice or has taken all reasonable steps to serve a copy of the notice on that partner; or

(b) the court considers it just and equitable to dispense with such requirements as to service; section 8A(1).

Further, under section 8A(2) where Ground 14A in Schedule 2 is added to a notice under section 8 with the leave of the court after proceedings for possession are begun and the partner who has left the dwelling-house as mentioned in that ground is not a party to the proceedings, the court shall not continue to entertain the proceedings unless:

(a) the landlord or, in the case of joint landlords, at least one of them has served a notice under subsection (3) on the partner who has left or has taken all reasonable steps to serve such a notice on that partner; or

(b) the court considers it just and equitable to dispense with the requirement of such a notice.

A notice for these purposes must:

(a) state that proceedings for the possession of the dwelling-house have begun;

(b) specify the ground or grounds on which possession is being sought; and

(c) give particulars of the ground or grounds.

6.2 Notices relating to recovery of possession

6.2.1 Notices that may be given in respect of Grounds 1 to 5

Grounds 1, 2, 3, 4 and 5 make provision for the giving of a notice in writing by a landlord. Part IV of Schedule 2 sets out the additional provisions relating to such a notice.

Where there are joint landlords a notice by one at least is sufficient. Where there are immediately successive tenants of substantially the same dwelling-house then a valid notice in writing given at the commencement of the first tenancy applies equally to later tenancies. However, a landlord may exclude the operation of that provision by giving a further notice at the commencement of the later tenancy that it is not one in respect of which possession can be recovered on the ground in question.

In addition, there are certain minor consequential provisions to note:

First, so far as Ground 1 is concerned the reference in paragraph (b) thereof to the reversion on the tenancy is both a reference to the reversion on the earlier tenancy and to that of any relevant later tenancy. Second, so far as Ground 3 or 4 is concerned any second or subsequent tenancy in relation to which the notice has effect shall be treated for the purposes of that ground as starting at the beginning of the tenancy in respect of which the notice was actually given. Third, any reference in Grounds 1 to 5 to a notice being given not later than the beginning of the tenancy is a reference to its being given not later than the day on which the tenancy is entered into. Thus, the provisions of section 45(2) do not apply. It is to be noted that Section 45(2) provides

> Subject to paragraph 11 of Schedule 2 to this Act, any reference in this part of the Act to the beginning of a tenancy is a reference to the day on which, under the terms of any lease, agreement or other document, the tenant is entitled to possession under the tenancy.

6.3 Pre-1996 Act assured shorthold tenancies: pre-tenancy notice

6.3.1 Requirement of pre-tenancy notice

In the case of pre-1996 Act assured shorthold tenancies section 20 of the 1988 Act provides that an assured tenancy which is not one to which section 19A applies is an assured shorthold tenancy if, *inter alia*, a notice is served which states, *inter alia*, that the assured tenancy is to be a shorthold tenancy; section 20(2)(d). In the context of the Landlord and Tenant Act 1954 Pt II the House of Lords has held in *Mannai Investment Co Ltd* v *Eagle Star Life Assurance Co Ltd* [1997] 1 EGLR 57 that a 'reasonable recipient' test was to be applied in interpreting the validity of a notice. The decision in *Mannai* was applied in *York* v *Casey* [1998] 2 EGLR 85 where the Court of Appeal held that the error relating to the termination date in the section 20 notice was evident and that a 'reasonable recipient' would not have been misled. In *York* in 1996 the plaintiff-owners of the subject property sought to let the same through agents, K. On August 17 1997 Mrs C expressed her interest in taking the letting on a six month shorthold tenancy. On September 6 1996 K wrote to Mr & Mrs C confirming the landlord's instructions to offer an assured shorthold tenancy for six months from September 28 1996. K also enclosed a notice in the standard form which conformed with the prescribed notice for an assured shorthold tenancy under section 20(1)(c). The notice incorrectly stated the termination date of the tenancy as 'September 6'. While the notice gave the names of both plaintiffs as the landlords the tenancy agreement only stated one of the names and the agreement was not signed by the plaintiffs. A section 21 notice was served in which both plaintiffs were described as landlords and possession sought. The Court of Appeal held that the error relating to the termination date in the section 20 notice was evident, preceding the commencement date and being plainly the date of the notice. The letter accompanying the notice was unambiguous as to the fact that a six month certain tenancy was contemplated. A reasonable recipient would understand that the last payment for May 1997 would be reduced to reflect the loss of three days.

The courts have considered the operation of the section 20 provisions on numerous occasions. In *Symons* v *Warren* [1995] CLY 177 an assured shorthold notice in the prescribed form had been delivered to the tenant before the tenancy was entered into but such notice had not been signed by the landlord or his agent and the landlord's name was mis-spelt. District Judge Jones, sitting at Clerkenwell County Court held, *inter alia*, that the failure to identify the landlord properly in the section 20 notice and the failure by either the landlord or his agent to sign such notice invalidated it. In such circumstances the tenant was an assured tenant of the premises.

The question in *Lomas* v *Atkinson* (1993) Legal Action September p16 was as to the status of a section 20 notice served by the landlord. However, the notice did not contain the preamble giving details of the ways in which a tenant could obtain advice. The assistant recorder held, *inter alia*, that the notice was defective so that the tenancy in question was an assured tenancy. In *Stevens* v *Lamb* (1996) Legal Action March p12 the agents of the landlord purported to serve a section 20 notice, but although they used the prescribed form they failed to include the landlord's name and address or telephone number. The county court judge held that the landlord's section 20 notice was defective. It is to be noted that in *Boyle* v *Verrall* [1996] EGCS 144 the Court of Appeal accepted that where a landlord failed to comply with the requirements of a section 20 notice it had created an assured tenancy.

In *Panayi* v *Roberts* [1993] 2 EGLR 51 there was an error as to the termination date in the notice given before the grant of the purported assured shorthold tenancy. The Court of Appeal held that the prescribed form requires the specification of the date on which the tenancy in respect of which the notice is served both commences and ends and a notice which gives a wrong date is not 'substantially to the same effect' as the prescribed form. The form predicates the insertion of the correct date for the tenancy and a notice with an incorrect date is not substantially to the same effect as a notice with a correct date and, accordingly, the appellant was not granted an assured shorthold tenancy. In *Brewer* v *Andrews* [1997] EGCS 19 the Court of Appeal held that the judge at first instance had correctly applied the decision in *Panayi* v *Roberts* in holding that two defects in the section 20 notice, namely the wrong date and a minor omission from the form, did not invalidate the notice.

In *Bedding* v *McCarthy* [1994] 2 EGLR 40 the landlord served a notice under section 20 and the tenant entered into possession on the afternoon of the same day. The Court of Appeal held that the section 20 notice had been validly served and that in computing a period of time no regard was to be paid to fractions of a day. The absence of the requisite date invalidated the notice in *Patel* v *Rodrigo* (1997) Legal Action June p20 where the county court judge held that the absence of the date invalidated the notice so that the tenant held an assured tenancy. The landlord served an undated section 20 notice on the prospective joint tenants in *Wakefield-Wylde* v *Fraser* (1998) Legal Action July 11 and the county court judge held that the notice was valid and there was no question of the tenants being misled. In *Demetriou* v *Panayi* [1998] 7 CL 377 P agreed to take a tenancy of premises and paid a deposit but no agreement was signed nor section 20 notice given. P's brother subsequently visited the premises and signed the section 20 notice and agreement for P. The county court judge held that P held an assured tenancy as the requirements of section 20 were not fulfilled. In *Clickex Ltd* v *McCann* [1999] 2 EGLR 63 the section 20 notice incorrectly stated the dates of commencement and termination and the Court of Appeal held that the two defects invalidated the notice. In *Quinlan* v *Amann* [1999] 78 P&CR D30 the section 20 notice was served on March 25 and the tenancy agreement was entered into on March 26 but the lease stated that the 12-month term ran from April 1. The Court of Appeal held that both documents were to be construed together and were not inconsistent.

In *Campbell* v *Chu* [1999] 4 CL 416 the landlord's agent entered into a tenancy agreement with the proposed tenant and served a section 20 notice stating that the landlord would be an intermediate agent who had given instructions to let. The county court judge held that an agent for an undisclosed principal can grant a tenancy: the section 20 notice was valid. The decision in *Chu* was not followed by the county court in *Gill* v *Cremadez* [2000] 6 CL 470 where the landlord's agent served a section 20 notice on C but included the agent's name instead of that of the landlord. The county court judge held that the section 20 notice was invalid for failure to comply with the statutory requirements. The omission of the prescribed information was held to invalidate the section 20 notice in *Manel* v *Memon* [2000] 2 EGLR 40. The Court of Appeal held that a section 20 noitce which did not contain the prescribed information to take legal assistance or advice was invalid. The decision in *York* v *Casey* [1998] 2 EGLR 25 was applied in *Charalambous* v *Pesman* [2001] Legal Action January p26 where the section 20 form left the name and address of the landlord blank. The deputy district judge held that the omissions meant that the notice was not 'substantially to the same effect as the prescribed form'.

6.3.2 Service of a pre-tenancy notice

In *Demetriou* v *Panayi* [1998] 7 CL 377 the county court held that section 20(2)(c) was not satisfied by service by the landlord's agent on the tenant. In *Yenula Properties Ltd* v *Naidu* [2001] 31 EG 100 (C.S) Lloyd J held that there was no reason why a section 20 notice could not be validly served upon a duly authorised agent of the tenant nor was there, on the facts, anything to suggest that the authority given to the tenant's agent did not extend to accepting such service.

Chapter 7

Grounds of possession

7.1 Mandatory grounds of possession

7.1.1 Introduction

Section 7 of and Schedule 2 to the 1988 Act provide a code for obtaining possession which differs significantly from that contained in the 1977 Rent Act governing regulated tenancies. Grounds for possession are divided into those in which the court has no discretion and those in which it has. The former are set out in Part I Schedule 2 as Grounds 1–8; the latter are set out in Part II as Grounds 9–16. Once the court is satisfied that any Part I Ground is established the court must make an order for possession. In the case, however, of Part II grounds, the position remains as it is under Part I of Schedule 15 to the 1977 Act so that even though the court is satisfied that a ground is established it may only make an order if it considers it reasonable to do so.

By section 12, an order for possession under Schedule 2 obtained by misrepresentation or concealment of material facts may result in the landlord being ordered to pay the former tenant such sum as appears sufficient as compensation for damage or loss sustained by him as a result of that order.

The order for possession cannot take effect at a time when the dwelling-house is let as an assured fixed term tenancy save in respect of Ground 2 or 8 in Part I of Schedule 2 or of any of the grounds in Part II other than Ground 16 and the terms of the tenancy make provision for it to be brought to an end on the ground in question (whether that provision takes the form of a provision for re-entry, for forfeiture, determination by notice or otherwise).

However, where a fixed term tenancy has ended, any statutory periodic tenancy which has arisen on the ending of the fixed term tenancy shall end (without any notice and regardless of the period) on the day on which the order for possession takes place.

7.2 Ground 1: Dwelling-house required by landlord for own occupation

Not later than the beginning of the tenancy the landlord gave notice in writing to the tenant that possession might be recovered on this ground or the court is of the opinion that it is just and equitable to dispense with the requirement of notice and (in either case):

(a) at some time before the beginning of the tenancy, the landlord who is seeking possession or, in the case of joint landlords seeking possession, at least one of them, occupied the dwelling-house as his only or principal home; or

(b) the landlord who is seeking possession or, in the case of joint landlords seeking possession, at least one of them requires the dwelling-house as his or his spouse's only or principal home and neither the landlord (or, in the case of joint landlords, any one of them) nor any other person who, as landlord, derived title under the landlord who gave the notice mentioned above acquired the reversion on the tenancy for money or money's worth.

In *Boyle* v *Verrall* [1996] EGCS 144, in 1987 B purchased a freehold flat and had a tenancy of a small country cottage and intended to keep the flat for use by her or her husband or both as their London home if and when one or both of them again secured work in London. B decided to let the flat unfurnished until it was required and on March 30 1993 she let to V at a rent of £650 per month, later increased to £700. B intended to create an assured shorthold tenancy under section 20, terminable by B on notice at or after the end of the agreed period. However, in error she failed to serve on him a completed section 20 notice with the result that she created an assured tenancy under section 1 of the 1988 Act, terminable only on one of a number of grounds specified in Schedule 2 to the Act. V knew at the time of her mistake and deliberately took advantage of it by failing to draw it to her attention. B claimed that she was entitled to terminate the tenancy on Ground 1 in Schedule 2, namely that she required the property as a principal home for her husband. She maintained that she had, before entering into the tenancy agreement, notified V in writing that she might require possession for that reason. In proceedings brought by B for possession of the property, the court refused to make the order sought on the basis that this was not an 'exceptional case' which justified dispensing with the written notice under section 20. The Court of Appeal held, *inter alia*, that Ground 1 of Schedule 2 to the 1988 Act, if established by a landlord, entitled him to possession and the judge had no discretion. The landlord did not even have to show that his requirement of the property for use as his or his spouse's principal home was reasonable as all that he had to establish was that he *bona fide* wanted, and genuinely had, the intention of using the property for that purpose. Discretion only came into play where a landlord did not serve the requisite written notice at the time of entering into the tenancy and the court had to consider whether it was 'just and equitable' to dispense with the requirements. In determining what was just and equitable for that purpose the court should look at all the circumstances of the case: see *Bradshaw* v *Baldwin-Wiseman* [1985] 1 EGLR 123. If oral notice was given when a tenancy was granted, it might, with or without other circumstances, be an important factor favouring dispensation. However, it did not follow that oral notice was a prerequisite of such a decision. Nor was the absence of oral notice a reason for restricting dispensation to circumstances only where an 'exceptional case' for it could be shown. In this case the judge had had regard to most but not all the relevant circumstances, but gave the wrong weight to some of them and had, in any event, wrongly placed a test of exceptionality to them. In all the circumstances it was just and equitable to dispense with the requirement of written notice. The decision in *Boyle* v *Verrall* was followed in *Mustafa* v *Ruddock* [1997] EGCS 87 where the Court of Appeal held that greater weight was to be given to the plaintiff's family situation and the fact that the form of agreement warned the tenant that no security of tenure was intended to be given.

To succeed under this ground the landlord, or in the case of joint landlords at least one of them, must establish that the dwelling-house is required as his or his spouse's only or principal home. The reversion to the assured tenancy sought to be ended must not have been acquired for money or money's worth. The notice required to be given should identify the ground under which possession might be recovered and the occasion therefor and stress that a court order if necessary might be sought. The words 'at some time' in (a) indicates that the landlord's previous occupation need not be immediately prior to the granting of the assured tenancy.

7.3 Ground 2: Possession required for mortgagee

The dwelling-house is subject to a mortgage granted before the beginning of the tenancy and:

(a) the mortgagee is entitled to exercise a power of sale conferred on him by the mortgage or by section 101 of the Law of Property Act 1925; and

(b)   the mortgagee requires possession of the dwelling-house for the purpose of disposing of it with vacant possession in exercise of that power; and

(c)   either notice was given as mentioned in Ground 1 above or the court is satisfied that it is just and equitable to dispense with the requirement of notice

and for the purposes of this ground 'mortgage' includes a charge and 'mortgagee' shall be construed accordingly.

The notice required is that mentioned in Ground 1. In this context it is to be noted that section 7(1) provides that as regards assured tenancies nothing in the Act relates to proceedings for possession of a dwelling-house which are brought by a mortgagee, within the meaning of the Law of Property Act 1925, who has lent money on the security of the assured tenancy.

7.4 Ground 3: Dwelling-house let for holiday purposes

The tenancy is a fixed term tenancy for a term not exceeding eight months and:

(a)   not later than the beginning of the tenancy the landlord gave notice in writing to the tenant that possession might be recovered on this ground; and

(b)   at some time within the period of twelve months ending with the beginning of the tenancy, the dwelling-house was occupied under a right to occupy it for a holiday.

7.5 Ground 4: Dwelling-house required for student letting

The tenancy is a fixed term tenancy for a term not exceeding twelve months and:

(a)   not later than the beginning of the tenancy the landlord gave notice in writing to the tenant that possession might be recovered on this ground; and

(b)   at some time within the period of twelve months ending with the beginning of the tenancy, the dwelling-house was let on a tenancy falling within paragraph 8 of Schedule 1 to this Act.

7.6 Ground 5: Dwelling-house required for occupation by a minister of religion

The dwelling-house is held for the purpose of being available for occupation by a minister of religion as a residence from which to perform the duties of his office and:

(a) not later than the beginning of the tenancy the landlord gave notice in writing to the tenant that possession might be recovered on this ground; and

(b) the court is satisfied that the dwelling-house is required for occupation by a minister of religion as such a residence.

7.7 Ground 6: Intention to demolish or reconstruct

The landlord who is seeking possession or, if that landlord is a registered housing association or charitable housing trust, a superior landlord intends to demolish or reconstruct the whole or a substantial part of the dwelling-house or to carry out substantial works on the dwelling-house or any part thereof or any building of which it forms part and the following conditions are fulfilled:

(a) the intended work cannot reasonably be carried out without the tenant giving up possession of the dwelling-house because:

   (i) the tenant is not willing to agree to such a variation of the terms of the tenancy as would give such access and other facilities as would permit the intended work to be carried out, or

   (ii) the nature of the intended work is such that no such variation is practicable, or

   (iii) the tenant is not willing to accept an assured tenancy of such part only of the dwelling-house (in this sub-paragraph referred to as 'the reduced part') as would leave in the possession of his landlord so much of the dwelling-house as would be reasonable to enable the intended work to be carried out and, where appropriate, as would give such access and other facilities over the reduced part as would permit the intended work to be carried out, or

   (iv) the nature of the intended work is such that such a tenancy is not practicable; and

(b) either the landlord seeking possession acquired his interest in the dwelling-house before the grant of the tenancy or that interest was in existence at the time of that grant and neither the landlord (or, in the case of joint landlords, any of them) nor any person who, alone or jointly with others, has acquired that interest since that time acquired it for money or money's worth; and

(c) the assured tenancy on which the dwelling-house is let did not come into being by virtue of any provision of Schedule 1 to the Rent Act 1977, as amended by Part I of Schedule 4 to this Act or, as the case may be, section 4 of the Rent (Agriculture) Act 1976, as amended by Part II of that Schedule.

For the purposes of this ground if, immediately before the grant of the tenancy, the tenant to whom it was granted or, if it was granted to joint tenants, any of them was the tenant or one of the joint tenants of the dwelling-house concerned under an earlier assured tenancy, or, as the case may be, under a tenancy to which Schedule 10 to the Local Government and Housing Act 1989 applied, any reference in paragraph (b) above to the grant of the tenancy is a reference to the grant of that earlier assured tenancy, or as the case may be, to the grant of the tenancy to which the said Schedule 10 applied.

For the purposes of this ground 'registered housing association' has the same meaning as in the Housing Associations Act 1985 and 'charitable housing trust' means a housing trust, within the meaning of that Act, which is a charity, within the meaning of the Charities Act 1993.

It is to be noted that Ground 6 has a number of similarities to the provisions in sections 30(1)(f) and 31A of the Landlord and Tenant Act 1954 Part II and the following discussion is based on authorities under those provisions.

In *Cunliffe* v *Goodman* [1950] 2 KB 237 (which was a decision on section 18(1) of the Landlord and Tenant Act 1927) Asquith LJ at p253 said:

An 'intention' to my mind connotes a state of affairs which the party 'intending' – I will call him X – does more than merely contemplate: it connotes a state of affairs which, on the contrary, he decides so far as in him lies, to bring about, and which in point of possibility, he has a reasonable prospect of being able to bring about by his own act of volition.

Further, at p254 he said:

Not merely is the 'intention' unsatisfied if the person professing it has too many hurdles to overcome, or too little control of events; it is equally inappropriate if at the material date that person is in effect not deciding to proceed but feeling his way and reserving his decision until he shall be in possession of financial data sufficient to enable him to determine whether the payment will be commercially worthwhile...

In the case of neither scheme did she form a settled intention to proceed. Neither project moved out of the zone of contemplation – out of the sphere of the tentative, the provisional and the exploratory – into the valley of decision.

This definition was approved for the purposes of paragraph (f) of section 30(1) by Viscount Simmonds in *Betty's Cafés Ltd* v *Phillips Furnishing Stores Ltd* (1958) 171 EG 319.

Under the 1988 Act the landlord is in a position to ensure that the action for possession comes on for hearing at a time of his choosing and this was not necessarily the case under Part II of the 1954 Act, particularly where the tenancy was brought to an end by a tenant's request under section 26. It is no doubt partly because the landlord can select the time at which his application for possession will come on that the 1988 Act does not contain provisions similar to those contained in section 31(2) of the 1954 Act.

The words 'to demolish or reconstruct the whole or a substantial part of the dwelling-house or to carry out substantial works on the dwelling-house or any part thereof or any building of which it forms part' are to be contrasted with the words in paragraph (f) of section 30(1) of the 1954 Act, namely: 'to demolish or reconstruct the premises comprised in the holding or a substantial part of those premises or to carry out substantial work of construction on the holding or part thereof.'

On the paragraph (f) wording the Court of Appeal held in *Cadle (Percy E) & Co Ltd* v *Jacmarch Properties Ltd* (1956) 168 EG 669 that the word 'reconstruct' meant a physical rebuilding following a measure of demolition of the premises comprised in the holding. A mere change of identity was not enough. Further, in *Cook* v *Mott* (1961) 178 EG 637, the Court of Appeal considered that reconstruction postulated a demolition in whole or in part of an existing structure but that 'construction' embraced new or additional work. The nature of the substantial works in Ground 6 is not restricted to works of construction as they are in paragraph (f).

It is suggested that where a landlord wishes to carry out substantial works on a block of flats he owns and possession is necessary of the whole building although in fact no work will be done on the premises comprised in a particular assured tenancy this ground will be available to him. This, however, is subject to the effect of certain conditions to which Ground 6 is subject which are considered below. The terms of condition (b) to Ground 6 are to be noted so that a landlord who derives his title on intestacy or under a will by virtue of a gift will be unaffected.

The terms of the assured tenancy may include a provision giving the landlord the required access and other facilities to enable him to reconstruct or carry out substantial works. In such a case a landlord will not be able to establish Ground 6 in any event; *Heath* v *Drown* (1972) 224 EG 231. Where the tenancy agreement if varied to include such terms would enable the landlord to enter and execute the works but the tenant is not willing to accept such variation then Ground 6 will be available to the landlord. Where a variation of the tenancy terms still would not enable the landlord to execute the works then the landlord may proceed under this ground.

It is suggested that the circumstances envisaged in condition (a)(iii) are likely to arise infrequently. A tenancy comprising less in the way of accommodation than the original tenancy ('the reduced part') would probably only be acceptable to a tenant whose family had grown smaller. In any case where condition (a) applies the landlord must establish that he could not reasonably have carried out the intended works without obtaining possession.

By section 11 where a court makes an order for possession on this ground the landlord has to pay a sum equal to the reasonable expense likely to be incurred by the tenant in removing from the dwelling-house. If there is a dispute as to the amount of such sum it is to be determined by agreement between the landlord and the tenant or, in default of agreement, by the court.

7.8 Ground 7: Possession required of inherited periodic tenancy

The tenancy was a periodic tenancy (including a statutory periodic tenancy) which has devolved under the will or intestacy of the former tenant and the proceedings for the recovery of possession are begun not later than twelve months after the death of the former tenant or, if a court so directs, after the date on which, in the opinion of the court, the landlord or, in the case of joint landlords, any one of them became aware of the former tenant's death.

For the purpose of this ground, the acceptance by the landlord of rent from a new tenant after the death of a former tenant shall not be regarded as creating a new periodic tenancy, unless the landlord agrees in writing to a change (as compared with the tenancy before the death) in the amount of the rent, the period of the tenancy, the premises which are let or any other term of the tenancy.

On the coming to an end of a fixed term assured tenancy other than by virtue of an order of the court or a surrender or other action on the part of the tenant the fixed term tenancy becomes a periodic tenancy pursuant to section 5 and is defined as a statutory periodic tenancy and is a tenancy to which this ground for possession may apply.

For the purposes of Ground 7, the acceptance by the landlord of rent from a tenant after the death of the former tenant is not to be regarded as creating a new periodic tenancy, unless the landlord agrees in writing to a change (as compared with the terms of the tenancy before the death) in the amount of rent, the period of the tenancy, the premises which are let or any other terms of the tenancy. By Ground 7 a tenant who has inherited a periodic tenancy will lose his tenancy so long as the landlord commences proceedings within the times laid down. Provision is made in the case of joint landlords. In *Osada* v *Shepping* [2000] 2 EGLR 38 Mrs O was the widow of Mr O who died on May 19 1998. Under an agreement of May 1992 Mr O became the tenant of a dwelling-house and, as the landlords were unable to establish that all the formalities for the creation of an assured shorthold tenancy had been complied with, held under an assured tenancy. The landlords became aware of the death of Mr O not later than May 31 1998. It was accepted that the tenancy had devolved to Mrs O under the will or intestacy of her husband. On February 17 1999 a notice under section 8 of the 1988 Act was served. On June 2 1999 the landlords issued a summons seeking an order for possession. The landlord argued that for the purposes of ground 7 of Schedule 2 to the 1988 Act 'proceedings for recovery of possession' is satisfied by the service of the section 8 notice. For ground 7 proceedings must be begun not later than 12 months after the death of the former tenant or, if the court so directs, after the date on which in the opinion of the court the landlord became aware of the former tenant's death. The Court of Appeal held that 'proceedings for the recovery of possession' meant court proceedings and not the service of a section 8 notice. The landlord was not entitled to recover possession as the proceedings had been issued too late.

7.9 Ground 8: Arrears of rent

Both at the date of the service of the notice under section 8 of this Act relating to proceedings for possession and at the date of the hearing:
(a)   If rent is payable weekly or fortnightly, at least eight weeks rent is unpaid;
(b)   If rent is payable monthly, at least two months' rent is unpaid;
(c)   If rent is paid quarterly, at least one quarter's rent is more than three months in arrears; and
(d)   If rent is payable yearly, at least three months' rent is more than three months in arrears;
and for the purposes of this ground 'rent' means rent lawfully due from the tenant.

If the defendant has paid off the arrears or paid off sufficient of the arrears to bring himself outside the provisions of Ground 8 the court has no discretion and must dismiss the application for possession under this Ground. However, the landlord may be entitled to possession under Ground 10 or 11.

In *Marath* v *MacGillivray* [1996] EGCS 22 the landlords lived abroad and the appellant was the tenant of a basement flat under a tenancy agreement for an assured shorthold tenancy for a term of six months under section 20 of the Housing Act 1988. On March 9 1995 the respondent landlords obtained an order for possession and the tenant appealed alleging, *inter alia*: (i) failure to comply with section 8 of the 1988 Act; (ii) failure to comply with section 48 of the Landlord and Tenant Act 1987; and (iii) estoppel on the ground of arrears of rent. The Court of Appeal held that section 8 was satisfied if it was clear to the tenant that, by the notice, the landlord was alleging that more than three months' rent arrears was due at the date of the notice and that there was some method whereby the tenant could ascertain what was alleged to be due. It was quite clear that the tenant was alleged to be over three months in arrears and information was given to enable a calculation to be made of how much was due. A notice served by the landlord's son as 'acting agent' included his name and address and gave the required information and therefore complied with section 48.

The question of whether the rent was lawfully due was considered in *Vignouelle* v *Bhardi and Rugova* (1999) Legal Action August p28 where the landlord claimed possession for arrears of rent amounting to £22,230 but most of the arrears were due to the refusal of the local authority to pay housing benefit. The county court held that Ground 8 could not be applied and the claim for possession was dismissed as the only reason the landlord had not received the monies due was due to an issue on her side.

In *Drew-Morgan* v *Hamid-Zadeh* [1999] 2 EGLR 13 a first floor flat was owned by the plaintiff-landlord and occupied by the defendant tenant under an assured shorthold tenancy. The landlord commenced proceedings for possession and the county court judge held, *inter alia*, (i) that section 48 of the Landlord and Tenant Act 1987 had been satisfied; (ii) ground 11 of schedule 2 to the Housing Act 1988 had been made out; and (iii) it was reasonable to make the possession order under section 7(4) of the 1988 Act. The Court of Appeal held, *inter alia*, that the landlord's notice under section 21 of the 1988 Act was sufficient to satisfy section 48 of the 1987 Act. A notice satisfied section 48 even where it did not state that the address was one at which notices could be served. An application for possession did not satisfy the requirements of a section 48 notice. It has been held by the Court of Appeal in *Artesian Residential Investments Ltd* v *Beck* [1999] 2 EGLR 30 that once a mandatory possession order under Ground 8 has been made the tenant has no entitlement to relief. In *Bessa Plus plc v Lancaster* [1997] EGCS 42 B was the registered proprietor of the property in question and L was the tenant. The landlord received a housing benefit payment (which he returned) from the local authority housing department in respect of the rent, but which was made out in the name of the tenant's cohabiting partner. While the housing department agreed to reissue the payment, B received another payment in the name of the cohabiting partner which he returned whereupon the arrears were over three months' rent. The Court of Appeal held that B did not act unreasonably in rejecting a payment made on behalf of someone who was neither an agent for the tenant nor a party to the tenancy agreement which prohibited sharing occupancy. In *Capital Prime Plus* v *Wills* [1999] 31 HLR 926 the Court of Appeal held, *inter alia*, that when considering an enforcement application the only requirement was to establish whether the order had been made under a mandatory or discretionary ground. In *Stirling* v *Leadenhall Residential 2 Ltd* [2001] EWCA Civ 1011 the Court of Appeal held that an arrangement between the landlord and the assured tenant after the date of a possession order under Ground 8 to allow the tenant to continue exclusive occupation of the property on payment of money at the rate of the rent plus arrears by monthly payments neither created a new tenancy nor revived the former assured tenancy. The landlord could invoke the original possession order to recover possession of the property when the occupier failed to pay the rent arrears.

7.10 Discretionary grounds of possession

7.10.1 Introduction

The difference between the grounds for possession in Part I and those in Part II is that while in the former it is sufficient for the Court to be satisfied that a particular ground is made out, in the latter an order can only be made if the court is also satisfied that it is reasonable to make the order. In *Capital Prime Plus* v *Wills* [1999] 31 HLR 926 the Court of Appeal held, *inter alia*, that in considering an enforcement application the only requirement was to establish whether the order had been made under a mandatory or discretionary ground.

7.10.2 Reasonableness

The material time at which the question of reasonableness has to be considered is the date of the trial. The court is required to take all material circumstances into account and this will include every matter which affects either the landlord or the tenant in the dwelling-house as well as the interests of the public at large. What the court must not do is to ascertain whether or not the landlord's wish to obtain possession is reasonable as its task is to consider solely whether it is reasonable to make the order for possession if otherwise satisfied that the ground has been established. The conduct of the parties must be looked at and this includes the conduct of an agent of the landlord. Lack of candour in court may be a factor to be placed on the scales. If a landlord has accepted rent with knowledge of a breach by the tenant of his obligations this may be relevant. The court should consider the length of time that the tenant has resided in the dwelling-house.

In *Creswell* v *Hodgson* [1951] 1 KB 92 the Court of Appeal held that a judge had not erred in taking into account the fact that the landlord had intended to sell the dwelling-house with vacant possession if he obtained the order for possession. Where on the proper inter-pretation of the 1988 Act certain matters are excluded from consideration in respect of a particular ground of possession such matters do not fall for consideration on the issue of reasonableness.

7.11 Ground 9: Suitable alternative accommodation

'Suitable alternative accommodation is available for the tenant or will be available for him when the order for possession takes effect.' Part III of Schedule 2 further provides as follows:

1. For the purposes of Ground 9 above, a certificate of the local housing authority for the district in which the dwelling-house in question is situated, certifying that the authority will provide suitable alternative accommodation for the tenant by a date specified in the certificate, shall be conclusive evidence that suitable alternative accommodation will be available for him by that date.

2. Where no such certificate as is mentioned in paragraph 1 above is produced to the court, accommodation shall be deemed to be suitable for the purposes of Ground 9 above if it consists of either:
   (a) premises which are to be let as a separate dwelling such that they will then be let on an assured tenancy, other than:
       (i) a tenancy in respect of which notice is given not later

than the beginning of the tenancy that possession might be recovered on any of Grounds 1 to 5 above, or

    (ii) an assured shorthold tenancy, within the meaning of Chapter II of Part 1 of this Act, or

(b) premises to be let as a separate dwelling on terms which will, in the opinion of the court, afford to the tenant security of tenure reasonably equivalent to the security afforded by Chapter 1 of Part I of this Act in the case of an assured tenancy of a kind mentioned in sub-paragraph (a) above, and, in the opinion of the court, the accommodation fulfils the relevant conditions as defined in paragraph 3 below.

3.   (1) For the purposes of paragraph 2 above, the relevant conditions are that the accommodation is reasonably suitable to the needs of the tenant and his family as regards proximity to place of work, and either:

(a) similar as regards rental and extent to the accommodation afforded by the dwelling-houses provided in the neighbourhood by any local housing authority for persons whose needs as regards extent are, in the opinion of the court, similar to those of the tenant and of his family; or

(b) reasonably suitable to the means of the tenant and to the needs of the tenant and his family as regards extent and character; and

that if any furniture was provided for use under the assured tenancy in question, furniture is provided for use in the accommodation which is either similar to that so provided or is reasonably suitable to the needs of the tenant and his family.

(2) For the purposes of sub-paragraph (1)(a) above a certificate of a local housing authority stating:

(a) the extent of the accommodation afforded by dwelling-houses provided by the authority to meet the needs of tenants with families of such number as may be specified in the certificate, and

(b) the amount of the rent charged by the authority for dwelling-houses affording accommodation of that extent, shall be conclusive evidence of the facts so stated.

4.   Accommodation shall not be deemed to be suitable to the needs of the tenant and his family if the result of their occupation of the accommodation would be that it would be an overcrowded dwelling-house for the purposes of Part X of the Housing Act 1985.

5.   Any document purporting to be a certificate of a local housing authority named therein issued for the purposes of this Part of this Schedule and to be signed by the proper officer of that authority shall be received in evidence and, unless the contrary is shown, shall be deemed to be such a certificate without further proof.

> In this Part of this Schedule 'local housing authority' and 'district'
> in relation to such an authority, have the same meaning as in the
> Housing Act 1985.

This wording is different from that in section 30(1)(c) of the 1954
Act but it is identical to that in section 98(1) of the 1977 Act. Further,
the provisions of Part III of Schedule 2 to the 1988 Act as to suitable
accommodation are, mutatis mutandis, essentially identical to the
provisions of Part IV of the 1977 Act as amended by the 1988 Act,
the Housing (Consequential Provisions) Act 1985, the 1985 Act and
the 1986 Act. Thus, many decided cases under the Rent Acts may
be relevant on this ground. In *Gladyric Ltd* v *Collinson* [1983] 2 EGLR
98 Lawson LJ at p762 said:

> It was pointed out to Mr Miller in the course of argument that county
> court judges dealing with this kind of case cannot be expected to give
> long detailed judgments. Indeed it would not be in the interests of the
> administration of justice in the county court if they did. They have to
> get to the heart of the case as quickly as they can and make their
> findings on it. The heart of this case was whether or not the alternative
> accommodation which had been offered was suitable. The best way for
> a county court judge to decide whether it is or it is not is to listen to the
> evidence of the parties and have a view and having had a view, he is in
> a far better position than this court to decide whether the offered
> accommodation is suitable.

7.12 Ground 10: Unpaid rent

Some rent lawfully due from the tenant:
(a) is unpaid on the date on which proceedings for possession are
     begun; and
(b) except where subsection (1)(b) of section 8 of this Act applies, was
     in arrears at the date of service of the notice under that section
     relating to those proceedings.

This ground is to be contrasted with Ground 8 where no question of
reasonableness arises and Ground 11. There are four distinct relevant
times: (1) the date at which rent becomes payable; (2) the date on
which the notice required to be given by the landlord under section 8
is served; (3) the date on which the landlord commences his proceedings; and (4) the date of hearing. Ground 8 is primarily concerned
with (1) and (4). Ground 10 is primarily concerned with (1), (2) and
(3), while Ground 11 is concerned primarily with (1). However, as
regards Ground 10, if under section (8)(1)(b) the court dispenses with
the need of a notice then only (1) and (3) will be relevant.

7.13 Ground 11: Persistent delays in paying rent

Whether or not any rent is in arrears on the date on which proceedings for possession are begun, the tenant has persistently delayed paying rent which has become lawfully due.

In *Drew-Morgan* v *Hamid-Zadeh* [1999] 2 EGLR 13 the Court of Appeal upheld the decision at first instance that the landlord had satisfied Ground 11 of Schedule 2.

7.14 Ground 12: Breach of obligation

Any obligation of the tenancy (other than one relating to the payment of rent) has been broken or not performed.

This wording is to be contrasted with that of section 30(1)(c) of the 1954 Act: 'other substantial breaches by him of his obligations under the current tenancy or for any other reason connected with the tenant's use or management of the holding.' It is suggested that the absence of the word 'substantial' in Ground 12 will be balanced by the reasonableness requirement.

Any breach of an express or even an implied obligation will be sufficient. If, for example, the tenant is obliged not to sub-let, a sufficient breach will be established by an unlawful sub-letting. In *Paddington Churches -Housing Association* v *Boateng* (1999) Legal Action January p27 the assured tenancy agreement contained a term that the tenant

... agrees to participate in groups and individual programmes designed to assist with the tenant's resettlement.

The county court held that the clause was not binding on the tenant in landlord and tenant terms.

7.15 Ground 13: Deterioration of premises by waste or neglect

The condition of the dwelling-house or any of the common parts has deteriorated owing to acts of waste by, or the neglect or default of, the tenant or any other person residing in the dwelling-house and, in the case of an act of waste by, or the neglect or default of, a person lodging with the tenant or a sub-tenant of his, the tenant has not taken such steps as he ought reasonably to have taken for the removal of the lodger or sub-tenant.

For the purposes of this ground, 'common parts' means any part of a building comprising the dwelling-house and any other premises which the tenant is entitled under the terms of the tenancy to use in common with the occupiers of other dwelling-houses in which the landlord has an estate or interest.

No doubt both under the Rent 1977 Act and the 1988 Act a separate case or ground for waste is included since waste, neglect or default does not always amount to a breach of the tenant's other obligations under the tenancy.

7.16 Ground 14: Nuisance or annoyance

A new Ground 14 was substituted by the Housing Act 1996. The new ground 14 is as follows:

> The tenant or a person residing in or visiting the dwelling-house –
> (a)   has been guilty of conduct causing or likely to cause a nuisance or annoyance to a person residing, visiting or otherwise engaging in a lawful activity in the locality, or
> (b)   has been convicted of –
>   (i)   using the dwelling-house or allowing it to be used for immoral or illegal purposes, or
>   (ii)   an arrestable offence committed in, or in the locality of, the dwelling-house.

In *North British Housing Association Ltd* v *Sheridan* [1999] 78 P&CR D38 the tenancy agreement expressly limited the right of the landlords to repossess beyond the limitations imposed by Parliament so that the four weeks notice provided by the tenancy agreement had not been given and the landlord agreed only to use the Grounds stipulated in the tenancy agreement which stipulated the statutory grounds existing at the date of the agreement in 1994 but not, of necessity, incorporating the amendments made by the Housing Act 1996. The Court of Appeal held that it was not the purpose of the tenancy agreement to restrict the landlord forever to the statutory grounds in the Housing Act 1988. The intention of the provision was not to disentitle either party from relying on amended provisions.

7.17 Ground 14A: Domestic violence

A new ground 14A was inserted by the Housing Act 1996. The new ground 14A reads as follows:

> The dwelling-house was occupied (whether alone or with others) by a married couple or a couple living together as husband and wife and –

(a) one or both of the partners is a tenant of the dwelling-house,
(b) the landlord who is seeking possession is a registered social landlord or a charitable housing trust,
(c) one partner has left the dwelling-house because of violence or threats of violence by the other towards –
   (i)   that partner, or
   (ii) a member of the family of that partner who was residing with that partner immediately before the partner left, and
(d) the court is satisfied that the partner who has left is unlikely to return.

It is to be noted that for the purposes of this ground 'registered social landlord' and 'member of the family' have the same meaning as in Part I of the Housing Act 1996 and 'charitable housing trust' means a housing trust, within the meaning of the Housing Associations Act 1985, which is a charity within the meaning of the Charities Act 1993.

There are special provisions as to section 8 notices for the ground and these are discussed in Chapter 6.

7.18 Ground 15: Deterioration of furniture by ill-treatment

The condition of any furniture provided for use under the tenancy has, in the opinion of the court, deteriorated owing to ill-treatment by the tenant or any other person residing in the dwelling-house and, in the case of ill-treatment by a person lodging with a tenant or by a sub-tenant of his, the tenant has not taken such steps as he ought reasonably to have taken for the removal of the lodger or his sub-tenant.

In the case of a periodic tenancy which is silent one way or the other about sub-letting and the like and no premium has been paid there is by virtue of section 15 of the Act an implied term that except with the consent of the landlord, the tenant shall not assign sub-let or part with the possession in whole or in part of the premises. Further by subsection (2) it is provided that section 19 of the Landlord and Tenant Act 1927 (provisions as to covenants not to assign without licence or consent made subject to a provision to the effect that such licence or consent is not to be unreasonably withheld) shall not apply to such an implied term.

7.19 Ground 16: Former service tenant

The dwelling-house was let to the tenant in consequence of his employment by the landlord seeking possession or a previous landlord under the tenancy and the tenant has ceased to be in that employment.

7.20 Ground 17: Landlord induced by false statement

A new Ground 17 is inserted by the Housing Act 1996. Ground 17 reads as follows:

> The tenant is the person, or one of the persons to whom the tenancy was granted and the landlord was induced to grant the tenancy by a false statement made knowingly or recklessly by –
> (a)   the tenant, or
> (b)   a person acting at the tenant's instigation.

Chapter 8

Court proceedings

8.1 Court jurisdiction

The county court has jurisdiction to hear and determine any question arising under any provision of Chapters I to III and V or sections 27 and 28 of the 1988 Act other than a question falling within the jurisdiction of a rent assessment committee by virtue of any such provision: section 40(1). Where the county court is exercising jurisdiction in relation to proceedings in respect of an assured tenancy the court also has jurisdiction to hear and determine any other proceedings joined with those proceedings, notwithstanding that, without this conferral of jurisdiction, those other proceedings would be outside the court's jurisdiction.

8.2 Requirement as to court orders and powers of the court

Unless there is a surrender or other action by the tenant the landlord can only obtain possession consequent upon a court order in possession proceedings initiated by him. Section 9 gives the court wide powers in possession cases relating to assured tenancies in certain circumstances. These powers, however, do not arise where a mandatory ground for possession is established by a landlord under Part I of Schedule 2. By section 9(1) the court may adjourn proceedings for possession for such period or periods as it thinks fit. On the making of an order for possession or at any time before the execution of such an order the court may (a) stay or suspend execution of the order or (b) postpone the date of possession, for such period or periods as the court thinks just. However, if the court does so adjourn, stay, suspend or postpone the court is required, unless it considers that to do so would cause exceptional hardship to the tenant or would otherwise be unreasonable, to impose conditions with regard to payment by the tenant of arrears of rent (if any) and rent or payment in respect of rent or *mesne* profits (payments in respect of occupation after the termination of the tenancy) and may impose such other conditions as it thinks fit. Where such conditions are imposed but they are

complied with the court may then, if it thinks fit, discharge or
rescind any order previously made or stay or suspend the
execution of an order for possession or postpone the date of
possession. Provision is made for a spouse or former spouse having
rights of occupation under the Family Law Act 1996 under section
9(5A) in any case where:

(a) at a time when proceedings are brought for possession of a
     dwelling-house let on an assured tenancy–
     (i)   an order is in force under s.35 of the Family Law Act 1996
           conferring rights on a former spouse of the tenant, or
     (ii) an order is in force under s.36 of that Act conferring
           rights on a cohabitant or former cohabitant (within the
           meaning of that Act) of the tenant,
(b) that cohabitant, former cohabitant or former spouse is then in
     occupation of the dwelling-house, and
(c) the assured tenancy is terminated as a result of those
     proceedings,

the cohabitant, former cohabitant or former spouse shall have the
same rights in relation to, or in connection with, any such
adjournment as is referred to in sub-section (1) above or any such
stay, suspension or postponement as is referred to in subsection (2)
above as he or she would have if the rights conferred by the order
referred to in paragraph (a) above were not affected by the
termination of the tenancy. If at the time proceedings are brought
for possession, the dwelling-house is let on an assured tenancy and
the assured tenancy is terminated as a result of those proceedings,
the spouse or the former spouse so long as he or she remains in
occupation has the same rights in relation to or in connection with
any adjournment as is referred to in section 9(1) or any stay,
suspension or postponement as is referred to in section 9(2) as he or
she would have if those rights of occupation were not affected by
the termination of the tenancy.

8.3 Claims for possession

As from October 15 2001 Part 55 and Practice Direction 55 of the
Civil Procedure Rules come into force which provide for new rules
for standard possession claims and accelerated possession claims
of property let on assured shorthold tenancies. CPR Part 55 and PD
55 are reproduced as Appendix E. For ordinary possession claims
commenced on or after 15 October 2001 proceedings should

normally be brought in the county court and in the High Court in 'exceptional cases'.

The possession claim must:

(i)   identify the land to which the claim relates;
(ii) state whether the claim relates to residential property;
(iii) state the ground on which possession is claimed;
(iv) give full details about any mortgage or tenancy agreement; and
(v)   give details of every person who, to the best of the claimant's knowledge, is in possession of the property.

If the claim includes a claim for non-payment of rent the particulars of claim must set out:

(i)   the amount due at the start of the proceedings;
(ii) in schedule form, the dates when the arrears of rent arose, all amounts of rent due, the dates and amounts of all payments made and a running total of the arrears;
(iii) the daily rate of any rent and interest;
(iv) any previous steps taken to recover the arrears of rent with full details of any court proceedings; and
(v)   any relevant information about the defendant's circumstances. In particular: (a) whether the defendant is in receipt of social security benefits; and (b) whether any payments are made on his behalf directly to the claimant under the Social Security Contributions and Benefits Act 1992.

The court will fix a date for the hearing when it issues the claim form which will be not less that 28 days from the date of issue. The standard period between the issue of the claim form and the hearing will be not more than eight weeks. The claim form and defence must be in the prescribed form. The claim form and particulars of claim must be served not less than 21 days before the date of the hearing. No acknowledgement of service is required. The defendant should file a defence within 14 days of service of the particulars of claim. Where the defendant does not file a defence, he may take part in any hearing but the court may take his failure to do so into account when deciding what order to make about costs. CPR Part 12 relating to default judgment does not apply.

At the initial hearing, or any adjournment of that hearing, the court may decide the claim or give case management directions. Where the claim is genuinely disputed on grounds which appear to be substantial, case management directions will include the allocation of the claim to a track or directions to enable it to be allocated. In allocating, the court shall have regard, *inter alia*, to the amount of any arrears or rent, the importance to the defendant of retaining possession of the land and the importance of vacant possession to the claimant.

8.4 Accelerated possession claims

There are new rules for accelerated possession claims of property let on an assured shorthold tenancy commenced on or after October 15 2001. In such a case a claimant may bring a possession claim where the claim is brought under section 21 of the 1988 Act to recover possession of residential property let under an assured shorthold tenancy and all the conditions listed in CPR Rule 55.12 are satisfied. The conditions are as follows:

(a) the tenancy and any agreement for the tenancy were entered into on or after 15 January 1989;

(b) the only purpose of the claim is to recover possession of the property and no other claim is made;

(c) the tenancy did not immediately follow an assured tenancy which was not an assured shorthold tenancy;

(d) the tenancy fulfilled the conditions provided by section 19A or 20(1)(a) to (c) of the 1988 Act;

(e) the tenancy –

(i) was the subject of a written agreement;

(ii) arises by virtue of section 5 of the 1988 Act but follows a tenancy that was the subject of a written agreement; or

(iii) relates to the same or substantially the same property let to the same tenant and on the same terms (though not necessarily as to rent or duration) as a tenancy which was the subject of a written agreement; and

(f) a notice in accordance with sections 21(1) or 21(4) of the 1988 Act was given to the tenant in writing.'

The claim must use the revised claim form (Form N5B) and the defence must use Form N11B. A defendant who wishes to oppose the claim or seek a postponement of possession beyond the two weeks must file this defence within 14 days after service of the claim form. Where a judge is satisfied that the claim form was served and the claimant has established that he is entitled to recover possession under section 21 of the 1988 Act he will make an order for possession without requiring the attendance of the parties whether or not the defendant seeks a postponement of possession on the ground of exceptional hardship under section 89 of the Housing Act 1980. In a claim in which the judge is satisfied that the defendant has shown exceptional hardship, he will only postpone possession without directing a hearing under rule 55.18(1) if –

(i) he considers that possession should be given up 6 weeks after the date of the order or, if the defendant has requested postponement to an earlier date, on that date; and

(ii) the claimant indicated on his claim form that he would be content for the court to make such an order without a hearing.

In all other cases if the defendant seeks a postponement of possession under section 89 of the Housing Act 1980, the judge will direct a hearing. If, at that hearing, the judge is satisfied that exceptional hardship would be caused by requiring possession to be given up by the date in the order of possession, he may vary that order so that possession is to be given up at a later date. That later date may be no later than six weeks after the making of the order for possession on the papers (see section 89 of the Housing Act 1980).

Chapter 9

Assured agricultural occupancies

9.1 Introduction

A modified form of assured tenancy was introduced by Part III of the 1988 Act in the form of assured agricultural occupancies which are defined in section 24(1) of that Act as being a 'tenancy or licence of a dwelling-house' which (a) complies with the qualifying conditions outlined in section 24(1)(a); and (b) by virtue of any provision of Schedule 3 of the Act, the agricultural worker condition is for the time being fulfilled with respect to the dwelling-house subject to the tenancy or licence. A tenancy or licence for the purpose of section 24(1)(a) or (b) is either: (a) an assured tenancy which is not an assured shorthold tenancy; or (b) a tenancy which is not an assured tenancy merely by reason of being excluded by paragraphs 3, 3A, 3B (tenancies at low rent) or 7 (tenancies of agricultural holdings) in Schedule 1 to the 1988 Act; or (c) a licence under which a person has exclusive possession of a dwelling-house as a separate dwelling and which, if it conferred a sufficient interest in land, would be a tenancy satisfying the tests in (a) and (b) (above). Section 24(2A) is inserted by the Housing Act 1996 to the effect that a tenancy is an excepted tenancy for the purposes of these provisions if it is a tenancy of an agricultural holding within the meaning of the Agricultural Holdings Act 1986 or a farm business tenancy within the meaning of the Agricultural Tenancies Act 1995.

9.2 Agricultural worker condition

For the agreement to form an assured agricultural occupancy not only must the agreement amount to a 'tenancy' or 'licence' within the meaning of section 24(1)(a), 2(a)(b)(c) of the 1988 Act but also the agricultural worker condition must be satisfied with respect to such a tenancy or licence. The qualifying conditions to satisfy the agricultural worker condition are contained in Schedule 3 to the 1988 Act which itself refers to Schedule 3 to the Rent (Agriculture) Act 1976 for determining the following:

    (a)   whether a person is a qualifying worker;

    (b)   whether a person is incapable of whole-time work in agriculture, or work in agriculture as a permit worker, in consequence of a qualifying injury or disease; and

    (c)   whether a dwelling-house is in qualifying ownership.

By virtue of Schedule 3 to the 1988 Act the agricultural worker condition is satisfied with respect to a dwelling-house subject to a relevant tenancy or licence if (para 2):

    (a)   the dwelling-house is or has been in qualifying ownership at any time during the subsistence of the tenancy or licence (whether or not it was at that time a relevant tenancy or licence); and

    (b)   the occupier or, where there are joint occupiers, at least one of them:

        (i)   is a qualifying worker or has been a qualifying worker at any time during the subsistence of the tenancy or licence (whether or not it was at that time a relevant tenancy or licence); or

        (ii)   is incapable of whole-time work in agriculture or work in agriculture as a permit worker in consequence of a qualifying injury or disease.

At this stage it is useful to note the definitions of 'qualifying owner-ship', 'qualifying worker' and 'incapable of whole-time work in agriculture' contained in Schedule 3 to the Rent (Agriculture) Act 1976. In general, the definitions to be applied are as follows, although the reader should refer to the whole of Schedule 3 to the 1976 Act to satisfy himself that the conditions are satisfied.

9.2.1 *Qualifying worker*

    1.   A person is a qualifying worker for the purposes of this Act at any time if, at that time, he has worked whole-time in agriculture, or has worked in agriculture as a permit worker, for not less than 91 out of the last 104 weeks.

9.2.2 *Incapable of whole-time work in agriculture, or work in agriculture as a permit worker, in consequence of a qualifying injury or disease:*

    2.–(1)A person is, for the purposes of this Act, incapable of full-time work in agriculture in consequence of a qualifying injury or disease if:

        (a)   he is incapable of such work in consequence of:

(i) an injury or disease prescribed in relation to him, by reason of his employment in agriculture, under section 76(2) of the Social Security Act 1975, or

(ii) an injury caused by an accident arising out of and in the course of his employment in agriculture, and

(b) at the time when he became so incapable, he was employed in agriculture as a whole-time worker.

(2) A person is, for the purposes of this Act, incapable of work in agriculture as a permit worker in consequence of a qualifying injury or disease if:

(a) he is incapable of such work in consequence of any such injury or disease as is mentioned in sub-paragraph (1) above, and

(b) at the time when he became so incapable he was employed in agriculture as a permit worker.

(3) Where:

(a) A person has died in consequence of any such injury or disease as is mentioned in sub-paragraph (1) above, and

(b) immediately before his death, he was employed in agriculture as a whole-time worker, or as a permit worker,

he shall be regarded for the purposes of this Act as having been, immediately before his death, incapable of full-time work in agriculture, or work in agriculture as a permit worker, in consequence of a qualifying injury or disease.

9.2.3 *Dwelling-house in qualifying ownership*

3.(1) A dwelling-house in relation to which a person ('the occupier') has a licence or tenancy is in qualifying ownership for the purposes of this Act at any time if, at that time, the occupier is employed in agriculture and the occupier's employer either:

(a) is the owner of the dwelling-house; or

(b) has made arrangements with the owner of the dwelling-house for it to be used as housing accommodation for persons employed by him in agriculture.

There are provisions for satisfying the agricultural worker conditions where the qualifying worker is deceased and immediately before his death the widow or widower was residing in the dwelling-house (para 3(1)(b)(2) of Schedule 3) or in the case of succession by the qualifying member of the previous qualifying occupier's family (namely not the widow or widower), such a member of the family is the qualifying member of the family if:

(a) on the death of the previous qualifying occupier there was no qualifying widow or widower; and

(b)   the member of the family was residing in the dwelling-house with the previous qualifying occupier at the time of, and for the period of two years before his death.

9.3 Determination of rent by rent assessment committee

By virtue of section 24(4) of the 1988 Act the provisions of section 14 as to the determination of rent by a rent assessment committee are applied to assured agricultural occupancies. It is to be noted that under section 24(3) of the 1988 Act every assured agricultural occupancy which is not an assured tenancy is to be treated as if it were such a tenancy subject to the provisions of sections 24 to 26 of the 1988 Act.

9.4 Security of tenure

The security of tenure provisions applicable to assured agricultural occupancies are contained in section 25 and Schedule 2 of the 1988 Act. If a statutory periodic tenancy arises on the coming to an end of an assured agricultural occupancy it is an assured agricultural occupancy as long as, under Schedule 3, the agricultural worker condition is for the time being fulfilled and, if no rent was payable under the assured agricultural occupancy, the provisions of section 5(3)(d) are to be read as if the rent under the periodic tenancy was a monthly one; section 25(1)(b) of the 1988 Act. The grounds of possession are as contained in Part II of Schedule 2 to the 1988 Act save that Ground 16 is not available against the tenant or licensee under the assured agricultural occupancy. However, it is to be noted that Part III of Schedule 2, dealing with the provision of suitable alternative accommodation, is applicable. If the tenant under an agreed agricultural occupancy gives notice to terminate his employment then, notwithstanding anything in any agreement or otherwise, that notice does not constitute a notice to quit as respects the assured agricultural occupancy; section 25(5) of the 1988 Act. Finally, there are provisions in section 27 of the Rent (Agriculture) Act 1976 for rehousing agricultural workers by local housing authorities where:

(a)   vacant possession is or will be needed of a dwelling-house which is subject to a protected occupancy or statutory tenancy, or which is let subject to a tenancy to which subsection (1) applies, in order to house a person who is or is to be employed in agriculture by the applicant, and that person's family;

(b) the applicant is unable to provide, by any reasonable means, suitable alternative accommodation for the occupier of the dwelling-house; and

(c) the authority ought, in the interests of efficient agriculture, to provide the suitable alternative accommodation.

These provisions are applied to assured agricultural occupancies by virtue of section 26 of the 1988 Act.

For the prescribed forms see Appendix D.

Chapter 10

Statutory succession

10.1 In respect of assured tenancies under section 17

Under section 17 a tenancy vests in a spouse and does not devolve upon him or her under the tenant's will or on an intestacy but these provisions do not apply to fixed term tenancies where the ordinary law relating to devolution by will or on an intestacy remains unaffected. Although a contractual periodic tenancy can devolve by will or on an intestacy it was obviously considered desirable that both contractual and statutory periodic tenancies should be dealt with in the same manner. For the purposes of these provisions the original tenancy must always be an assured tenancy.

The surviving spouse must at the time of the tenant's death have been occupying the dwelling-house as his or her only or principal home. A spouse within the section is given a wide meaning: namely, a person who was living with the tenant as his or her wife or husband.

The succession protected by this section is given only once to a tenancy. Thus, if in his lifetime the dead tenant inherited a fixed term assured tenancy under a will or on an intestacy or had vested in him a periodic tenancy by virtue of this section no further protection is afforded. Provisions are also made for the position of a joint tenancy.

The loss of protection is extended to what is called a 'new tenancy'. Where the circumstances are those set out in the penultimate paragraph and the successor tenant is granted alone or jointly with others a tenancy consisting of a dwelling-house or a tenancy of a dwelling-house which is substantially the same as that dwelling-house and there is no break in occupation between the end of the succeeded tenancy and the new tenancy, there is no protection.

10.2 In respect of certain tenancies previously protected by the Rent Act 1977 or the Rent (Agriculture) Act 1976

Section 39 of and Schedule 4 to the 1988 Act contain important provisions which result in certain persons who would have become statutory tenants under the Rent Act on the death of an original or first successor tenant becoming entitled instead to an assured tenancy. These provisions are important because the tenant will not be entitled to the rent control protection he would have enjoyed as a statutory tenant and the grounds on which the landlord will become entitled to possession are also significantly different. Further, persons who might have become statutory tenants on succession lose their protection altogether.

Under paragraph 2(1) of Part I of Schedule 1 to the 1977 Act as amended there may be a maximum of two transmissions on death; first on the death of an original tenant, the second on the death of the first successor. In each case, at least since the relevant provisions of the 1980 Act came into force, the surviving spouse of the deceased tenant succeeds if he or she was residing with her or him at death. If, however, there is no surviving spouse a member of the tenant's family may succeed providing he or she was residing with the tenant at the time of her or his death and for six months preceding the tenant's death. Under the 1988 Act, on the death of an original tenant or a first successor which occurs after January 14 1989 significantly different rules apply to those applying before that date.

Where the death is that of the original tenant Part I of Schedule 1 to the 1977 Act has effect subject to the amendments in Part I to Schedule 4 to the 1988 Act. Where, however, it is the first successor who dies, Part I of Schedule 1 to the 1977 Act has effect subject to the amendments in paragraphs 5 to 9 of Part I of Schedule 4 to the 1988 Act. So that the effect of the amendments may be appreciated Part I of Schedule 1 to the 1977 Act with the amendments of Part I of Schedule 4 to the 1988 Act is printed as Appendix B.

Provision is made defining a spouse of a deceased original tenant. Where there is no such spouse a member of the family may succeed but he or she must have been residing in the dwelling-house at the time of the death and for the period of two years before the death. Transitional provisions are made where the original tenant dies within 18 months of January 15 1989. When the first successor was a protected tenant at the time of his death then a surviving spouse and a member of the family are both treated in like manner to that of a member of the family on the death of the original tenant.

In the case of an original occupier within the meaning of section 4 of the 1976 Act (statutory tenants and tenancies) who dies after January 14 1989 that section has effect subject to the amendments in

Part II of Schedule 4 to the 1988 Act. That section contains provisions not dissimilar to those contained in Part I of Schedule 1 to the 1977 Act in so far as they relate to successors on the death of an original tenant. The amendment to section 4 on the death of an occupier after January 14 1989 results in a person who is entitled to possession becoming entitled to an assured tenancy. Again for an understanding of the position section 4 is printed as amended in Appendix B.

The periodic assured tenancy to which such a successor becomes entitled is one:

(a) taking effect in possession immediately after the death of the protected or statutory tenant or protected occupier called 'the predecessor' on whose death the successor became so entitled;

(b) deemed to have been granted to the successor by the person who, immediately before the death of the predecessor, was the landlord of the predecessor under his tenancy;

(c) under which the premises which are let are the same dwelling-house as, immediately before his death, the predecessor occupied under his tenancy;

(d) under which the periods of the tenancy are the same as those for which rent was last payable by the predecessor under his tenancy;

(e) under which subject to section 13 (increase of rent under assured periodic tenancies), section 14 (determination of rent by rent assessment committee) and section 15 (the limited prohibition on assignment etc. without consent) the other terms are the same as those on which, under his tenancy, the predecessor occupied the dwelling-house immediately before his death; and

(f) which for the purposes of section 13(2) (landlord's notice for the purpose of securing an increase in rent) is treated as a statutory periodic tenancy.

In paragraphs (b) to (c) 'under his tenancy' in relation to the predecessor means under his protected tenancy or protected occupancy or in his capacity as a statutory tenant.

If immediately before the death of the predecessor, the landlord might have recovered possession of the dwelling-house under Case 19 of Schedule 15 to the 1977 Act (dwelling-house let under a protected shorthold tenancy or is treated under section 55 of the 1980 Act as having been so let) the assured periodic tenancy to which the successor becomes entitled is to be an assured shorthold tenancy (whether or not it fulfils the conditions in section 20(1) – definition of assured shorthold tenancies).

If immediately before his death, the predecessor was a protected occupier or statutory tenant within the meaning of the 1976 Act the assured periodic tenancy to which the successor becomes entitled shall be an assured agricultural occupancy (whether or not it fulfils the conditions of section 24(1) – definition of assured agricultural occupancies).

Provision is also made where a protected or statutory tenant or protected tenant (the predecessor) was a tenant under a fixed term tenancy. Section 6 (fixing of terms of statutory periodic tenancy) is to apply in relation to the assured periodic tenancy to which the successor becomes entitled on the predecessor's death but subject to certain modifications.

For any reference to a statutory periodic tenancy there is to be substituted a reference to the assured periodic tenancy to which the successor becomes so entitled. The definition of 'the former tenancy' in section 6(1)(a) is omitted. The definition of 'implied terms' means the terms of the tenancy which have effect by virtue of section 39(6)(e) not section 5(3)(e).

Finally, for any reference to the coming to an end of the former tenancy there is to be substituted a reference to the date of the predecessor's death.

10.3 Summary of the succession rules under the Rent Act 1977

In summary, a statutory tenancy by succession under the 1977 Act can be claimed as follows:

(a)   the surviving spouse of a protected or statutory tenant remains (as previously) the statutory tenant of the dwelling-house by succession (if and so long as he continues to occupy the dwelling-house as a residence). A person living with the deceased tenant 'as his or her wife or husband' is now treated as the spouse of the tenant.

(b)   where the tenant is survived by a family member other than his or her spouse that family member is only entitled to an assured tenancy and that member must have lived in the dwelling-house with the deceased for 2 years immediately prior to death.

(c)   where the surviving spouse of the deceased tenant (not other family members) dies a member of both the first successor's family and the original tenant's family may succeed to an assured tenancy by succession but must have resided with the first success-ion in the dwelling-house for 2 years prior to latter's death.

(d)   No succession is possible where the first succession was by a
family member other than the deceased's spouse.

In the context of these provisions the House of Lords has held that
the surviving partner of a same-sex relationship can fall within the
definition of a member of the family for the purpose of the
succession provisions but canot be considered a surviving spouse;
Fitzpatrick v *Sterling Housing Association* [2000] 32 HLR 178

Chapter 11

Miscellaneous provisions

11.1 Provisions as to reversions on assured tenancies: section 18

Where a dwelling-house is lawfully let on an assured tenancy and the landlord is himself a tenant under a superior tenancy which ends, the assured tenancy nevertheless continues as a tenancy held of the person whose interest would, apart from such continuance entitle him to actual possession of the dwelling-house at that time. These provisions do not apply when by virtue of the application of Schedule 1 the landlord's interest would result in the tenancy not being an assured one.

Provision is also made for the position where an assured periodic tenancy (including a statutory periodic tenancy) continues beyond the beginning of the tenancy which was granted whether before or after the commencement of the Act, so as to begin on or after the date on which the fixed term tenancy came to an end (being then followed by a statutory periodic tenancy) or a day on which, apart from the 1988 Act, a periodic tenancy could have been brought to an end by the landlord by a notice to quit. The reversionary tenancy is to have effect as though it had been granted subject to the periodic tenancy.

11.2 Access for repairs: section 16

Section 16 provides that it shall be an implied term of every assured tenancy that the tenant shall afford to the landlord access to the dwelling-house let on the tenancy and all reasonable facilities for executing on the premises any repairs which the landlord is entitled to execute.

11.3 Payment of removal expenses in certain cases: section 11

Where a landlord recovers possession on the mandatory ground that he intends to demolish or reconstruct the whole or a substantial part of the building (Ground 6) or on the discretionary ground of offering suitable alternative accommodation (Ground 9) the landlord must pay to the tenant a sum equal to the reasonable expenses likely to be incurred by the tenant in removing from the dwelling-house.

If the parties cannot agree the sum the court must determine it. If not paid, the tenant can recover the sum as a civil debt due from the landlord.

11.4 Limited prohibition on assignment: section 15

In the case of an assured periodic tenancy a term is implied that the tenant shall not assign the tenancy (in whole or in part) nor sub-let or part with possession of the whole or any part of the dwelling-house without the landlord's consent; section 15(1). In such a case the implied proviso under section 19 of the Landlord and Tenant Act 1927, namely that consent cannot be unreasonably withheld, does not apply; section 15(2).

It is to be noted that the implied term under section 15(1) of the 1988 Act does not apply in the case of a periodic tenancy which is not a statutory periodic tenancy or an assured periodic tenancy arising under Schedule 10 to the Local Government and Housing Act 1989 if there is a provision (whether contained in the tenancy or not) prohibiting or permitting (absolutely or conditionally) assigning, subletting or parting with possession or there is a provision requiring a premium to be paid on the grant or renewal of the tenancy: section 15(3)(a),(b).

11.5 'Beginning of a tenancy': section 45(2)

Section 45(2) provides that subject to paragraph 11 of Schedule 2 (special provisions regarding a landlord's notice in writing in respect of Grounds 1–5) any reference in sections 1–45 to the beginning of a tenancy is a reference to the day on which the tenancy is entered into or, if it is later, the date on which, under the terms of any lease, agreement or other document, the tenant is entitled to possession under the tenancy.

11.6 Compensation for misrepresentation or concealment: section 12

Section 12 provides that where a landlord obtains an order for possession of a dwelling-house let on an assured tenancy on one or more of the grounds in Schedule 2 and it is subsequently made to appear to the court that the order was obtained by a misrepresentation or concealment of material facts that court may order the landlord to pay to the former tenant such sum as appears sufficient as compensation for damage or loss sustained by that tenant as a result of the order.

These provisions do not apply where the landlord of a fixed term tenancy obtains an order for possession not on one or more of the grounds set out in Schedule 2 but pursuant to the powers in the tenancy exercised by him to determine the tenancy in certain circumstances. The words 'concealment of material facts', as was made clear by Scott LJ in *Thorne* v *Smith* [1947] KB 307, emanate from *uberrimae fidei* contracts and in these circumstances the standard of conduct demanded of a landlord is utmost good faith. The cause of action afforded by the section is additional to and not in substitution of common law remedies such as an action for deceit: *French* v *Lowen* (1925) 105 EG 491. Both causes of action can be joined in one proceedings. Innocent misrepresentation can be sufficient for the purposes of this section. Damages are compensatory not punitive: *Engleheart* v *Catford* (1926) 108 EG 731 (CA).

11.7 Restriction on levy of distress for rent: section 19

Section 19(1) of the 1988 Act provides that subject to the County Courts Act 1984 no distress for the rent of any dwelling-house let on an assured tenancy shall be levied except with the leave of the county court. Where an application is made to the county court for leave to distrain, the county court has the same powers with respect of adjournment, stay, suspension, postponement and otherwise as are conferred on the court by section 9 in relation to proceedings for possession of such a dwelling-house.

Appendix A

Relevant sections of the Housing Act 1988

PART I
RENTED ACCOMMODATION
CHAPTER I
ASSURED TENANCIES
Meaning of assured tenancy etc.

Assured tenancies

1.–(1) A tenancy under which a dwelling-house is let as a separate dwelling is for the purposes of this Act an assured tenancy if and so long as–

   (*a*)   the tenant or, as the case may be, each of the joint tenants is an individual; and

   (*b*)   the tenant or, as the case may be, at least one of the joint tenants occupies the dwelling-house as his only or principal home; and

   (*c*)   the tenancy is not one which, by virtue of subsection (2) or subsection (6) below, cannot be an assured tenancy.

(2) Subject to subsection (3) below, if and so long as a tenancy falls within any paragraph in Part I of Schedule 1 to this Act, it cannot be an assured tenancy; and in that Schedule–

   (*a*)   'tenancy' means a tenancy under which a dwelling-house is let as a separate dwelling;

   (*b*)   Part II has effect for determining the rateable value of a dwelling-house for the purposes of Part I; and

   (*c*)   Part III has effect for supplementing paragraph 10 in Part I.

[(2A)] The Secretary of State may by order replace any amount referred to in paragraphs 2 and 3A of Schedule 1 to this Act by such amount as is specified in the order; and such an order shall be made by statutory instrument which shall be subject to annulment in pursuance of a resolution of either House of Parliament.]

(3) Except as provided in Chapter V below, at the commencement of this Act, a tenancy–

   (*a*)   under which a dwelling-house was then let as a separate dwelling, and (*b*)   which immediately before that commencement was an assured tenancy for the purposes of sections 56 to 58 of the Housing Act 1980 (tenancies granted by approved bodies),

shall become an assured tenancy for the purposes of this Act.

(4) In relation to an assured tenancy falling within subsection (3) above–

(*a*)   Part I of Schedule 1 to this Act shall have effect subject to subsection (5) below as if it consisted only of paragraphs 11 and 12; and

(*b*)   sections 56 to 58 of the Housing Act 1980 (and Schedule 5 to that Act) shall not apply after the commencement of this Act.

(5) In any case where–

(*a*)   immediately before the commencement of this Act the landlord under a tenancy is a fully mutual housing association, and

(*b*)   at the commencement of this Act the tenancy becomes an assured tenancy by virtue of subsection (3) above,

then, so long as that association remains the landlord under that tenancy (and under any statutory periodic tenancy which arises on the coming to an end of that tenancy), paragraph 12 of Schedule 1 to this Act shall have effect in relation to that tenancy with the omission of sub-paragraph (1)(*h*).

(6) [repealed]

(7) [repealed]

Letting of a dwelling-house together with other land

2.–(1) If, under a tenancy, a dwelling-house is let together with other land then, for the purposes of this Part of this Act,–

(*a*)   if and so long as the main purpose of the letting is the provision of a home for the tenant or, where there are joint tenants, at least one of them, the other land shall be treated as part of the dwelling-house; and

(*b*)   if and so long as the main purpose of the letting is not as mentioned in paragraph (a) above, the tenancy shall be treated as not being one under which a dwelling-house is let as a separate dwelling.

(2) Nothing in subsection (1) above affects any question whether a tenancy is precluded from being an assured tenancy by virtue of any provision of Schedule 1 to this Act.

Tenant sharing accommodation with persons other than landlord

3.–(1) Where a tenant has the exclusive occupation of any accommodation (in this section referred to as 'the separate accommodation') and–

(*a*) the terms as between the tenant and his landlord on which he holds the separate accommodation include the use of other accommodation (in this section referred to as 'the share accommodation') in common with another person or other persons, not being or including the landlord, and

(*b*) by reason only of the circumstances mentioned in paragraph (a) above, the separate accommodation would not, apart from this section, be a dwelling-house let on an assured tenancy,

the separate accommodation shall be deemed to be a dwelling-house let on an assured tenancy and the following provisions of this section shall have effect.

(2) For the avoidance of doubt it is hereby declared that where, for the purpose of determining the rateable value of the separate accommodation, it is necessary to make an apportionment under Part II of Schedule 1 to this Act, regard is to be had to the circumstances mentioned in subsection (1)(a) above.

(3) While the tenant is in possession of the separate accommodation, any term of the tenancy terminating or modifying, or providing for the termination or modification of, his right to the use of any of the shared accommodation which is living accommodation shall be of no effect.

(4) Where the terms of the tenancy are such that, at any time during the tenancy, the persons in common with whom the tenant is entitled to the use of the shared accommodation could be varied or their number could be increased, nothing in subsection (3) above shall prevent those terms from having effect so far as they relate to any such variation or increase.

(5) In this section 'living accommodation' means accommodation of such a nature that the fact that it constitutes or is included in the shared accommodation is sufficient, apart from this section, to prevent the tenancy from constituting an assured tenancy of a dwelling-house.

Certain sublettings not to exclude any part of sub-lessor's premises from assured tenancy

4.–(1) Where the tenant of a dwelling-house has sub-let a part but not the whole of the dwelling-house, then, as against his landlord or any superior landlord, no part of the dwelling-house shall be treated as excluded from being a dwelling-house let on an assured tenancy by reason only that the terms on which any person claiming under the tenant holds any part of the dwelling-house include the use of accommodation in common with other persons. (2) Nothing in this section affects the rights against, and liabilities to, each other of the tenant and any person claiming under him, or of any two such persons.

Security of tenure

Security of tenure

5.–(1) An assured tenancy cannot be brought to an end by the landlord except by obtaining an order of the court in accordance with the following provisions of this Chapter or Chapter II below or, in the case of a fixed term tenancy which contains power for the landlord to determine the tenancy in certain circumstances, by the exercise of that power and, accordingly, the service by the landlord of a notice to quit shall be of no effect in relation to a periodic assured tenancy.

(2) If an assured tenancy which is a fixed term tenancy comes to an end otherwise than by virtue of–

(*a*)   an order of the court, or

(*b*)   a surrender or other action on the part of the tenant,

then, subject to section 7 and Chapter II below, the tenant shall be entitled to remain in possession of the dwelling-house let under that tenancy and, subject to subsection (4) below, his right to possession shall depend upon a periodic tenancy arising by virtue of this section.

(3)   The periodic tenancy referred to in subsection (2) above is one–

(*a*)   taking effect in possession immediately on the coming to an end of the fixed term tenancy;

(*b*)   deemed to have been granted by the person who was the landlord under the fixed term tenancy immediately before it came to an end to the person who was then the tenant under that tenancy;

(*c*)   under which the premises which are let are the same dwelling-house as was let under the fixed term tenancy;

(*d*)   under which the periods of the tenancy are the same as those for which rent was last payable under the fixed term tenancy; and

(*e*)   under which, subject to the following provisions of this Part of this Act, the other terms are the same as those of the fixed term tenancy immediately before it came to an end, except that any term which makes provision for determination by the landlord or the tenant shall not have effect while the tenancy remains an assured tenancy.

(4) The periodic tenancy referred to in subsection (2) above shall not arise if, on the coming to an end of the fixed term tenancy,the tenant is entitled, by virtue of the grant of another tenancy, to possession of the same or substantially the same dwelling-house as was let to him under the fixed term tenancy.

(5) If, on or before the date on which a tenancy is entered into or is deemed to have been granted as mentioned in subsection (3)(b) above, the person who is to be the tenant under that tenancy–

(*a*)   enters into an obligation to do any act which (apart from this sub-section) will cause the tenancy to come to an end at a time when it is an assured tenancy, or

(*b*)   executes, signs or gives any surrender, notice to quit or other document which (apart from this subsection) has the effect of bringing the tenancy to an end at a time when it is an assured tenancy,

the obligation referred to in paragraph (*a*) above shall not be enforceable or, as the case may be, the surrender, notice to quit or other document referred to in paragraph (*b*) above shall be of no effect.

(6) If, by virtue of any provision of this Part of this Act, Part I of Schedule 1 to this Act has effect in relation to a fixed term tenancy as if it consisted only of paragraphs 11 and 12, that Part shall have the like effect in relation to any periodic tenancy which arises by virtue of this section on the coming to an end of the fixed term tenancy.

(7) Any reference in this Part of this Act to a statutory periodic tenancy is a reference to a periodic tenancy arising by virtue of this section.

Fixing of terms of statutory period tenancy

6.–(1) In this section, in relation to a statutory periodic tenancy,–

(a) 'the former tenancy' means the fixed term tenancy on the coming to an end of which the statutory periodic tenancy arises; and

(b) 'the implied terms' means the terms of the tenancy which have effect by virtue of section 5(3)(e) above, other than terms as to the amount of the rent;

but nothing in the following provisions of this section applies to a statutory periodic tenancy at a time when, by virtue of paragraph 11 or paragraph 12 in Part I of Schedule 1 to this Act, it cannot be an assured tenancy.

(2) Not later than the first anniversary of the day on which the former tenancy came to an end, the landlord may serve on the tenant, or the tenant may serve on the landlord, a notice in the prescribed form proposing terms of the statutory periodic tenancy different from the implied terms and, if the landlord or the tenant considers it appropriate, proposing an adjustment of the amount of the rent to take account of the proposed terms.

(3) Where a notice has been served under subsection (2) above,–

(a) within the period of three months beginning on the date on which the notice was served on him, the landlord or the tenant, as the case may be, may, by an application in the prescribed form, refer the notice to a rent assessment committee under subsection (4) below;

and

(b) if the notice is not so referred, then, with effect from such date, not falling within the period referred to in paragraph (a) above, as may be specified in the notice, the terms proposed in the notice shall become terms of the tenancy in substitution for any of the implied terms dealing with the same subject matter and the amount of the rent shall be varied in accordance with any adjustment so proposed.

(4) Where a notice under subsection (2) above is referred to a rent assessment committee, the committee shall consider the terms proposed in the notice and shall determine whether those terms, or some other terms (dealing with the same subject matter as the proposed terms), are such as, in the committee's opinion, might reasonably be expected to be found in an assured periodic tenancy of the dwelling-house concerned, being a tenancy–

(a) which begins on the coming to an end of the former tenancy; and

(b) which is granted by a willing landlord on terms which, except in so far as they relate to the subject matter of the proposed terms, are those of the statutory periodic tenancy at the time of the committee's consideration.

(5) Whether or not a notice under subsection (2) above proposes an adjustment of the amount of the rent under the statutory periodic tenancy, where a rent assessment committee determine any terms under sub-section (4) above, they shall, if they consider it appropriate, specify such an adjustment to take account of the terms so determined.

(6) In making a determination under subsection (4) above, or specifying an adjustment of an amount of rent under subsection (5) above, there shall be disregarded any effect on the terms or the amount of the rent attributable to granting of a tenancy to a sitting tenant.

(7) Where a notice under subsection (2) above is referred to a rent assessment committee, then, unless the landlord and the tenant otherwise agree, with effect from such date as the committee may direct–

(*a*)   the terms determined by the committee shall become terms of the statutory periodic tenancy in substitution for any of the implied terms dealing with the same subject matter; and

(*b*)   the amount of the rent under the statutory periodic tenancy shall be altered to accord with any adjustment specified by the committee;

but for the purposes of paragraph (*b*) above the committee shall not direct a date earlier than the date specified, in accordance with subsection (3)(*b*) above, in the notice referred to them.

(8) Nothing in this section requires a rent assessment committee to continue with a determination under subsection (4) above if the landlord and tenant give notice in writing that they no longer require such a determination or if the tenancy has come to an end.

Orders for possession

7.–(1) The court shall not make an order for possession of a dwelling-house let on an assured tenancy except on one or more of the grounds set out in Schedule 2 to this Act; but nothing in this Part of this Act relates to proceedings for possession of such a dwelling-house which are brought by a mortgagee, within the meaning of the Law of Property Act 1925, who has lent money on the security of the assured tenancy.

(2) The following provisions of this section have effect, subject to section 8 below, in relation to proceedings for the recovery of possession of a dwelling-house let on an assured tenancy.

(3) If the court is satisfied that any of the grounds in Part I of Schedule 2 to this Act is established then, subject to [subsections (5A) and (6)] below, the court shall make an order for possession.

(4) If the court is satisfied that any of the grounds in Part II of Schedule 2 to this Act is established, then, subject to [subsections (5A) and (6)] below, the court may make an order for possession if it considers it reasonable to do so.

(5) Part III of Schedule 2 to this Act shall have effect for supplementing Ground 9 in that Schedule and Part IV of that Schedule shall have effect in relation to notices given as mentioned in Grounds 1 to 5 of that Schedule.

[(5A) The court shall not make an order for possession of a dwelling-house let on an assured periodic tenancy arising under Schedule 10 to the Local Government and Housing Act 1989 on any of the following grounds, that is to say,–

(a)   Grounds 1, 2 and 5 in Part I of Schedule 2 to this Act;

(b)   Ground 16 in Part II of that Schedule; and

(c)   if the assured periodic tenancy arose on the termination of a former 1954 Act tenancy, within the meaning of the said Schedule 10, Ground 6 in Part I of Schedule 2 to this Act.]

(6) The court shall not make an order for possession of a dwelling-house to take effect at a time when it is let on an assured fixed term tenancy unless–

(a)   the ground for possession is Ground 2 or Ground 8 in Part I of Schedule 2 to this Act or any of the grounds in Part II of that Schedule, other than Ground 9 or Ground 16; and

(b)   the terms of the tenancy make provision for it to be brought to an end on the ground in question (whether that provision takes the form of a provision for re-entry, for forfeiture, for determination by notice or otherwise).

(7) Subject to the preceding provisions of this section, the court may make an order for possession of a dwelling-house on grounds relating to a fixed term tenancy which has come to an end; and where an order is made in such circumstances, any statutory periodic tenancy which has arisen on the ending of the fixed term tenancy shall end (without any notice and regardless of the period) on the day on which the order takes effect.

Notice of proceedings for possession

8.–(1) The court shall not entertain proceedings for possession of a dwelling-house let on an assured tenancy unless–

(a)   the landlord or, in the case of joint landlords, at least one of them has served on the tenant a notice in accordance with this section and the proceedings are begun within the time limits stated in the notice in accordance with [subsections (3) to (4B) below]; or

(b)   the court considers it just and equitable to dispense with the requirement of such a notice.

(2) The court shall not make an order for possession on any of the grounds in Schedule 2 to this Act unless that ground and particulars of it are specified in the notice under this section; but the grounds specified in such a notice may be altered or added to with the leave of the court.

(3) A notice under this section is one in the prescribed form informing the tenant that–

(a)   the landlord intends to begin proceedings for possession of the dwelling-house on one or more of the grounds specified in the notice; and

(b)   those proceedings will not begin earlier than a date specified in the notice [in accordance with subsections (4) to (4B) below]; and

(c)   those proceedings will not begin later than twelve months from the date of service of the notice.

(4) If a notice under this section specifies in accordance with subsection (3)(a) above Ground 14 in Schedule 2 to this Act (whether with or without other grounds), the date specified in the notice as mentioned in subsection (3)(b) above shall not be earlier than the date of the service of the notice.

[(4A) If a notice under this section specifies in accordance with subsection (3)(a) above, any of Grounds 1, 2, 5 to 7, 9 and 16 in Schedule 2 to this Act (whether without other grounds or with any ground other than Ground 14),the date specified in the notice as mentioned in subsection (3)(b) above shall not be earlier than–

(a)   two months from the date of service of the notice; and

(b)   if the tenancy is a periodic tenancy, the earliest date on which, apart from section 5(1) above, the tenancy could be brought to an end by a notice to quit given by the landlord on the same date as the date of service of the notice under this section.

(4B) In any other case, the date specified in the notice as mentioned in subsection (3)(b) above shall not be earlier than the expiry of the period of two weeks from the date of the service of the notice.]

(5) The court may not exercise the power conferred by subsection (1) (b) above if the landlord seeks to recover possession on Ground 8 in Schedule 2 to this Act.

(6) Where a notice under this section–

(a)   is served at a time when the dwelling-house is let on a fixed term tenancy, or

(b)   is served after a fixed term tenancy has come to an end but relates (in whole or in part) to events occurring during that tenancy,

the notice shall have effect notwithstanding that the tenant becomes or has become tenant under a statutory periodic tenancy arising on the coming to an end of the fixed term tenancy.

Additional notice requirements: ground of domestic violence

[**8A.**–(1) Where the ground specified in a notice under section 8 (whether with or without other grounds) is Ground 14A in Schedule 2 to this Act and the partner who has left the dwelling-house as mentioned in that ground is not a tenant of the dwelling-house, the court shall not entertain proceedings for possession of the dwelling-house unless–

(a)   the landlord or, in the case of joint landlords, at least one of them has served on the partner who has left a copy of the notice or has taken all reasonable steps to serve a copy of the notice on that partner, or

(b)   the court considers it just and equitable to dispense with such requirements as to service.

(2) Where Ground 14A in Schedule 2 to this Act is added to a notice under section 8 with leave of the court after proceedings for possession are begun and the partner who has left the dwelling-house as mentioned in that ground is not a party to the proceedings, the court shall not continue to entertain the proceedings unless–

(a)   the landlord or, in the case of joint landlords, at least one of them has served a notice under subsection (3) below on the partner who has left or has taken all reasonable steps to serve such a notice on that partner, or

(b)   the court considers it just and equitable to dispense with the requirement of such a notice.

(3) A notice under this subsection shall–

(a)   state that proceedings for the possession of the dwelling-house have begun,

(b)   specify the ground or grounds on which possession is being sought, and

(c)   give particulars of the ground or grounds.]

Extended discretion of court in possession claims

9.–(1) Subject to subsection (6) below, the court may adjourn for such period or periods as it thinks fit proceedings for possession of a dwelling-house let on an assured tenancy.

(2) On the making of an order for possession of a dwelling-house let on an assured tenancy or at any time before the execution of such an order, the court, subject to subsection (6) below, may–

(a)   stay or suspend execution of the order, or

(b)   postpone the date of possession,

for such period or periods as the court thinks just.

(3) On any such adjournment as is referred to in subsection (1) above or on any such stay, suspension or postponement as is referred to in subsection (2) above, the court, unless it considers that to do so would cause exceptional hardship to the tenant or would otherwise be unreasonable, shall impose conditions with regard to payment by the tenant of arrears of rent (if any) and rent or payments in respect of occupation after the termination of the tenancy (*mesne* profits) and may impose such other conditions as it thinks fit.

(4) If any such conditions as are referred to in subsection (3) above are complied with, the court may, if it thinks fit, discharge or rescind any such order as is referred to in subsection (2) above.

(5) In any case where–

(a)   at a time when proceedings are brought for possession of a dwelling-house let on an assured tenancy, the tenant's spouse or former spouse, having [matrimonial home rights under Part VI of the Family Law Act 1996] is in occupation of the dwelling-house, and

(b)   the assured tenancy is terminated as a result of those proceedings, the spouse or former spouse, so long as he or she remains in occupation, shall have the same rights in relation to, or in connection with, any such adjournment as is referred to in subsection (1) above or any such stay, suspension or postponement as is referred to in subsection (2) above, as he or she would have if [those matrimonial home rights] were not affected by the termination of the tenancy.

(5A) In any case where–

(a)   at a time when proceedings are brought for possession of a dwelling-house let on an assured tenancy–

    (i)   an order is in force under s.35 of the Family Law Act 1996 conferring rights on a former spouse of the tenant, or

    (ii) an order is in force under s.36 of that Act conferring rights on a cohabitant or former cohabitant (within the meaning of that Act) of the tenant,

(b)   that cohabitant, former cohabitant or former spouse is then in occupation of the dwelling-house, and

(c)   the assured tenancy is terminated as a result of those proceedings,

the cohabitant, former cohabitant or former spouse shall have the same rights in relation to, or in connection with, any such adjournment as is referred to in subsection (1) above or any such stay, suspension or postponement as is referred to in subsection (2) above as he or she would have if the rights conferred by the order referred to in paragraph (a) above were not affected by the termination of the tenancy.]

(6) This section does not apply if the court is satisfied that the landlord is entitled to possession of the dwelling-house–

(*a*)   on any of the grounds in Part I of Schedule 2 to this Act; or

(*b*)   by virtue of subsection (1) or subsection (4) of section 31 below.

Special provisions applicable to shared accommodation

10.–(1) This section applies in a case falling within subsection (1) of section 3 above and expressions used in this section have the same meaning as in that section.

(2) Without prejudice to the enforcement of any order made under subsection (3) below, while the tenant is in possession of the separate accommodation, no order shall be made for possession of any of the shared accommodation, whether on the application of the immediate landlord of the tenant or on the application of any person under whom that landlord derives title, unless a like order has been made, or is made at the same time, in respect of the separate accommodation; and the provisions of section 6 above shall have effect accordingly.

(3) On the application of the landlord, the court may make such order as it thinks just either–

(*a*) terminating the right of the tenant to use the whole or any part of the shared accommodation other than living accommodation; or

(*b*) modifying his right to use the whole or any part of the shared accommodation, whether by varying the persons or increasing the number of persons entitled to the use of that accommodation or otherwise.

(4) No order shall be made under subsection (3) above so as to effect any termination or modification of the rights of the tenant which, apart from section 3(3) above, could not be effected by or under the terms of the tenancy.

Payment of removal expenses in certain cases

11.–(1) Where a court makes an order for possessing of a dwelling-house let on an assured tenancy on Ground 6 or Ground 9 in Schedule 2 to this Act (but not on any other ground), the landlord shall pay to the tenant a sum equal to the reasonable expenses likely to be incurred by the tenant in removing from the dwelling-house.

(2) Any question as to the amount of the sum referred in subsection (1) above shall be determined by agreement between the landlord and the tenant or, in default of agreement, by the court.

(3) Any sum payable to a tenant by virtue of this section shall be recoverable as a civil debt due from the landlord.

Compensation for misrepresentation or concealment

12. Where a landlord obtains an order for possession of a dwelling-house let on an assured tenancy on one or more of the grounds in Schedule 2 to this Act and it is subsequently made to appear to the court that the order was obtained by misrepresentation or concealment of material facts, the court may order the landlord to pay to the former tenant such sum as appears sufficient as compensation for damage or loss sustained by that tenant as a result of the order.

Rent and other terms

Increase of rent under assured periodic tenancies

13.–(1) This section applies to–

(*a*) a statutory periodic tenancy other than one which, by virtue of paragraph 11 or paragraph 12 in Part I of Schedule I to this Act, cannot for the time being be an assured tenancy; and

(b)   any other periodic tenancy which is an assured tenancy, other than one in relation to which there is a provision, for the time being binding on the tenant, under which the rent for a particular period of the tenancy will or may be greater than the rent for an earlier period.

(2) For the purpose of securing an increase in the rent under a tenancy to which this section applies, the landlord may serve on the tenant a notice in the prescribed form proposing a new rent to take effect at the beginning of a new period of the tenancy specified in the notice, being a period beginning not earlier than–

(a)   the minimum period after the date of the service of the notice; and

(b)   except in the case of a statutory periodic tenancy, the first anniversary of the date on which the first period of the tenancy began; and

(c)   if the rent under the tenancy has previously been increased by virtue of a notice under this subsection or a determination under section 14 below, the first anniversary of the date on which the increased rent took effect.

(3) The minimum period referred to in subsection (2) above is–

(a)   in the case of a yearly tenancy, six months;

(b)   in the case of a tenancy where the period is less than a month, one month; and

(c)   in any other case, a period equal to the period of the tenancy.

(4) Where a notice is served under subsection (2) above, a new rent specified in the notice shall take effect as mentioned in the notice unless, before the beginning of the new period specified in the notice,–

(a)   the tenant by an application in the prescribed form refers the notice to a rent assessment committee; or

(b)   the landlord and the tenant agree on a variation of the rent which is different from that proposed in the notice or agree that the rent should not be varied.

(5) Nothing in this section (or in section 14 below) affects the right of the landlord and the tenant under an assured tenancy to vary by agreement any term of the tenancy (including a term relating to rent).

Determination of rent by rent assessment committee

14.–(1) Where, under subsection (4)(a) of section 13 above, a tenant refers to a rent assessment committee a notice under subsection (2) of that section, the committee shall determine the rent at which, subject to subsections (2) and (4) below, the committee consider that the dwelling-house concerned might reasonably be expected to be let in the open market by a willing landlord under an assured tenancy–

 (a) which is a periodic tenancy having the same periods as those of the tenancy to which the notice relates;

 (b) which begins at the beginning of the new period specified in the notice;

 (c) the terms of which (other than relating to the amount of the rent) are the same as those of the tenancy to which the notice relates; and

 (d) in respect of which the same notices, if any, have been given under any of Grounds 1 to 5 of Schedule 2 to this Act, as have been given (or have effect as if given) in relation to the tenancy to which the notice relates.

(2) In making a determination under this section, there shall be disregarded–

 (a) any effect on the rent attributable to the granting of a tenancy to sitting tenant;

 (b) any increase in the value of the dwelling-house attributable to a relevant improvement carried out by a person who at the time it was carried out was the tenant, if the improvement–

  (i) was carried out otherwise than in pursuance of an obligation to his immediate landlord, or

  (ii) was carried out pursuant to an obligation to his immediate landlord being an obligation which did not relate to the specific improvement concerned but arose by reference to consent given to the carrying out of that improvement; and

 (c) any reduction in the value of the dwelling-house attributable to a failure by the tenant to comply with any terms of the tenancy.

(3) For the purposes of subsection (2)(b) above, in relation to a notice which is referred by a tenant as mentioned in subsection (1) above, an improvement is a relevant improvement if either it was carried out during the tenancy to which the notice relates or the following conditions are satisfied, namely–

(*a*) that it was carried out not more than twenty-one years before the date of service of the notice; and

(*b*) that, at all times during the period beginning when the improvement was carried out and ending on the date of service of the notice, the dwelling-house has been let under an assured tenancy; and

(*c*) that, on the coming to an end of an assured tenancy at any time during that period, the tenant (or, in the case of joint tenants, at least one of them) did not quit.

[(3A) In making a determination under this section in any case where under Part I of the Local Government Finance Act 1992 the landlord or a superior landlord is liable to pay council tax in respect of a hereditament ('the relevant hereditament') of which the dwelling-house forms part, the rent assessment committee shall have regard to the amount of council tax which, as at the date on which the notice under section 13(2) above was served, was set by the billing authority–

(*a*) for the financial year in which that notice was served, and

(*b*) for the category of dwellings within which the relevant hereditament fell on that date,

but any discount or other reduction affecting the amount of council tax payable shall be disregarded.

(3B) In subsection (3A) above–

(*a*) 'hereditament' means a dwelling within the meaning of Part I of the Local Government Finance Act 1992,

(*b*) 'billing authority' has the same meaning as in that Part of that Act, and

(*c*) 'category of dwellings' has the same meaning as in section 30(1) and (2) of that Act.]

(4) In this section 'rent' does not include any service charge, within the meaning of section 18 of the Landlord and Tenant Act 1985, but, subject to that, includes any sums payable by the tenant to the landlord on account of the use of furniture [in respect of council tax] or for any of the matters referred to in subsection (1)(*a*) of that section, whether or not those sums are separate from the sums payable for the occupation of the dwelling-house concerned or are payable under separate agreements.

(5) Where any rates in respect of the dwelling-house concerned are borne by the landlord or a superior landlord, the rent assessment committee shall make their determination under this section as if the rates were not so borne.

(6) In any case where–

(a)   a rent assessment committee have before them at the same time the reference of a notice under section 6(2) above relating to a tenancy (in this subsection referred to as 'the section 6 reference') and the reference of a notice under section 13(2) above relating to the same tenancy (in this subsection referred to as 'the section 13 reference'), and

(b)   the date specified in the notice under section 6(2) above is not later than the first day of the new period specified in the notice under section 13(2) above, and

(c)   the committee propose to hear the two references together, the committee shall make a determination in relation to the section 6 reference before making their determination in relation to the section 13 reference and, accordingly, in such a case the reference in subsection (1)(c) above to the terms of the tenancy to which the notice relates shall be construed as a reference to those terms as varied by virtue of the determination made in relation to the section 6 reference.

(7) Where a notice under section 13(2) above has been referred to a rent assessment committee, then, unless the landlord and the tenant otherwise agree, the rent determined by the committee (subject, in a case where subsection (5) above applies, to the addition of the appropriate amount in respect of rates) shall be the rent under the tenancy with effect from the beginning of the new period specified in the notice or, if it appears to the rent assessment committee that that would cause undue hardship to the tenant, with effect from such later date (not being later than the date the rent is determined) as the committee may direct.

(8) Nothing in this section requires a rent assessment committee to continue with their determination of a rent for a dwelling-house if the landlord and tenant give notice in writing that they no longer require such a determination or if the tenancy has come to an end.

[(9) This section shall apply in relation to an assured shorthold tenancy as if in subsection (1) the reference to an assured tenancy were a reference to an assured shorthold tenancy.]

[Interim increase before April 1, 1994 of rent under assured periodic tenancies in certain cases where landlord liable for council tax

14A.– In any case where–

(a)   under Part I of the Local Government Finance Act 1992 the landlord of a dwelling-house let under an assured tenancy

to which section 13 above applies or a superior landlord is
liable to pay council tax in respect of a dwelling (within the
meaning of that Part of that Act) which includes that
dwelling-house,

(*b*)   under the terms of the tenancy (or an agreement collateral
to the tenancy) the tenant is liable to make payments to the
landlord in respect of council tax,

(*c*)   the case falls within subsection (2) or subsection (3) below,
and

(*d*)   no previous notice under this subsection has been served in
relation to the dwelling-house,

the landlord may serve on the tenant a notice in the prescribed
form proposing an increased rent to take account of the tenant's
liability to make payments to the landlord in respect of council tax,
such increased rent to take effect at the beginning of a new period
of the tenancy specified in the notice being a period beginning not
earlier than one month after the date on which the notice was
served.

(2) The case falls within this subsection if–

(*a*)   the rent under the tenancy has previously been increased by
virtue of a notice under section 13(2) above or a
determination under section 14 above, and

(*b*)   the first anniversary of the date on which the increased rent
took effect has not yet occurred.

(3) The case falls within this subsection if a notice has been
served under section 13(2) above before April 1, 1993 but no
increased rent has taken effect before that date.

(4) No notice may be served under subsection (1) above after
March 31, 1994.

(5) Where a notice is served under subsection (1) above, the new
rent specified in the notice shall take effect as mentioned in the
notice unless, before the beginning of the new period specified in
the notice–

(*a*)   the tenant by an application in the prescribed form refers
the notice to a rent assessment committee, or

(*b*)   the landlord and the tenant agree on a variation of the rent
which is different from that proposed in the notice or agree
that the rent should not be varied.

(6) Nothing in this section (or in section 14B below) affects the
right of the landlord and the tenant under an assured tenancy to
vary by agreement any term of the tenancy (including a term
relating to rent).

Interim determination of rent by rent assessment committee

14B.–(1) Where, under subsection (5)(a) of section 14A above, a tenant refers to a rent assessment committee a notice under subsection (1) of that section, the committee shall determine the amount by which, having regard to the provisions of section 14(3A) above, the existing rent might reasonably be increased to take account of the tenant's liability to make payments to the landlord in respect of council tax.

(2) Where a notice under section 14A(1) above has been referred to a rent assessment committee, then, unless the landlord and the tenant otherwise agree, the existing rent shall be increased by the amount determined by the committee with effect from the beginning of the new period specified in the notice or, if it appears to the committee that that would cause undue hardship to the tenant, with effect from such later date (not being later than the date the increase is determined) as the committee may direct.

(3) In any case where–

(a)   a rent assessment committee have before them at the same time the reference of a notice under section 13(2) above relating to a tenancy (in this subsection referred to as 'the section 13 reference') and the reference of a notice under section 14A()1) above relating to the same tenancy (in this subsection referred to as 'the section 14A reference'); and

(b)   the committee propose to hear the two references together, the committee shall make a determination in relation to the section 13 reference before making their determination in relation to the section 14A reference, and if in such a case the date specified in the notice under section 13(2) above is later than the date specified in the notice under section 14A(1) above, the rent determined under the section 14A reference shall not take effect until the date specified in the notice under section 13(2).

(4) In this section 'rent' has the same meaning as in section 14 above; and section 14(4) above applies to a determination under this section as it applies to a determination under that section.]

Limited prohibition on assignment etc. without consent

15.–(1) Subject to subsection (3) below, it shall be an implied term of every assured tenancy which is a periodic tenancy that, except with the consent of the landlord, the tenant shall not–

(a)   assign the tenancy (in whole or in part); or

(b)   sub-let or part with possession of the whole or any part of the dwelling-house let on the tenancy.

(2) Section 19 of the Landlord and Tenant Act 1927 (consents to assign not to be unreasonably withheld etc.) shall not apply to a term which is implied into an assured tenancy by subsection (1) above.

(3) In the case of a periodic tenancy which is not a statutory periodic tenancy [or an assured periodic tenancy arising under Schedule 10 to the Local Government and Housing Act 1989]2 subsection (1) above does not apply if–

(a)   there is a provision (whether contained in the tenancy or not) under which the tenant is prohibited (whether absolutely or conditionally) from assigning or sub-letting or parting with possession or is permitted (whether absolutely or conditionally) to assign, sub-let or part with possession; or

(b)   a premium is required to be paid on the grant or renewal of the tenancy.

(4) In subsection (3)(b) above 'premium' includes–

(a)   any fine or other like sum;

(b)   any other pecuniary consideration in addition to rent; and

(c)   any sum paid by way of deposit, other than one which does not exceed one-sixth of the annual rent payable under the tenancy immediately after the grant or renewal in question.

Access for repairs

16. It shall be an implied term of every assured tenancy that the tenant shall afford to the landlord access to the dwelling-house let on the tenancy and all reasonable facilities for executing therein any repairs which the landlord is entitled to execute.

Miscellaneous

Succession to assured periodic tenancy by spouse

17.–(1) In any case where–

(a)   the sole tenant under an assured periodic tenancy dies, and

(b)   immediately before the death, the tenant's spouse was occupying the dwelling-house as his or her only or principal home, and

(c)   the tenant was not himself a successor, as defined in subsection (2) or subsection (3) below,

then, on the death, the tenancy vests by virtue of this section in the spouse (and, accordingly, does not devolve under the tenant's will or intestacy).

(2) For the purposes of this section, a tenant is a successor in relation to a tenancy if–

(a)   a tenancy became vested in him either by virtue of this section or under the will or intestacy of a previous tenant; or

(b)   at some time before the tenant's death the tenancy was a joint tenancy held by himself and one or more other persons and, prior to his death, he became the sole tenant by survivorship; or

(c)   he became entitled to the tenancy as mentioned in section 39(5) below.

(3) For the purposes of this section, a tenant is also a successor in relation to a tenancy (in this subsection referred to as 'the new tenancy') which was granted to him (alone or jointly with others) if–

(a)   at some time before the grant of the new tenancy, he was, by virtue of subsection (2) above, a successor in relation to an earlier tenancy of the same or substantially the same dwelling-house as is let under the new tenancy; and

(b)   at all times since he became such a successor he has been a tenant (alone or jointly with others) of the dwelling-house which is let under the new tenancy or of a dwelling-house which is substantially the same as that dwelling-house.

(4) For the purposes of this section, a person who was living with the tenant as his or her wife or husband shall be treated as the tenant's spouse.

(5) If, on the death of the tenant, there is, by virtue of subsection (4) above, more than one person who fulfils the condition in subsection (1)(b) above, such one of them as may be decided by agreement or, in default of agreement, by the county court shall be treated as the tenant's spouse for the purposes of this section.

Provisions as to reversions on assured tenancies

18.–(1) If at any time–

(a)   a dwelling-house is for the time being lawfully let on an assured tenancy, and

(b)   the landlord under the assured tenancy is himself a tenant under a superior tenancy; and

(c)   the superior tenancy comes to an end,

then, subject to subsection (2) below, the assured tenancy shall continue in existence as a tenancy held of the person whose interest would, apart from the continuance of the assured tenancy, entitle him to actual possession of the dwelling-house at that time.

(2) Subsection (1) above does not apply to an assured tenancy if the interest which, by virtue of that subsection, would become that of the landlord, is such that, by virtue of Schedule 1 to this Act, the tenancy could not be an assured tenancy.

(3) Where, by virtue of any provision of this Part of this Act, an assured tenancy which is a periodic tenancy (including a statutory periodic tenancy) continues beyond the beginning of a reversionary tenancy which was granted (whether before, on or after the commencement of this Act) so as to begin on or after–

(a)   the date on which the previous contractual assured tenancy came to an end, or

(b)   a date on which, apart from any provision of this Part, the periodic tenancy could have been brought to an end by the landlord by notice to quit,

the reversionary tenancy shall have effect as if it had been granted subject to the periodic tenancy.

(4) The reference in subsection (3) above to the previous contractual assured tenancy applies only where the periodic tenancy referred to in that subsection is a statutory periodic tenancy and is a reference to the fixed-term tenancy which immediately preceded the statutory periodic tenancy.

Restriction on levy of distress for rent

19.–(1) Subject to subsection (2) below, no distress for the rent of any dwelling-house let on an assured tenancy shall be levied except with the leave of the county court; and, with respect to any application for such leave, the court shall have the same powers with respect to adjournment, stay, suspension, postponement and otherwise as are conferred by section 9 above in relation to proceedings for possession of such a dwelling-house.

(2) Nothing in subsection (1) above applies to distress levied under section 102 of the County Courts Act 1984.

CHAPTER II
ASSURED SHORTHOLD TENANCIES

[Assured shorthold tenancies: post-Housing Act 1996 tenancies

19A. An assured tenancy which–

(a)   is entered into on or after the day on which section 96 of the

Housing Act 1996 comes into force (otherwise than pursuant to a contract made before that day), or

(b)   comes into being by virtue of section 5 above on the coming to an end of an assured tenancy within paragraph (a) above,

is an assured shorthold tenancy unless it falls within any paragraph in Schedule 2A to this Act.]

[Assured shorthold tenancies: pre-Housing Act 1996 tenancies

20.–(1) Subject to subsection (3) below, an assured tenancy which is not one to which section 19A above applies is an assured shorthold tenancy if–

(*a*)   it is a fixed term tenancy granted for a term certain of not less than six months,

(*b*)   there is no power for the landlord to determine the tenancy at any time earlier than six months from the beginning of the tenancy, and

(*c*)   a notice in respect of it is served as mentioned in subsection (2) below.]

(2) The notice referred to in subsection (1)(c) above is one which–

(*a*)   is in such form as may be prescribed;

(*b*)   is served before the assured tenancy is entered into;

(*c*)   is served by the person who is to be the landlord under the assured tenancy on the person who is to be the tenant under that tenancy;
and

(*d*)   states that the assured tenancy to which it relates is to be a shorthold tenancy.

(3) Notwithstanding anything in subsection (1) above, where–

(*a*)   immediately before a tenancy (in this subsection referred to as 'the new tenancy') is granted, the person to whom it is granted or, as the case may be, at least one of the persons to whom it is granted was a tenant under an assured tenancy which was not a shorthold tenancy, and

(*b*)   the new tenancy is granted by the person who, immediately before the beginning of the tenancy, was the landlord under the assured tenancy referred to in paragraph (a) above,

the new tenancy cannot be an assured shorthold tenancy.

(4) Subject to subsection (5) below, if, on the coming to an end of an assured shorthold tenancy (including a tenancy which was an assured shorthold but ceased to be assured before it came to an end), a new tenancy of the same or substantially the same premises

comes into being under which the landlord and the tenant are the same as at the coming to an end of the earlier tenancy, then, if and so long as the new tenancy is an assured tenancy, it shall be an assured shorthold tenancy, whether or not it fulfils the conditions in paragraphs (a) to (c) of subsection (1) above.

(5) Subsection (4) above does not apply if, before the new tenancy is entered into (or, in the case of a statutory periodic tenancy, takes effect in possession), the landlord serves notice on the tenant that the new tenancy is not to be a shorthold tenancy.

[(5A) Subsections (3) and (4) above do not apply where the new tenancy is one to which section 19A above applies.]

(6) In the case of joint landlords–

(a)   the reference in subsection (2)(c) above to the person who is to be the landlord is a reference to at least one of the persons who are to be joint landlords; and

(b)   the reference in subsection (5) above to the landlord is a reference to at least one of the joint landlords.

(7) [repealed]

[Post-Housing Act 1996 tenancies: duty of landlord to provide statement as to terms of tenancy

20A.–(1) Subject to subsection (3) below, a tenant under an assured shorthold tenancy to which section 19A above applies may, by notice in writing, require the landlord under that tenancy to provide him with a written statement of any term of the tenancy which–

(a)   falls within subsection (2) below, and

(b)   is not evidenced in writing.

(2) The following terms of a tenancy fall within this subsection, namely–

(a)   the date on which the tenancy began or, if it is a statutory periodic tenancy or a tenancy to which section 39(7) below applies, the date on which the tenancy came into being,

(b)   the rent payable under the tenancy and the dates on which that rent is payable,

(c)   any term providing for a review of the rent payable under the tenancy, and

(d)   in the case of a fixed term tenancy, the length of the fixed term.

(3) No notice may be given under subsection (1) above in relation to a term of the tenancy if–

(a)   the landlord under the tenancy has provided a statement of that term in response to an earlier notice under that subsection given by the tenant under the tenancy, and

(b)   the term has not been varied since the provision of the statement referred to in paragraph (a) above.

(4) A landlord who fails, without reasonable excuse, to comply with a notice under subsection (1) above within the period of 28 days beginning with the date on which he received the notice is liable on summary conviction to a fine not exceeding level 4 on the standard scale.

(5) A statement provided for the purposes of subsection (1) above shall not be regarded as conclusive evidence of what was agreed by the parties to the tenancy in question.

(6) Where–

(a)   a term of a statutory periodic tenancy is one which has effect by virtue of section 5(3)(e) above, or

(b)   a term of a tenancy to which subsection (7) of section 39 below applies is one which has effect by virtue of subsection (6)(e) of that section,

subsection (1) above shall have effect in relation to it as if paragraph (b) related to the term of the tenancy from which it derives.

(7) In subsections (1) and (3) above–

(a)   references to the tenant under the tenancy shall, in the case of joint tenants, be taken to be references to any of the tenants, and

(b)   references to the landlord under the tenancy shall, in the case of joint landlords, be taken to be references to any of the landlords.]

Recovery of possession on expiry or termination of assured shorthold tenancy

21.–(1) Without prejudice to any right of the landlord under an assured shorthold tenancy to recover possession of the dwelling-house let on the tenancy in accordance with Chapter I above, on or after the coming to an end of an assured shorthold tenancy which was fixed term tenancy, a court shall make an order for possession of the dwelling-house if it is satisfied–

(a)   that the assured shorthold tenancy has come to an end and no further assured tenancy (whether shorthold or not) is for the time being in existence, other than [an assured shorthold periodic tenancy (whether statutory or not)] and

(*b*)   the landlord or, in the case of joint landlords, at least one of
them has given to the tenant not less than two months'
notice [in writing] stating that he requires possession of the
dwelling-house.

(2) A notice under paragraph (b) of subsection (1) above may be
given before or on the day on which the tenancy comes to an end;
and that sub-section shall have effect notwithstanding that on the
coming to an end of the fixed term tenancy a statutory periodic
tenancy arises.

(3) Where a court makes an order for possession of a dwelling-
house by virtue of subsection (1) above, any statutory periodic
tenancy which has arisen on the coming to an end of the assured
shorthold tenancy shall end (without further notice and regardless
of the period) on the day on which the order takes effect.

(4) Without prejudice to any such right as is referred to in
subsection (1) above, a court shall make an order for possession of
a dwelling-house let on an assured shorthold tenancy which is a
periodic tenancy if the court is satisfied–

(*a*)   that the landlord or, in the case of joint landlords, at least
one of them has given to the tenant a notice [in writing]
stating that, after a date specified in the notice, being the
last day of a period of the tenancy and not earlier than two
months after the date the notice was given, possession of
the dwelling-house is required by virtue of this section; and

(*b*)   that the date specified in the notice under paragraph (a)
above is not earlier than the earliest day on which, apart
from section 5(1) above, the tenancy could be brought to an
end by a notice to quit given by the landlord on the same
date as the notice under paragraph (a) above.

[(5) Where an order for possession under subsection (1) or (4)
above is made in relation to a dwelling-house let on a tenancy to
which section 19A above applies, the order may not be made so as
to take effect earlier than–

(*a*)   in the case of a tenancy which is not a replacement tenancy,
six months after the beginning of the tenancy, and

(*b*)   in the case of a replacement tenancy, six months after the
beginning of the original tenancy.

(6) In subsection (5)(b) above, the reference to the original
tenancy is–

(*a*)   where the replacement tenancy came into being on the
coming to an end of a tenancy which was not a replacement
tenancy, to the immediately preceding tenancy, and

(b)   where there have been successive replacement tenancies, to the tenancy immediately preceding the first in the succession of replacement tenancies.

(7) For the purposes of this section, a replacement tenancy is a tenancy–

(a)   which comes into being on the coming to an end of an assured shorthold tenancy, and

(b)   under which, on its coming into being–

(i)   the landlord and tenant are the same as under the earlier tenancy as at its coming to an end, and

(ii)   the premises let are the same or substantially the same as those let under the earlier tenancy as at that time.]

Reference of excessive rents to rent assessment committee

22.–(1) Subject to section 23 and subsection (2) below, the tenant under an assured shorthold tenancy may make an application in the prescribed form to a rent assessment committee for a determination of the rent which, in the committee's opinion, the landlord might reasonably be expected to obtain under the assured shorthold tenancy.

(2) No application may be made under this section if–

(a)   the rent payable under the tenancy is a rent previously determined under this section;

[(aa) the tenancy is one to which section 19A above applies and more than six months have elapsed since the beginning of the tenancy or, in the case of a replacement tenancy, since the beginning of the original tenancy; or]

(b)   the tenancy is an assured shorthold tenancy falling within subsection (4) of section 20 above (and, accordingly, is one in respect of which notice need not have been served as mentioned in subsection (2) of that section).

(3) Where an application is made to a rent assessment committee under subsection (1) above with respect to the rent under an assured shorthold tenancy, the committee shall not make such a determination as is referred to in that subsection unless they consider–

(a)   that there is a sufficient number of similar dwelling-houses in the locality let on assured tenancies (whether shorthold or not); and

(b)   that the rent payable under the assured shorthold tenancy in question is significantly higher than the rent which the landlord might reasonably be expected to be able to obtain under the tenancy, having regard to the level of rents payable under the tenancies referred to in paragraph (a) above.

(4) Where, on an application under this section, a rent assessment committee make a determination of a rent for an assured shorthold tenancy–

(*a*)   the determination shall have effect from such date as the committee may direct, not being earlier than the date of the application;

(*b*)   if, at any time on or after the determination takes effect, the rent which, apart from this paragraph would be payable under the tenancy exceeds the rent so determined, the excess shall be irrecoverable from the tenant; and

(*c*)   no notice may be served under section 13(2) above with respect to a tenancy of the dwelling-house in question until after the first anniversary of the date on which the determination takes effect.

(5) Subsections (4), (5) and (8) of section 14 above apply in relation to a determination of rent under this section as they apply in relation to a determination under that section and, accordingly, where subsection (5) of that section applies, any reference in subsection (4)(b) above to rent is a reference to rent exclusive of the amount attributable to rates.

[(5A) Where–

(*a*)   an assured tenancy ceases to be an assured shorthold tenancy by virtue of falling within paragraph 2 of Schedule 2A to this Act, and

(*b*)   at the time when it so ceases to be an assured shorthold tenancy there is pending before a rent assessment committee an application in relation to it under this section,

the fact that it so ceases to be an assured shorthold tenancy shall, in relation to that application, be disregarded for the purposes of this section.

(6) In subsection (2)(aa) above, the references to the original tenancy and to a replacement tenancy shall be construed in accordance with subsections (6) and (7) respectively of section 21 above.]

Termination of rent assessment committee's functions

23.–(1) If the Secretary of State by order made by statutory instrument so provides, section 22 above shall not apply in such cases or to tenancies or dwelling-houses in such areas or in such other circumstances as may be specified in the order.

(2) An order under this section may contain such transitional, incidental and supplementary provisions as appear to the Secretary of State to be desirable.

(3) No order shall be made under this section unless a draft of the order has been laid before, and approved by a resolution of, each House of Parliament.

CHAPTER III
ASSURED AGRICULTURAL OCCUPANCIES

Assured agricultural occupancies

24.–(1) A tenancy or licence of a dwelling-house is for the purposes of this Part of this Act an 'assured agricultural occupancy' if–

- (*a*) it is of a description specified in subsection (2) below; and
- (*b*) by virtue of any provision of Schedule 3 to this Act the agricultural worker condition is for the time being fulfilled with respect to the dwelling-house subject to the tenancy or licence and is not an excepted tenancy.

(2) The following are the tenancies and licences referred to in subsection (1)(a) above–

- (*a*) an assured tenancy which is not an assured shorthold tenancy;
- (*b*) a tenancy which does not fall within paragraph (a) above by reason only of paragraph 3, 3A, 3B or paragraph 7 of Schedule 1 to this Act [or more than one of those paragraphs] [and is not an excepted tenancy]; and
- (*c*) a licence under which a person has the exclusive occupation of a dwelling-house as a separate dwelling and which, if it conferred a sufficient interest in land to be a tenancy, would be a tenancy falling within paragraph (a) or paragraph (b) above.

[(2A) For the purposes of subsection (2)(b) above, a tenancy is an excepted tenancy if it is–

- (*a*) a tenancy of an agricultural holding within the meaning of the Agricultural Holdings Act 1986 in relation to which that Act applies, or
- (*b*) a farm business tenancy within the meaning of the Agricultural Tenancies Act 1995.]

(3) For the purposes of Chapter I above and the following

provisions of this Chapter, every assured agricultural occupancy which is not an assured tenancy shall be treated as if it were such a tenancy and any reference to a tenant, a landlord or any other expression appropriate to a tenancy shall be construed accordingly; but the provisions of Chapter I above shall have effect in relation to every assured agricultural occupancy subject to the provisions of this Chapter.

(4) Section 14 above shall apply in relation to an assured agricultural occupancy as if in subsection (1) of that section the reference to an assured tenancy were a reference to an assured agricultural occupancy.

Security of tenure

25.–(1) If a statutory periodic tenancy arises on the coming to an end of an assured agricultural occupancy–

(a)   it shall be an assured agricultural occupancy as long as, by virtue of any provision of schedule 3 to this Act, the agricultural worker condition is for the time being fulfilled with respect to the dwelling-house in question; and

(b)   if no rent was payable under the assured agricultural occupancy which constitutes the fixed term tenancy referred to in subsection (2) of section 5 above, subsection (3)(d) of that section shall apply as if for the words 'the same as those for which rent was last payable under' there were substituted 'monthly beginning on the day following the coming to an end of.'

(2) In its application to an assured agricultural occupancy, Part II of Schedule 2 to this Act shall have effect with the omission of Ground 16.

(3) In its application to an assured agricultural occupancy, Part III of Schedule 2 to this Act shall have effect as if any reference in paragraph 2 to an assured tenancy included a reference to an assured agricultural occupancy.

(4) If the tenant under an assured agricultural occupancy gives notice to terminate his employment then, notwithstanding anything in any agreement or otherwise, that notice shall not constitute a notice to quit as respects the assured agricultural occupancy.

(5) Nothing in subsection (4) above affects the operation of an actual notice to quit given in respect of an assured agricultural occupancy.

Rehousing of agricultural workers etc.

26.–(1) In section 27 of the Rent (Agriculture) Act 1976 (rehousing: applications to housing authority)–
- (a) in subsection (1)(a) after 'statutory tenancy' there shall be inserted 'or an assured agricultural occupancy'; and
- (b) at the end of subsection (3) there shall be added 'and assured agricultural occupancy has the same meaning as in Chapter III of Part I of the Housing Act 1988.

CHAPTER V
PHASING OUT OF RENT ACTS AND OTHER TRADITIONAL PROVISIONS

New protected tenancies and agricultural occupancies restricted to special cases

34.–(1) A tenancy which is entered into on or after the commencement of this Act cannot be a protected tenancy, unless–
- (a) it is entered into in pursuance of a contract made before the commencement of this Act; or
- (b) it is granted to a person (alone or jointly with others) who, immediately before the tenancy was granted, was a protected or statutory tenant and is so granted by the person who at that time was the landlord (or one of the joint landlords) under the protected or statutory tenancy; or
- (c) it is granted to a person (alone or jointly with others) in the following circumstances–
  - (i) prior to the grant of the tenancy, an order for possession of a dwelling-house was made against him (alone or jointly with others) on the court being satisfied as mentioned in section 98(1)(a) of, or Case 1 in Schedule 16 to, the Rent Act 1977 or Case 1 in Schedule 4 to the Rent (Agriculture) Act 1976 (suitable alternative accommodation available); and
  - (ii) the tenancy is of the premises which constitute the suitable alternative accommodation as to which the court was so satisfied; and
  - (iii) in the proceedings for possession the court considered that, in the circumstances, the grant of an assured tenancy would not afford the required security and, accordingly, directed that the tenancy would be a protected tenancy; or
- (d) [it is a tenancy under which the interest of the landlord was

at the time the tenancy was granted held by a new town corporation, within the meaning of section 80 of the Housing Act 1985, and, before the date which has effect by virtue of paragraph (a) or paragraph (b) of subsection (4) of section 38 below, ceased to be so held by virtue of a disposal by the Commission for the New Towns made pursuant to a direction under section 37 of the New Towns Act 1981.]

(2) In subsection (1)(b) above 'protected tenant' and 'statutory tenant' do not include–

(*a*)   a tenant under a protected shorthold tenancy;

(*b*)   a protected or statutory tenant of a dwelling-house which was let under a protected shorthold tenancy which has ended before the commencement of this Act and in respect of which at that commencement either there has been no grant of a further tenancy or any grant of a further tenancy has been to the person who, immediately before the grant, was in possession of the dwelling-house as a protected or statutory tenant;

and in this subsection 'protected shorthold tenancy' includes a tenancy which, in proceedings for possession under Case 19 in Schedule 15 to the Rent Act 1977, is treated as a protected shorthold tenancy.

(3) In any case where–

(*a*)   by virtue of subsections (1) and (2) above, a tenancy entered into on or after the commencement of this Act is an assured tenancy, but

(*b*)   apart from subsection (2) above, the effect of subsection (1)(b) above would be that the tenancy would be a protected tenancy, and

(*c*)   the landlord and the tenant under the tenancy are the same as at the coming to an end of the protected or statutory tenancy which, apart from subsection (2) above, would fall within subsection (1)(b) above,

the tenancy shall be an assured shorthold tenancy (whether or not [in the case of a tenancy to which the provision applies] it fulfils the conditions in section 20(1) above) unless, before the tenancy is entered into, the landlord serves notice on the tenant that it is not to be a shorthold tenancy.

(4) A licence or a tenancy which is entered into on or after the commencement of this Act cannot be a relevant licence or relevant tenancy for the purposes of the Rent (Agriculture) Act 1976 (in this subsection referred to as 'the 1976 Act') unless–

(a) it is entered into in pursuance of a contract made before the commencement of this Act; or

(b) it is granted to a person (alone or jointly with others) who, immediately before the licence or tenancy was granted, was a protected occupier or statutory tenant, within the meaning of the 1976 Act, and is so granted by the person who at that time was the landlord or licensor (or one of the joint landlords or licensors) under the protected occupancy or statutory tenancy in question.

(5) Except as provided in subsection (4) above, expressions used in this section have the same meaning as in the Rent Act 1977.

Removal of special regimes for tenancies of housing associations etc.

35.–(1) In this section 'housing association tenancy' has the same meaning as in Part VI of the Rent Act 1977.

(2) A tenancy which is entered into on or after the commencement of this Act cannot be a housing association tenancy unless–

(a) it is entered into in pursuance of a contract made before the commencement of this Act; or

(b) it is granted to a person (alone or jointly with others) who, immediately before the tenancy was granted, was a tenant under a housing association tenancy and is so granted by the person who at that time was the landlord under that housing association tenancy; or

(c) it is granted to a person (alone or jointly with others) in the following circumstances–

    (i) prior to the grant of the tenancy, an order for possession of a dwelling-house was made against him (alone or jointly with others) on the court being satisfied as mentioned in paragraph (b) or paragraph (c) of subsection (2) of section 84 of the Housing Act 1985; and

    (ii) the tenancy is of the premises which constitute the suitable accommodation as to which the court was so satisfied; and

    (iii) in the proceedings for possession the court directed that the tenancy would be a housing association tenancy; or

(d) [it is a tenancy under which the interest of the landlord was at the time the tenancy was granted held by a new town corporation, within the meaning of section 80 of the

Housing Act 1985, and, before the date which has effect by virtue of paragraph (a) or paragraph (b) of subsection (4) of section 38 below, ceased to be so held by virtue of a disposal by the Commission for the New Towns made pursuant to a direction under section 37 of the New Towns Act 1981.]

(3) Where, on or after the commencement of this Act, a [registered social landlord, within the meaning of the Housing Act 1985 (see s.5(4) and (5) of the Act] grants a secure tenancy pursuant to an obligation under section 554 (2A) of the Housing Act 1985 (as set out in Schedule 17 to this Act) then, in determining whether that tenancy is a housing association tenancy, it shall be assumed for the purposes only of section 86(2)(b) of the Rent Act 1977 (tenancy would be a protected tenancy but for section 15 or 16 of that Act) that the tenancy was granted before the commencement of this Act.

(4) [Subject to section 38(4A) below] a tenancy or licence which is entered into on or after the commencement of this Act cannot be a secure tenancy unless–

(a)   the interest of the landlord belongs to a local authority, a new town corporation or an urban development corporation, all within the meaning of section 80 of the Housing Act 1985 [or a housing action trust established under Part III of this Act]; or

(b)   the interest of the landlord belongs to a housing co-operative within the meaning of section 27B of the Housing Act 1985 (agreements between local housing authorities and housing co-operatives) and the tenancy or licence is of a dwelling-house comprised in a housing co-operative agreement falling within that section; or

(c)   it is entered into in pursuance of a contract made before the commencement of this Act; or

(d)   it is granted to a person (alone or jointly with others) who, immediately before it was entered into, was a secure tenant and is so granted by the body which at that time was the landlord or licensor under the secure tenancy; or

(e)   it is granted to a person (alone or jointly with others) in the following circumstances–

(i)   prior to the grant of the tenancy or licence, an order for possession of a dwelling-house was made against him (alone or jointly with others) on the court being satisfied as mentioned in paragraph (b) or paragraph (c) of subsection (2) of section 84 of the Housing Act 1985; and

(ii) the tenancy or licence is of the premises which constitute the suitable accommodation as to which the court was so satisfied; and

(iii) in the proceedings for possession the court considered that, in the circumstances, the grant of an assured tenancy would not afford the required security and, accordingly, directed that the tenancy or licence would be a secure tenancy; or

(*f*) it is granted pursuant to an obligation under section 554(2A) of the Housing Act 1985 (as set out in Schedule 17 to this Act).

(5) If, on or after the commencement of this Act, the interest of the landlord under a protected or statutory tenancy becomes held by a housing association, a housing trust, [or the Housing Corporation] [or, where that interest becomes held by him as a result of the exercise by him of functions under Part III of the Housing Associations Act 1985, the Secretary of State] nothing in the preceding provisions in this section shall prevent the tenancy from being a housing association tenancy or a secure tenancy and, accordingly, in such a case section 80 of the Housing Act 1985 (and any enactment which refers to that section) shall have effect without regard to the repeal of provisions of that section effected by this Act.

(6) In subsection (5) above 'housing association' and 'housing trust' have the same meaning as in the Housing Act 1985.

New restricted contracts limited to transitional cases

36.–1 A tenancy or other contract entered into after the commencement of this Act cannot be a restricted contract for the purposes of the Rent Act 1977 unless it is entered into in pursuance of a contract made before the commencement of this Act.

(2) If the terms of a restricted contract are varied after this Act comes into force then, subject to subsection (3) below,–

(*a*) if the variation affects the amount of the rent which, under the contract, is payable for the dwelling in question the contract shall be treated as a new contract entered into at the time of the variation (and subsection (1) above shall have effect accordingly); and

(*b*) if the variation does not affect the amount of the rent which, under the contract, is so payable, nothing in this section shall affect the determination of the question whether the variation is such as to give rise to a new contract.

(3) Any reference in subsection (2) above to a variation affecting the amount of the rent which, under a contract, is payable for a dwelling does not include a reference to–

(a)   a reduction or increase effected under section 78 of the Rent Act 1977 (power of rent tribunal); or

(b)   a variation which is made by the parties and has the effect of making the rent expressed to be payable under the contract the same as the rent for the dwelling which is entered in the registered under section 79 of the Rent Act 1977.

(4) In subsection (1) of section 81A of the Rent Act 1977 (cancellation of registration of rent relating to a restricted contract) paragraph (a) (no cancellation until two years have elapsed since the date of the entry) shall cease to have effect.

(5) In this section 'rent' has the same meaning as in Part V of the Rent Act 1977.

No further assured tenancies under Housing Act 1980

37.–(1) A tenancy which is entered into on or after the commencement of this Act cannot be an assured tenancy for the purposes of sections 56 to 58 of the Housing Act 1980 (in this section referred to as a '1980 Act tenancy').

(2) In any case where–

(a)   before the commencement of this Act, a tenant under a 1980 Act tenancy made an application to the court under section 24 of the Landlord and Tenant Act 1954 (for the grant of a new tenancy), and

(b)   at the commencement of this Act the 1980 Act tenancy is continuing by virtue of that section or of any provision of Part IV of the said Act of 1954,

section 1(3) of this Act shall not apply to the 1980 Act tenancy.

(3) If, in a case falling within subsection (2) above, the court makes an order for the grant of a new tenancy under section 29 of the Landlord and Tenant Act 1954, that tenancy shall be an assured tenancy for the purposes of this Act.

(4) In any case where–

(a)   before the commencement of this Act a contract was entered into for the grant of a 1980 Act tenancy, but

(b)   at the commencement of this Act the tenancy had not been granted,

the contract shall have effect as a contract for the grant of an assured tenancy (within the meaning of this Act).

(5) In relation to an assured tenancy falling within subsection (3) above or granted pursuant to a contract falling within subsection (4) above, Part I of Schedule 1 to this Act shall have effect as if it consisted only of paragraphs 11 and 12; and, if the landlord granting the tenancy is a fully mutual housing association, then, so long as that association remains the landlord under that tenancy (and under any statutory periodic tenancy which arises on the coming to an end of that tenancy), the said paragraph 12 shall gave effect in relation to that tenancy with the omission of subparagraph (1)(h).

(6) Any reference in this section to a provision of the Landlord and Tenant Act 1954 is a reference only to that provision as applied by section 58 of the Housing Act 1980.

Transfer of existing tenancies from public to private sector

38.–(1) The provisions of subsection (3) below apply in relation to a tenancy which was entered into before, or pursuant to a contract made before the commencement of this Act if,–

(a)   at that commencement or, if it is later, at the time it is entered into, the interest of the landlord is held by a public body (within the meaning of subsection (5) below); and

(b)   at some time after that commencement, the interest of the landlord ceases to be so held.

(2) The provisions of subsection (3) below also apply in relation to a tenancy which was entered into before, or pursuant to a contract made before, the commencement of this Act if,–

(a)   at the commencement of this Act or, if it is later, at the time it is entered into, it is a housing association tenancy; and

(b)   at some time after that commencement, it ceases to be such a tenancy.

(3) [Subject to subsections (4), (4A) and (4B) below] on and after the time referred to in subsection (1)(b) or, as the case may be, subsection (2)(b) above–

(a)   the tenancy shall not be capable of being a protected tenancy, a protected occupancy or a housing association tenancy;

(b)   the tenancy shall not be capable of being a secure tenancy unless (and only at a time when) the interest of the landlord under the tenancy is (or is again) held by a public body; and

(c)   paragraph 1 of Schedule 1 to this Act shall not apply in relation to it, and the question whether at any time thereafter it becomes (or remains) an assured tenancy shall be determined accordingly.

(4) In relation to a tenancy under which, at the commencement of this Act or, if it is later, at the time the tenancy is entered into, the interest of the landlord is held by a new town corporation, within the meaning of section 80 of the Housing Act 1985 [and which subsequently ceases to be so held by virtue of a disposal by the Commission for the New Towns made pursuant to a direction under section 37 of the New Towns Act 1981], subsections (1) and (3) above shall have effect as if any reference in subsection (1) above to the commencement of this Act were a reference to–

(a) the date on which expires the period of two years beginning on the day this Act is passed; or

(b) if the Secretary of State by order made by statutory instrument within that period so provides, such other date (whether earlier or later) as may be specified by the order for the purposes of this subsection.

[(4A) Where, by virtue of a disposal falling within subsection (4) above and made before the date which has effect by virtue of paragraphs (a) or paragraph (b) of that subsection, the interest of the landlord under a tenancy passes to [a registered social landlord (within the meaning of the Housing Act 1985) (see section 5(4) and (5) of that Act)] then, notwithstanding anything in subsection (3) above, so long as the tenancy continues to be held by a body which would have been specified in subsection (1) of section 80 of the Housing Act 1985 if the repeal of provisions of that section effected by this Act had not been made, the tenancy shall continue to be a secure tenancy and to be capable of being a housing association tenancy.]

[(4B) Where, by virtue of a disposal by the Secretary of State made in the exercise by him of functions under Part III of the Housing Associations Act 1985, the interest of the landlord under a secure tenancy passes to a registered social landlord (within the meaning of the Housing Act 1985) then, notwithstanding anything in subsection (3) above, so long as the tenancy continues to be held by a body which would have been specified in subsection (1) of section 80 of the Housing Act 1985 if the repeal of provisions of that section effected by this Act had not been made, the tenancy shall continue to be a secure tenancy and to be capable of being a housing association tenancy.]

(5) For the purposes of this section, the interest of a landlord under a tenancy is held by a public body at a time when–

(*a*)	it belongs to a local authority, a new town corporation or an urban development corporation, all within the meaning of section 80 of the Housing Act 1985; or

(*b*)	it belongs to a housing action trust established under Part III of this Act; or

(*c*)	it belongs to the Development Board for Rural Wales; or

(*d*)	it belongs to Her Majesty in right of the Crown or to a government department or is held in trust for Her Majesty for the purposes of a government department.

(6) In this section–

(*a*)	'housing association tenancy' means a tenancy to which Part VI of the Rent Act 1977 applies;

(*b*)	'protected tenancy' has the same meaning as in that Act; and

(*c*)	'protected occupancy' has the same meaning as in the Rent (Agriculture) Act 1976.

Statutory tenants: succession

39.–(1) In section 2(1)(b) of the Rent Act 1977 (which introduces the provisions of Part 1 of Schedule 1 to that Act relating to statutory tenants by succession) after the words 'statutory tenant of a dwelling-house' there shall be inserted 'or, as the case may be, is entitled to an assured tenancy of a dwelling-house by succession.'

(2) Where the person who is the original tenant, within the meaning of Part I of Schedule 1 to the Rent Act 1977, dies after the commencement of this Act, that Part shall have effect subject to the amendments in Part 1 of Schedule 4 to this Act.

(3) Where subsection (2) above does not apply but the person who is the first successor, within the meaning of Part I of Schedule 1 to the Rent Act 1977, dies after the commencement of this Act, that Part shall have effect subject to the amendments in paragraphs 5 to 9 of Part I of Schedule 4 to this Act.

(4) In any case where the original occupier, within the meaning of section 4 of the Rent (Agriculture) Act 1976 (statutory tenants and tenancies) dies after the commencement of this Act, that section shall have effect subject to the amendments in Part II of Schedule 4 to this Act.

(5) In any case where, by virtue of any provision of–

(*a*)	Part I of Schedule 1 to the Rent Act 1977, as amended in accordance with subsection (2) or subsection (3) above, or

(*b*)	section 4 of the Rent (Agriculture) Act 1976, as amended in accordance with subsection (4) above, a person (in the following provisions of this section referred to as 'the successor') becomes entitled to an assured tenancy of a dwelling-house by succession, that tenancy shall be a periodic tenancy arising by virtue of this section.

(6) Where, by virtue of subsection (5) above, the successor becomes entitled to an assured periodic tenancy, that tenancy is one–

(a)   taking effect in possession immediately after the death of the protected or statutory tenant or protected occupier (in the following provisions of this section referred to as 'the predecessor:) on whose death the successor became so entitled;

(b)   deemed to have been granted to the successor by the person who, immediately before the death of the predecessor, was the landlord of the predecessor under his tenancy;

(c)   under which the premises which are let are the same dwelling-house as, immediately before his death, the predecessor occupied under his tenancy;

(d)   under which the periods of the tenancy are the same as those for which rent was last payable by the predecessor under his tenancy;

(e)   under which, subject to sections 13 to 15 above, the other terms are the same as those on which, under his tenancy, the predecessor occupied the dwelling-house immediately before his death; and

(f)   which, for the purposes of section 13(2) above, is treated as a statutory periodic tenancy;

and in paragraphs (b) to (e) above 'under his tenancy', in relation to the predecessor, means under his protected tenancy or protected occupancy or in his capacity as a statutory tenant.

(7) If, immediately before the death of the predecessor, the landlord might have recovered possession of the dwelling-house under Case 19 in Schedule 15 to the Rent Act 1977, the assured periodic tenancy to which the successor becomes entitled shall be an assured shorthold tenancy (whether or not [in the case of a tenancy to which the provision applies] it fulfils the conditions in section 20(1) above).

(8) If, immediately before his death, the predecessor was a protected occupier or statutory tenant within the meaning of the Rent (Agriculture) Act 1976, the assured periodic tenancy to which the successor becomes entitled shall be an assured agricultural occupancy (whether or not it fulfils the conditions in section 24(1) above).

(9) Where, immediately before his death, the predecessor was a tenant under a fixed term tenancy, section 6 above shall apply in relation to the assured periodic tenancy to which the successor becomes entitled on the predecessor's death subject to the following modifications–

(*a*) for any reference to a statutory periodic tenancy there shall be substituted a reference to the assured periodic tenancy to which the successor becomes so entitled;

(*b*) in subsection (1) of that section, paragraph (a) shall be omitted and the reference in paragraph (b) to section 5(3)(e) above shall be construed as a reference to subsection (6)(e) above; and

(*c*) for any reference to the coming to an end of the former tenancy there shall be substituted a reference to the date of the predecessor's death.

(10) If and so long as a dwelling-house is subject to an assured tenancy to which the successor has become entitled by succession, section 7 above and Schedule 2 to this Act shall have effect subject to the modifications in Part III of Schedule 4 to this Act; and in that Part 'the predecessor' and 'the successor' have the same meaning as in this section.

CHAPTER VI
GENERAL PROVISIONS

Jurisdiction of county courts

40.–(1) A county court shall have jurisdiction to hear and determine any question arising under any provision of–

(*a*) Chapters I to III and V above, or

(*b*) sections 27 and 28 above,

other than a question falling within the jurisdiction of a rent assessment committee by virtue of any such provision.

(2) [repealed]

(3) Where any proceedings under any provision mentioned in subsection (1) above are being taken in a county court, the court shall have jurisdiction to hear and determine any other proceedings joined with those proceedings, notwithstanding that, apart from this subsection, those other proceedings would be outside the court's jurisdiction.

(4) [repealed]

(5) [repealed]

Rent assessment committees: procedure and information powers

41.–(1) [...]

(2) The rent assessment committee to whom a matter is referred under Chapter I or Chapter II above may by notice in the prescribed form served on the landlord or the tenant require him to give to the committee, within such period of not less than fourteen days from the service of the notice as may be specified in the notice, such information as they may reasonably require for the purposes of their functions.

(3) If any person fails without reasonable excuse to comply with a notice served on him under subsection (2) above, he shall be liable on summary conviction to a fine not exceeding level 3 on the standard scale.

(4) Where an offence under subsection (3) above committed by a body corporate is proved to have been committed with the consent or connivance of, or to be attributable to any neglect on the part of, any director, manager or secretary or other similar officer of the body corporate or any person who was purporting to act in any such capacity, he as well as the body corporate shall be guilty of that offence and shall be liable to be proceeded against and punished accordingly.

[Amounts attributable to services

41A. In order to assist authorities to give effect to the housing benefit scheme under Part VII of the Social Security and Benefits Act 1992, where a rent is determined under section 14 or 22 above, the rent assessment committee shall note in their determination the amount (if any) of the rent which, in the opinion of the committee, is fairly attributable to the provision of services, except where that amount is in their opinion negligible; and the amount so noted may be included in the information specified in an order under section 42 below.]

[Provision of information as to exemption from council tax

41B. A billing authority within the meaning of Part I of the Local Government Finance Act 1992 shall, if so requested in writing by a rent officer or rent assessment committee in connection with his or their functions under any enactment, inform the rent officer or rent assessment committee in writing whether or not a particular dwelling (within the meaning of Part I of the Local Government Finance Act 1992) is, or was at any time specified in the request, an exempt dwelling for the purposes of that Part of that Act.']

Information as to determination of rents

42.–(1) The President of every rent assessment panel shall keep and make publicly available, in such manner as is specified in an order made by the Secretary of State, such information as may be so specified with respect to rents under assured tenancies and assured agricultural occupancies which have been the subject of references or applications to, or determinations by, rent assessment committees.

(2) A copy of any information certified under the hand of an officer duly authorised by the President of the rent assessment panel concerned shall be receivable in evidence in any court and in any proceedings.

(3) An order under subsection (1) above–

(a)   may prescribe the fees to be charged for the supply of a copy, including a certified copy, of any of the information kept by virtue of that subsection; and

(b)   may make different provision with respect to different cases or descriptions of case, including different provision for different areas.

(4) The power to make an order under subsection (1) above shall be exercisable by statutory instrument which shall be subject to annulment in pursuance of a resolution of either House of Parliament.

Powers of local authorities for purposes of giving information

43. In section 149 of the Rent Act 1977 (which, among other matters, authorises local authorities to publish information for the benefit of landlords and tenants with respect to their rights and duties under certain enactments), in subsection (1)(a) after sub-paragraph (iv) there shall be inserted–

'(v) Chapters I to III of Part I of the Housing Act 1988'.

Application to Crown Property

44.–(1) Subject to paragraph 11 of Schedule I to this Act and subsection (2) below, Chapters I to IV above apply in relation to premises in which there subsists, or at any material time subsisted, a Crown interest as they apply in relation to premises in relation to which no such interest subsists or ever subsisted.

(2) In Chapter IV above–

(*a*)   sections 27 and 28 do not bind the Crown; and

(*b*)   the remainder binds the Crown to the extent provided for in section 10 of the Protection from Eviction Act 1977.

(3) In this section 'Crown interest' means an interest which belongs to Her Majesty in right of the Crown or of the Duchy of Lancaster or to the Duchy of Cornwall, or to a government department, or which is held in trust for Her Majesty for the purposes of a government department.

(4) Where an interest belongs to Her Majesty in right of the Duchy of Lancaster, then, for the purposes of Chapters I to IV above, the Chancellor of the Duchy of Lancaster shall be deemed to be the owner of the interest.

Interpretation of Part I

45.–(1) In this Part of this Act, except where the context otherwise requires,–

'dwelling-house' may be a house or part of a house;

'fixed term tenancy' means any tenancy other than a periodic tenancy,

'fully mutual housing association' has the same meaning as in Part I of the Housing Associations Act 1985;

'landlord' includes any person from time to time deriving title under the original landlord and also includes, in relation to a dwelling-house, any person other than a tenant who is, or but for the existence of assured tenancy would be, entitled to possession of the dwelling-house;

'let' includes 'sub-let'

'prescribed' means prescribed by regulations made by the Secretary of State by statutory instrument;

'rates' includes water rates and charges but does not include an owner's drainage rate, as defined in section 63(2)(a) of the Land Drainage Act 1976;

'secure tenancy' has the meaning assigned by section 79 of the Housing Act 1985;

'statutory periodic tenancy' has the meaning assigned by section 5(7) above, 'tenancy' includes a sub-tenancy and an agreement for a tenancy or sub-tenancy, and

'tenant' includes a sub-tenant and any person deriving title under the original tenant or sub-tenant.

(2) Subject to paragraph 11 of Schedule 2 to this Act, any reference in this Part of this Act to the beginning of a tenancy is a reference to the day on which the tenancy is entered into or, if it is later, the day on which, under the terms of any lease, agreement or other document, the tenant is entitled to possession under the tenancy.

(3) Where two or more persons jointly constitute either the landlord or the tenant in relation to a tenancy, then, except where this Part of this Act otherwise provides, any reference to the landlord or to the tenant is a reference to all the persons who jointly constitute the landlord or the tenant, as the case may require.

(4) For the avoidance of doubt, it is hereby declared that any reference in this Part of this Act (however expressed) to a power for a landlord to determine a tenancy does not include a reference to a power of re-entry or forfeiture for breach of any term or condition of the tenancy.

(5) Regulations under subsection (1) above may make different provision with respect to different cases or descriptions of case, including different provision for different areas.

SCHEDULES

Section 1

SCHEDULE 1
TENANCIES WHICH CANNOT BE ASSURED TENANCIES

PART I
THE TENANCIES
Tenancies entered into before commencement

1. A tenancy which is entered into before, or pursuant to a contract made before, the commencement of this Act.

Tenancies of dwelling-houses with high rateable values

[2.–(1) A tenancy–
(a)　which is entered into on or after April 1, 1990 (otherwise than, where the dwelling-house had a rateable value on March 31, 1990, in pursuance of a contract made before April 1, 1990), and

(b)   under which the rent payable for the time being is payable
      at a rate exceeding £25,000 a year.

(2) In sub-paragraph (1) 'rent' does not include any sum payable
by the tenant as it expressed (in whatever terms) to be payable in
respect of rates, [council tax,] services, management, repairs,
maintenance or insurance, unless it could not have been regarded
by the parties to the tenancy as a sum so payable.

2A. A tenancy–
(a)   which was entered into before April 1, 1990, or on or after
      that date in pursuance of a contract made before that date,
      and
(b)   under which the dwelling-house had a rateable value on
      March 31, 1990 which, if it is in Greater London, exceeded
      £1,500 and, if it is elsewhere, exceeded £750.]

Tenancies at a low rent

[3.   A tenancy under which for the time being no rent is payable.
3A. A tenancy–
(a)   which is entered into on or after April 1, 1990 (otherwise
      than, where the dwelling-house had a rateable value on
      March 31, 1990, in pursuance of a contract made before
      April 1, 1990), and
(b)   under which the rent payable for the time being is payable
      at a rate of, if the dwelling-house is in Greater London,
      £1,000 or less a year and, if it is elsewhere, £250 or less a year.
3B. A tenancy–
(a)   which was entered into before April 1, 1990 or, where the
      dwelling-house had a rateable value on March 31, 1990, on
      or after April 1, 1990 in pursuance of a contract made before
      that date, and
(b)   under which the rent for the time being payable is less than
      two-thirds of the rateable value of the dwelling-house on
      March 31, 1990.
3C. Paragraph 2(2) above applies for the purposes of paragraphs
3, 3A and 3B as it applies for the purposes of paragraph 2(1).]

Business tenancies

4. A tenancy to which Part II of the Landlord and Tenant Act
1954 applies (business tenancies).

Licensed premises

5. A tenancy under which the dwelling-house consists of or

comprises premises licensed for the sale of intoxicating liquors for consumption on the premises.

Tenancies of agricultural land

6.–(1) A tenancy under which agricultural land, exceeding two acres, is let together with the dwelling-house.

(2) In this paragraph 'agricultural land' has the meaning set out in section 26(3)(a) of the General Rate Act 1967 (exclusion of agricultural land and premises from liability for rating).

Tenancies of agricultural holdings etc

[7.–(1) A tenancy under which the dwelling-house–
(a)   is comprised in an agricultural holding, and
(b)   is occupied by the person responsible for the control (whether as tenant or as servant or agent of the tenant) of the farming of the holding.

(2) A tenancy under which the dwelling-house–
(a)   is comprised in the holding held under a farm business tenancy, and
(b)   is occupied by the person responsible for the control (whether as tenant or as servant or agent of the tenant) of the management of the holding.

(3) In this paragraph–
'agricultural holding' means any agricultural holding within the meaning of the Agricultural Holdings Act 1986 held under a tenancy in relation to which that Act applies, and

'farm business tenancy' and 'holding', in relation to such a tenancy, have the same meaning as in the Agricultural Tenancies Act 1995.]

Lettings to students

8.–(1) A tenancy which is granted to a person who is pursuing, or intends to pursue, a course of study provided by a specified educational institution and is so granted either by that institution or by another specified institution or body of persons.

(2) In sub-paragraph (1) above 'specified' means specified, or of a class specified, for the purposes of this paragraph by regulations made by the Secretary of State by statutory instrument.

(3) A statutory instrument made in the exercise of the power conferred by sub-paragraph (2) above shall be subject to annulment in pursuance of a resolution of either House of Parliament.

Holiday lettings

9. A tenancy the purpose of which is to confer on the tenant the right to occupy the dwelling-house for a holiday.

Resident landlords

10.–(1) A tenancy in respect of which the following conditions are fulfilled–

(a) that the dwelling-house forms part only of a building and, except in a case where the dwelling-house also forms part of a flat, the building is not a purpose-built block of flats; and

(b) that, subject to Part III of this Schedule, the tenancy was granted by an individual who, at the time when the tenancy was granted, occupied as his only or principal home another dwelling-house which,–

(i) in the case mentioned in paragraph (a) above, also forms part of the flat; or

(ii) in any other case, also forms part of the building; and

(c) that, subject to Part III of this Schedule, at all times since the tenancy was granted the interest of the landlord under the tenancy has belonged to an individual who, at the time he owned that interest, occupied as his only or principal home another dwelling-house which,–

(i) in the case mentioned in paragraph (a) above, also formed part of the flat; or

(ii) in any other case, also formed part of the building; and

(d) that the tenancy is not one which is excluded from this sub-paragraph by sub-paragraph (3) below.

(2) If a tenancy was granted by two or more persons jointly, the reference in sub-paragraph (1)(b) above to an individual is a reference to any one of those persons and if the interest of the landlord is for the time being held by two or more persons jointly, the reference in sub-paragraph (1)(c) above to an individual is a reference to any one of those persons.

(3) A tenancy (in this sub-paragraph referred to as 'the new tenancy') is excluded from sub-paragraph (1) above if–

(a) it is granted to a person (alone, or jointly with others) who, immediately before it was granted, was a tenant under an assured tenancy (in this sub-paragraph referred to as 'the former tenancy') of the same dwelling-house or of another dwelling-house which forms part of the building in question: and

(b)   the landlord under the new tenancy and under the former tenancy is the same person or, if either of those tenancies is or was granted by two or more persons jointly, the same person is the landlord or one of the landlords under each tenancy.

Crown tenancies

11.–(1) A tenancy under which the interest of the landlord belongs to Her Majesty in right of the Crown or to a government department or is held in trust for Her Majesty for the purpose of a government department.

(2) The reference in sub-paragraph (1) above to the case where the interest of the landlord belongs to Her Majesty in right of the Crown does not include the case where that interest is under the management of the Crown Estate Commissioners [or is held by the Secretary of State as the result of the exercise by him of functions under Part III of the Housing Associations Act 1985].

Local authority tenancies etc.

12.–(1) A tenancy under which the interest of the landlord belongs to–
(a)   a local authority, as defined in sub-paragraph (2) below;
(b)   the Commission for the New Towns,
(c)   [repealed];
(d)   an urban development corporation established by an order under section 135 of the Local Government, Planning and Land Act 1980;
(e)   a development corporation, within the meaning of the New Towns Act 1981;
[(ee) the London Fire and Emergency Planning Authority];
(f)   an authority established under section 10 of the Local Government Act 1985 (waste disposal authorities);
(g)   a residuary body, within the meaning of the Local Government Act 1985; or
[(gg) The Residuary Body for Wales (Corff Gweddilliol Cymru)];
(h)   a fully mutual housing association; or
(i)   a housing action trust established under Part III of this Act.

(2) The following are local authorities for the purposes of sub-paragraph (1)(a) above–
(a)   the council of a county, county borough, district or London borough;
(b)   the Common Council of the City of London;
(c)   the Council of the Isles of Scilly;

(d)   the Broads Authority;
[(da)a National Park Authority];
(e)   the Inner London Education Authority;
(f)   a joint authority, within the meaning of the Local
      Government Act 1985; and
(g)   a police authority established under section 3 of the Police
      Act 1996, the Service Authority for the National Criminal
      Intelligence Service and the Service Authority for the
      National Crime Squad.

Accommodation for asylum-seekers

[12A.–Accommodation for asylum-seekers
(1) A tenancy granted by a private landlord under arrangements
for the provision of support for asylum-seekers or dependants of
asylum-seekers made under Part VI of the Immigration and
Asylum Act 1999.
(2) 'Private landlord' means a landlord who is not within section
80(1) of the Housing Act 1985.]

Transitional cases

13.–(1) A protected tenancy, within the meaning of the Rent Act
1977.
(2) A housing association tenancy, within the meaning of Part VI
of that Act.
(3) A secure tenancy.
(4) Where a person is a protected occupier of a dwelling-house,
within the meaning of the Rent (Agriculture) Act 1976, the relevant
tenancy, within the meaning of that Act, by virtue of which he
occupies the dwelling-house.

PART II
RATEABLE VALUES

14.–(1) The rateable value of a dwelling-house at any time shall
be ascertained for the purposes of Part I of this Schedule as
follows–
(a)   if the dwelling-house is a hereditament for which a rateable
      value is then shown in the valuation list, it shall be that
      rateable value;
(b)   if the dwelling-house forms part only of such a
      hereditament or consists of or forms part of more than one
      such hereditament, its rateable value shall be taken to be

such value as is found by a proper apportionment or aggregation of the rateable value or values so shown.

(2) Any question arising under this Part of this Schedule as to the proper apportionment or aggregation of any value or values shall be determined by the county court and the decision of that court shall be final.

15. Where, after the time at which the rateable value of a dwelling-house is material for the purposes of any provision of Part I of this Schedule, the valuation list is altered so as to vary the rateable value of the hereditament of which the dwelling-house consists (in whole or in part) or forms part and the alteration has effect from that time or from an earlier time, the rateable value of the dwelling-house at the material time shall be ascertained as if the value shown in the valuation list at the material time had been the value shown in the list as altered.

16. Paragraphs 14 and 15 above apply in relation to any other land which, under section 2 of this Act, is treated as part of a dwelling-house as they apply in relation to the dwelling-house itself.

PART III
PROVISIONS FOR DETERMINING APPLICATION OF PARAGRAPH 10 (RESIDENT LANDLORDS)

17.–(1) In determining whether the condition in paragraph 10(1)(c) above is at any time fulfilled with respect to a tenancy, there shall be disregarded–

(a) any period of not more than twenty-eight days, beginning with the date on which the interest of the landlord under the tenancy becomes vested at law and in equity in an individual who, during that period, does not occupy as his only or principal home another dwelling-house which forms part of the building or, as the case may be, flat concerned;

(b) if, within a period falling within paragraph (a) above, the individual concerned notifies the tenant in writing of his intention to occupy as his only or principal home another dwelling-house in the building or, as the case may be, flat concerned, the period beginning with the date on which the interest of the landlord under the tenancy becomes vested in that individual as mentioned in that paragraph and ending–

(i)   at the expiry of the period of six months beginning on that date, or

(ii) on the date on which that interest ceases to be so vested, or

      (iii)   on the date on which that interest becomes again vested in such an individual as is mentioned in paragraph 10(1)(c) or the condition in that paragraph becomes deemed to be fulfilled by virtue of paragraph 18(1) or paragraph 20 below, whichever is the earlier; and

  (c)   any period of not more than two years beginning with the date on which the interest of the landlord under the tenancy becomes, and during which it remains, vested–

      (i)   in trustees as such; or

      (ii) by virtue of section 9 of the Administration of Estates Act 1925, in [the Probate Judge or the Public Trustee].

(2) Where the interest of the landlord under a tenancy becomes vested at law and in equity in two or more persons jointly, of whom at least one was an individual, sub-paragraph (1) above shall have effect subject to the following modifications–

  (a)   in paragraph (a) for the words from 'an individual' to 'occupy' there shall be substituted 'the joint landlords if, during that period none of them occupies'; and

  (b)   in paragraph (b) for the words 'the individual concerned' there shall be substituted 'any of the joint landlords who is an individual' and for the words 'that individual' there shall be substituted 'the joint landlords'.

18.–(1) During any period when–

  (a)   the interest of the landlord under the tenancy referred to in paragraph 10 above is vested in trustees as such, and

  (b)   that interest is [repealed] held on trust for any person who or for two or more persons of whom at least one occupies as his only or principal home a dwelling-house which forms part of the building or, as the case may be, flat referred to in paragraph 10(1)(a),

the condition in paragraph 10(1)(c) shall be deemed to be fulfilled and accordingly, no part of that period shall be disregarded by virtue of paragraph 17 above.

(2) If a period during which the condition in paragraph 10(1)(c) is deemed to be fulfilled by virtue of sub-paragraph (1) above comes to an end on the death of a person who was in occupation of a dwelling-house as mentioned in paragraph (b) of that sub-paragraph, then, in determining whether that condition is at any time thereafter fulfilled, there shall be disregarded any period–

  (a)   which begins on the date of the death;

(b) during which the interest of the landlord remains vested as mentioned in sub-paragraph (1)(a) above; and

(c) which ends at the expiry of the period of two years beginning on the date of the death or on any earlier date on which the condition in paragraph 10(1)(c) becomes again deemed to be fulfilled by virtue of sub-paragraph (1) above.

19. In any case where–

(a) immediately before a tenancy comes to an end the condition in paragraph 10(1)(c) is deemed to be fulfilled by virtue of paragraph 18(1) above, and

(b) on the coming to an end of that tenancy the trustees in whom the interest of the landlord is vested grant a new tenancy of the same or substantially the same dwelling-house to a person (alone or jointly with others) who was the tenant or one of the tenants under the previous tenancy,

the condition in paragraph 10(1)(b) above shall be deemed to be fulfilled with respect to the new tenancy.

20.–(1) The tenancy referred to in paragraph 10 above falls within this paragraph if the interest of the landlord under the tenancy becomes vested in the personal representatives of a deceased person acting in that capacity.

(2) If the tenancy falls within this paragraph, the condition in paragraph 10(1)(c) shall be deemed to be fulfilled for any period, beginning with the date on which the interest becomes vested in the personal representatives and not exceeding two years, during which the interest of the landlord remains so vested.

21. Throughout any period which, by virtue of paragraph 17 or paragraph 18(2) above, falls to be disregarded for the purpose of determining whether the condition in paragraph 10(1)(c) is fulfilled with respect to a tenancy, no order shall be made for possession of the dwelling-house subject to that tenancy, other than an order which might be made if that tenancy were or, as the case may be, had been an assured tenancy.

22. For the purposes of paragraph 10 above, a building is a purpose-built block of flats if as constructed it contained, and it contains, two or more flats; and for this purpose 'flat' means a dwelling-house which–

(a) forms part only of a building; and

(b) is separated horizontally from another dwelling-house which forms part of the same building.

Section 7
SCHEDULE 2

GROUNDS FOR POSSESSION OF DWELLING-HOUSES LET ON ASSURED TENANCIES

PART I
GROUNDS ON WHICH COURT MUST ORDER POSSESSION

Ground 1

Not later than the beginning of the tenancy the landlord gave notice in writing to the tenant that possession might be recovered on this ground or the court is of the opinion that it is just and equitable to dispense with the requirement of notice and (in either case)–

(a)   at some time before the beginning of the tenancy, the landlord who is seeking possession or, in the case of joint landlords seeking possession, at least one of them occupied the dwelling-house as his only or principal home; or

(b)   the landlord who is seeking possession or, in the case of joint landlords seeking possession, at least one of them requires the dwelling-house as his or his spouse's only or principal home and neither the landlord (or, in the case of joint landlords, any one of them) nor any other person who, as landlord, derived title under the landlord who gave the notice mentioned above acquired the reversion on the tenancy for money or money's worth.

Ground 2

The dwelling-house is subject to a mortgage granted before the beginning of the tenancy and–

(a)   the mortgagee is entitled to exercise a power of sale conferred on him by the mortgage or by section 101 of the Law of Property Act 1925; and

(b)   the mortgagee requires possession of the dwelling-house for the purpose of disposing of it with vacant possession in exercise of that power; and

(c)   either notice was given as mentioned in Ground 1 above or the court is satisfied that it is just and equitable to dispense with the requirement of notice;

and for the purposes of this ground 'mortgage' includes a charge and 'mortgagee' shall be construed accordingly.

Ground 3

The tenancy is a fixed term tenancy for a term not exceeding eight months and–

(a)   not later than the beginning of the tenancy the landlord gave notice in writing to the tenant that possession might be recovered on this ground: and

(b)   at some time within the period of twelve months ending with the beginning of the tenancy, the dwelling-house was occupied under a right to occupy it for a holiday.

Ground 4

The tenancy is a fixed term tenancy for a term not exceeding twelve months and–

(a)   not later than the beginning of the tenancy the landlord gave notice in writing to the tenant that possession might be recovered on this ground; and

(b)   at some time within the period of twelve months ending with the beginning of the tenancy, the dwelling-house was let on a tenancy falling within paragraph 8 of Schedule 1 to this Act.

Ground 5

The dwelling-house is held for the purpose of being available for occupation by a minister of religion as a residence from which to perform the duties of his office and–

(a)   not later than the beginning of the tenancy the landlord gave notice in writing to the tenant that possession might be recovered on this ground; and

(b)   the court is satisfied that the dwelling-house is required for occupation by a minister of religion as such a residence.

Ground 6

The landlord who is seeking possession or, if that landlord is a [registered social landlord] or charitable housing trust, a superior landlord intends to demolish or reconstruct the whole or a substantial part of the dwelling-house or to carry out substantial works on the dwelling-house or any part thereof or any building of which it forms part and the following conditions are fulfilled–

(a)   the intended work cannot reasonably be carried out without the tenant giving up possession of the dwelling-house because–

(i)   the tenant is not willing to agree to such a variation of the terms of the tenancy as would give such access and other facilities as would permit the intended work to be carried out, or

(ii) the nature of the intended work is such that no such variation is practicable, or

(iii) the tenant is not willing to accept an assured tenancy of such part only of the dwelling-house (in this sub-paragraph referred to as 'the reduced part') as would leave in the possession of his landlord so much of the dwelling-house as would be reasonable to enable the intended work to be carried out and, where appropriate, as would give such access and other facilities over the reduced part as would permit the intended work to be carried out, or

(iv) the nature of the intended work is such that such a tenancy is not practicable; and

(b) either the landlord seeking possession acquired his interest in the dwelling-house before the grant of the tenancy or that interest was in existence at the time of that grant and neither that landlord (or, in the case of joint landlords, any of them) nor any other person who, alone or jointly with others, has acquired that interest since that time acquired it for money or money's worth; and

(c) the assured tenancy on which the dwelling-house is let did not come into being by virtue of any provision of Schedule I to the Rent Act 1977, as amended by Part I of Schedule 4 to this Act or, as the case may be, section 4 of the Rent (Agri-culture) Act 1976, as amended by Part 11 of that Schedule.

For the purposes of this ground, if, immediately before the grant of the tenancy, the tenant to whom it was granted or, if it was granted to joint tenants, any of them was the tenant or one of the joint tenants [of the dwelling-house concerned] under an earlier assured tenancy [or, as the case may be, under a tenancy to which Schedule 10 to the Local Government and Housing Act 1989 applied], any reference in paragraph (b) above to the grant of the tenancy is a reference to the grant of that earlier assured tenancy [or, as the case may be, to the grant of the tenancy to which the said Schedule 10 applied].

For the purposes of this ground ['registered social landlord' has the same meaning as in the Housing Act 1985 (see section 5(4) and (5) of that Act)] and 'charitable housing trust' means a housing

trust, within the the meaning of [the Housing Associations Act 1985], which is a charity, within meaning of [the Charities Act 1993].
   [... repealed]

Ground 7

The tenancy is a periodic tenancy (including a statutory periodic tenancy) which has devolved under the will or intestacy of the former tenant and the proceedings for the recovery of possession are begun not later than twelve months after the death of the former tenant or, if the court so directs, after the date on which, in the opinion of the court, the landlord or, in the case of joint landlords, any one of them became aware of the former tenant's death.

   For the purposes of this ground, the acceptance by the landlord of rent from a new tenant after the death of the former tenant shall not be regarded as creating a new periodic tenancy, unless the landlord agrees in writing to a change (as compared with the tenancy before the death) in the amount of the rent, the period of the tenancy, the premises which are let or any other term of the tenancy.

Ground 8

Both at the date of the service of the notice under section 8 of this Act relating to the proceedings for possession and at the date of the hearing–
   (a) if rent is payable weekly or fortnightly, at least [eight week's] rent is unpaid;
   (b) if rent is payable monthly, at least [two months'] rent is unpaid;
   (c) if rent is payable quarterly, at least one quarter's rent is more than three months in arrears; and
   (d) if rent is payable yearly, at least three months' rent is more than three months' rent in arrears;
and for the purpose of this ground 'rent' means rent lawfully due from the tenant.

PART II

GROUNDS ON WHICH COURT MAY ORDER POSSESSION

Ground 9

Suitable alternative accommodation is available for the tenant or will be available for him when the order for possession takes effect.

Ground 10

Some rent lawfully due from the tenant–
  (a) is unpaid on the date on which the proceedings for possession are begun; and
  (b) except where subsection (1)(b) of section 8 of this Act applies, was in arrears at the date of the service of the notice under that section relating to those proceedings.

Ground 11

Whether or not any rent is in arrears on the date on which proceedings for possession are begun, the tenant has persistently delayed paying rent which has become lawfully due.

Ground 12

Any obligation of the tenancy (other than one related to the payment of rent) has been broken or not performed.

Ground 13

The condition of the dwelling-house or any of the common parts has deteriorated owing to acts of waste by, or the neglect or default of, the tenant or any other person residing in the dwelling-house and, in the case of an act of waste by, or the neglect or default of, a person lodging with the tenant or a sub-tenant of his, the tenant has not taken such steps as he ought reasonably to have taken for the removal of the lodger or sub-tenant.

For the purposes of this ground, 'common parts' means any part of a building comprising the dwelling-house and any other premises which the tenant is entitled under the terms of the tenancy to use in common with the occupiers of other dwelling-houses in which the landlord has an estate or interest.

Ground 14

[The tenant or a person residing in or visiting the dwelling-house–
  (a) has been guilty of conduct causing or likely to cause a nuisance or annoyance to a person residing, visiting or otherwise engaging in a lawful activity in the locality, or
  (b) has been convicted of–
       (i) using the dwelling-house or allowing it to be used for immoral or illegal purposes, or
       (ii) an arrestable offence committed in, or in the locality of, the dwelling-house.]

[Ground 14A

The dwelling-house was occupied (whether alone or with others) by a married couple or a couple living together as husband and wife and–

(a) one or both of the partners is a tenant of the dwelling-house,

(b) the landlord who is seeking possession is a registered social landlord or a charitable housing trust,

(c) one partner has left the dwelling-house because of violence or threats of violence by the other towards–

    (i) that partner, or

    (ii) a member of the family of that partner who was residing with that partner immediately before the partner left, and

(d) the court is satisfied that the partner who has left is unlikely to return.

For the purposes of this ground 'registered social landlord' and 'member of the family' have the same meaning as in Part I of the Housing Act 1996 and 'charitable housing trust' means a housing trust, within the meaning of the Housing Associations Act 1985, which is a charity within the meaning of the Charities Act 1993.]

Ground 15

The condition of any furniture provided for use under the tenancy has, in the opinion of the court, deteriorated owing to ill–treatment by the tenant or any other person residing in the dwelling-house and, in the case of ill–treatment by a person lodging with the tenant or by a sub-tenant of his, the tenant has not taken such steps as he ought reasonably to have taken for the removal of the lodger or sub-tenant.

Ground 16

The dwelling-house was let to the tenant in consequence of his employment by the landlords seeking possession or a previous landlord under the tenancy and the tenant has ceased to be in that employment.

[For the purposes of this ground, at a time when the landlord is or was the Secretary of State, employment by a health services body, as defined in section 60(7) of the National Health Service and Community Care Act 1990, shall be regarded as employment by the Secretary of State.]

[*Ground 17*

The tenant is the person, or one of the persons, to whom the tenancy was granted and the landlord was induced to grant the tenancy by a false statement made knowingly or recklessly by–

(a)   the tenant, or

(b)   a person acting at the tenant's instigation.]

PART III
SUITABLE ALTERNATIVE ACCOMMODATION

1. For the purposes of Ground 9 above, a certificate of the local housing authority for the district in which the dwelling-house in question is situated, certifying that the authority will provide suitable alternative accommodation for the tenant by a date specified in the certificate, shall be conclusive evidence that suitable alternative accommodation will be available for him by that date.

2. Where no such certificate as is mentioned in paragraph 1 above is produced to the court, accommodation shall be deemed to be suitable for the purposes of Ground 9 above if it consists of either–

(a)   premises which are to be let as a separate dwelling such that they will then be let on an assured tenancy, other than–

(i)   a tenancy in respect of which notice is given not later than the beginning of the tenancy that possession might be recovered on any of Grounds 1 to 5 above, or

(ii)   an assured shorthold tenancy, within the meaning of Chapter II of Part I of this Act, or

(b)   premises to be let as a separate dwelling on terms which will, in the opinion of the court, afford to the tenant security of tenure reasonably equivalent to the security afforded by Chapter I of Part 1 of this Act in the case of an assured tenancy of a kind mentioned in sub-paragraph (a) above,

and, in the opinion of the court, the accommodation fulfils the relevant conditions as defined in paragraph 3 below.

3.–(1) For the purposes of paragraph 2 above, the relevant conditions are that the accommodation is reasonably suitable to the needs of the tenant and his family as regards proximity to place of work, and either–

(a)(b) reasonably suitable to the means of the tenant and to the needs of the tenant and his family as regards extent and character; and that if any furniture was provided for use under the assured tenancy in question, furniture is provided for use in the accommodation which is either similar to that so provided or is reasonably suitable to the needs of the tenant and his family.

(2) For the purposes of sub-paragraph (1)(a) above, a certificate of a local housing authority stating–

(a) the extent of the accommodation afforded by dwelling-houses provided by the authority to meet the needs of tenants with families of such number as may be specified in the certificate, and

(b) the amount of the rent charged by the authority for dwelling-houses affording accommodation of that extent,

shall be conclusive evidence of the facts so stated.

4. Accommodation shall not be deemed to be suitable to the needs of the tenant and his family if the result of their occupation of the accommodation would be that it would be an overcrowded dwelling-house for the purposes of Part X of the Housing Act 1985.

5. Any document purporting to be a certificate of a local housing authority named therein issued for the purposes of this Part of this Schedule and to be signed by the proper officer of that authority shall be received in evidence and, unless the contrary is shown, shall be deemed to be such a certificate without further proof.

6. In this Part of this Schedule 'local housing authority' and 'district', in relation to such an authority, have the same meaning as in the Housing Act 1985.

PART IV
NOTICES RELATING TO RECOVERY OF POSSESSION

7. Any reference in Grounds 1 to 5 in Part I of this Schedule or in the following provisions of this Part to the landlord giving a notice in writing to the tenant is, in the case of joint landlords, a reference to at least one of the joint landlords giving such a notice.

8.–(1) If, not later than the beginning of a tenancy (in this paragraph referred to as 'the earlier tenancy'), the landlord gives such a notice in writing to the tenant as is mentioned in any of Grounds 1 to 5 in Part I of this Schedule, then, for the purposes of the ground in question and any further application of this paragraph, that notice shall also have effect as if it had been given immediately before the beginning of any later tenancy falling within subparagraph (2) below.

(2) Subject to sub-paragraph (3) below, sub-paragraph (1) above applies to a later tenancy–

(a)   which takes effect immediately on the coming to an end of the earlier tenancy: and

(b)   which is granted (or deemed to be granted) to the person who was the tenant under the earlier tenancy immediately before it came to an end; and

(c)   which is of substantially the same dwelling-house as the earlier tenancy.

(3) sub-paragraph (1) above does not apply in relation to a later tenancy if, not later than the beginning of the tenancy, the landlord gave notice in writing to the tenant that the tenancy is not one in respect of which possession can be recovered on the ground in question.

9. Where paragraph 8(1) above has effect in relation to a notice given as mentioned in Ground I in Part I of this Schedule, the reference in paragraph (b) of that ground to the reversion on the tenancy is a reference to the reversion on the earlier tenancy and on any later tenancy falling within paragraph 8(2) above.

10. Where paragraph 8(1) above has effect in relation to a notice given as mentioned in Ground 3 or Ground 4 in Part I of this Schedule, any second or subsequent tenancy in relation to which the notice has effect shall be treated for the purpose of that ground as beginning at the beginning of the tenancy in respect of which the notice was actually given.

11. Any reference in Grounds 1 to 5 in Part I of this Schedule to a notice being given not later than the beginning of the tenancy is a reference to its being given not later than the day on which the tenancy is entered into and, accordingly, section 45(2) of this Act shall not apply to any such reference.

[SCHEDULE 2A

ASSURED TENANCIES: NON–SHORTHOLDS

Tenancies excluded by notice

1.–(1) An assured tenancy in respect of which a notice is served as mentioned in sub-paragraph (2) below.

(2) The notice referred to in sub-paragraph (1) above is one which–

(a)   is served before the assured tenancy is entered into,

(b)   is served by the person who is to be the landlord under the assured tenancy on the person who is to be the tenant under that tenancy, and

(c)   states that the assured tenancy to which it relates is not to be an assured shorthold tenancy.

2.–(1) An assured tenancy in respect of which a notice is served as mentioned in sub-paragraph (2) below.

(2) The notice referred to in sub-paragraph (1) above is one which–

(a)   is served after the assured tenancy has been entered into,

(b)   is served by the landlord under the assured tenancy on the tenant under that tenancy, and

(c)   states that the assured tenancy to which it relates is no longer an assured shorthold tenancy.

Tenancies containing exclusionary provision

3. An assured tenancy which contains a provision to the effect that the tenancy is not an assured shorthold tenancy.

Tenancies under section 39

4. An assured tenancy arising by virtue of section 39 above, other than one to which subsection (7) of that section applies.

Former secure tenancies

5. An assured tenancy which became an assured tenancy on ceasing to be a secure tenancy.

Tenancies under Schedule 10 to the Local Government and Housing Act 1989

6. An assured tenancy arising by virtue of Schedule 10 to the Local Government and Housing Act 1989 (security of tenure on ending of long residential tenancies).

Tenancies replacing non-shortholds

7.–(1) An assured tenancy which–

(a)   is granted to a person (alone or jointly with others) who, immediately before the tenancy was granted, was the tenant (or, in the case of joint tenants, one of the tenants) under an assured tenancy other than a shorthold tenancy ('the old tenancy'),

(b)   is granted (alone or jointly with others) by a person who was at that time the landlord (or one of the joint landlords) under the old tenancy, and

(c)   is not one in respect of which a notice is served as mentioned in sub-paragraph (2) below.

(2) The notice referred to in sub-paragraph, (1)(c) above is one which–

(a)   is in such form as may be prescribed,
(b)   is served before the assured tenancy is entered into,
(c)   is served by the person who is to be the tenant under the
       assured tenancy on the person who is to be the landlord
       under that tenancy (or, in the case of joint landlords, on at
       least one of the persons who are to be joint landlords), and
(d)   states that the assured tenancy to which it relates is to be a
       shorthold tenancy.
8. An assured tenancy which comes into being by virtue of
section 5 above on the coming to an end of an assured tenancy
which is not a shorthold tenancy.

Assured agricultural occupancies

9.–(1) An assured tenancy–
(a)   in the case of which the agricultural worker condition is, by
       virtue of any provision of Schedule 3 to this Act, for the time
       being fulfilled with respect to the dwelling-house subject to
       the tenancy, and
(b)   which does not fall within sub-paragraph (2) or (4) below.
(2) Assured tenancy falls within this sub-paragraph if–
(a)   before it is entered into, a notice–
       (i)   in such form as may be prescribed, and
       (ii)   stating that the tenancy is to be a shorthold tenancy, is
              served by the person who is to be the landlord under
              the tenancy on the person who is to be the tenant
              under it, and
(b)   it is not an excepted tenancy.
(3) For the purposes of sub-paragraph (2)(b) above, an assured
tenancy is an excepted tenancy if–
(a)   the person to whom it is granted or, as the case may be, at
       least one of the persons to whom it is granted was,
       immediately before it is granted, a tenant or licensee under
       an assured agricultural occupancy, and
(b)   the person by whom it is granted or, as the case may be, at
       least one of the persons by whom it is granted was,
       immediately before it is granted, a landlord or licensor
       under the assured agricultural occupancy referred to in
       paragraph (a) above.
(4) An assured tenancy falls within this sub-paragraph if it
comes into being by virtue of section 5 above on the coming to an
end of a tenancy falling within sub-paragraph (2) above.'.]

SCHEDULE 3
AGRICULTURAL WORKER CONDITIONS
Interpretation

1.–(1) In this Schedule–

'the 1976 Act' means the Rent (Agriculture) Act 1976;

'agriculture' has the same meaning as in the 1976 Act; and

'relevant tenancy or licence' means a tenancy or licence of a description specified in section 24(2) of this Act.

(2) In relation to a relevant tenancy or licence–

(a)   'the occupier' means the tenant or licensee; and

(b)   'the dwelling-house' means the dwelling-house which is let under the tenancy or, as the case may be, is occupied under the licence.

(3) Schedule 3 to the 1976 Act applies for the purposes of this Schedule as it applies for the purposes of that Act and, accordingly, shall have effect to determine–

(a)   whether a person is a qualifying worker:

(b)   whether a person is incapable of whole–time work in agriculture, or work in agriculture as a permit worker, in consequence of a qualifying injury or disease; and

(c)   whether a dwelling-house is in qualifying ownership.

The conditions

2. The agricultural worker condition is fulfilled with respect to a dwelling-house subject to a relevant tenancy or licence if–

(a)   the dwelling-house is or has been in qualifying ownership at any time during the subsistence of the tenancy or licence (whether or not it was at that time a relevant tenancy or licence); and

(b)   the occupier or, where there are joint occupiers, at least one of them–

(i)   is a qualifying worker or has been a qualifying worker at any time during the subsistence of the tenancy or licence (whether or not it was at that time a relevant tenancy or licence); or

(ii)   is incapable of whole–time work in agriculture or work in agriculture as a permit worker in consequence of a qualifying injury or disease.

3.–(1) The agricultural worker condition is also fulfilled with respect to a dwelling-house subject to a relevant tenancy or licence if–

(a) that condition was previously fulfilled with respect to the dwelling-house but the person who was then the occupier or, as the case may be, a person who was one of the joint occupiers (whether or not under the same relevant tenancy or licence) has died; and

(b) that condition ceased to be fulfilled on the death of the occupier referred to in paragraph (a) above (hereinafter referred to as 'the previous qualifying occupier'); and

(c) the occupier is either–
   (i) the qualifying widow or widower of the previous qualifying occupier; or
   (ii) the qualifying member of the previous qualifying occupier's family.

(2) For the purposes of sub-paragraph (1)(c)(i) above and sub-paragraph (3) below a widow or widower of the previous qualifying occupier of the dwelling-house is a qualifying widow or widower if she or he was residing in the dwelling-house immediately before the previous qualifying occupier's death.

(3) Subject to sub-paragraph (4) below, for the purposes of sub-paragraph (1)(c)(ii) above, a member of the family of the previous qualifying occupier of the dwelling-house is the qualifying member of the family if–

(a) on the death of the previous qualifying occupier there was no qualifying widow or widower; and

(b) the member of the family was residing in the dwelling-house with the previous qualifying occupier at the time of, and for the period of two years before, his death.

(4) Not more than one member of the previous qualifying occupier's family may be taken into account in determining whether the agricultural worker condition is fulfilled by virtue of this paragraph and, accordingly, if there is more than one member of the family–

(a) who is the occupier in relation to the relevant tenancy or licence, and

(b) who, apart from this sub-paragraph, would be the qualifying member of the family by virtue of sub-paragraph (3) above,

only that one of those members of the family who may be decided by agreement or, in default of agreement by the county court shall be the qualifying member.

(5) For the purposes of the preceding provisions of this paragraph a person who, immediately before the previous qualifying occupier's death, was living with the previous occupier

as his or her wife or husband shall be treated as the widow or widower of the previous occupier.

(6) If, immediately before the death of the previous qualifying occupier, there is, by virtue of sub-paragraph (5) above, more than one person who falls within sub-paragraph (1)(c)(i) above, such one of them as may be decided by agreement or, in default of agreement, by the county court shall be treated as the qualifying widow or widower for the purposes of this paragraph.

4. The agricultural worker condition is also fulfilled with respect to a dwelling-house subject to a relevant tenancy or licence if–

(a)   the tenancy or licence was granted to the occupier or, where there are joint occupiers, at least one of them in consideration of his giving up possession of another dwelling-house of which he was then occupier (or one of joint occupiers) under another relevant tenancy or licence; and

(b)   immediately before he gave up possession of that dwelling-house, as a result of his occupation the agricultural worker condition was fulfilled with respect to it (whether by virtue of paragraph 2 or paragraph 3 above or this paragraph);

and the reference in paragraph (a) above to a tenancy or licence granted to the occupier or at least one of joint occupiers includes a reference to the case where the grant is to him together with one or more other persons.

5.–(1) This paragraph applies where–

(a)   by virtue of any of paragraphs 2 to 4 above, the agricultural worker condition is fulfilled with respect to a dwelling-house subject to a relevant tenancy or licence (in this paragraph referred to as 'the earlier tenancy or licence'); and

(b)   another relevant tenancy or licence of the same dwelling-house (in this paragraph referred to as 'the later tenancy or licence') is granted to the person who, immediately before the grant, was the occupier or one of the joint occupiers under the earlier tenancy or licence and as a result of whose occupation the agricultural worker condition was fulfilled as mentioned in paragraph (a) above;

and the reference in paragraph (b) above to the grant of the later tenancy or licence to the person mentioned in that paragraph includes a reference to the case where the grant is to that person together with one or more other persons.

(2) So long as a person as a result of whose occupation of the dwelling-house the agricultural worker condition was fulfilled with respect to the earlier tenancy or licence continues to be the

occupier, or one of the joint occupiers, under the later tenancy or licence, the agricultural worker condition shall be fulfilled with respect to the dwelling-house.

(3) For the purposes of paragraphs 3 and 4 above and any further application of this paragraph, where sub-paragraph (2) above has effect, the agricultural worker condition shall be treated as fulfilled so far as concerns the later tenancy or licence by virtue of the same paragraph of this Schedule as was applicable (or, as the case may be, last applicable) in the case of the earlier tenancy or licence.

SCHEDULE 4
STATUTORY TENANTS: SUCCESSION

PART I
AMENDMENTS OF SCHEDULE 1 TO RENT ACT 1977

1. In paragraph 1 the words 'or, as the case may be, paragraph 3' shall be omitted.

2. At the end of paragraph 2 there shall be inserted the following sub-paragraphs–

'(2) For the purposes of this paragraph, a person who was living with the original tenant as his or her wife or husband shall be treated as the spouse of the original tenant.

(3) If, immediately after the death of the original tenant, there is, by virtue of sub-paragraph (2) above, more than one person who fulfils the conditions in sub-paragraph (1) above, such one of them as may be decided by agreement or, in default of agreement, by the county court shall be treated as the surviving spouse for the purposes of this paragraph.'

3. In paragraph 3–
   (a) after the words 'residing with him' there shall be inserted 'in the dwelling-house';
   (b) for the words 'period of 6 months' there shall be substituted 'period of 2 years'; and
   (c) for the words from 'the statutory tenant' onwards there shall be substituted 'entitled to an assured tenancy of the dwelling-house by succession'; and
   (d) at the end there shall be added the following sub-paragraph–

'(2) If the original tenant died within the period of 18 months beginning on the operative date, then, for the purposes of this paragraph, a person who was residing in the dwelling-house with the original tenant at the time of his death and for the period which began 6 months before the operative date and ended at the time of his death shall be taken to have been residing with the original tenant for the period of 2 years immediately before his death.'

4. In paragraph 4 the words 'or 3' shall be omitted.

5. In paragraph 5–

(a) for the words from 'or, as the case may be' to 'of this Act' there shall be substituted 'below shall have effect'; and

(b) for the words 'the statutory tenant' there shall be substituted 'entitled to an assured tenancy of the dwelling-house by succession'.

6. For paragraph 6 there shall be substituted the following paragraph–

'6.–(1) Where a person who–

(a) was a member of the original tenant's family immediately before that tenant's death, and

(b) was a member of the first successors family immediately before the first successor's death,

was residing in the dwelling-house with the first successor at the time of, and for the period of 2 years immediately before, the first successor's death, that person or, if there is more than one such person, such one of them as may be decided by agreement or, in default of agreement, by the county court shall be entitled to an assured tenancy of the dwelling-house by succession.

(2) If the first successor died within the period of 18 months beginning on the operative date, then, for the purposes of this paragraph, a person who was residing in the dwelling-house with the first successor at the time of his death and for the period which began 6 months before the operative date and ended at the time of his death shall be taken to have been residing with the first successor for the period of 2 years immediately before his death.'

7. Paragraph 7 shall be omitted.

8. In paragraph 10(1)(a) for the words 'paragraphs 6 or 7' there shall be substituted 'paragraph 6'.

9. At the end of paragraph 11 there shall be inserted the following paragraph–

'11A. In this Part of this Schedule 'the operative date' means the date on which Part I of the Housing Act 1988 came into force.'

PART II
AMENDMENTS OF SECTION 4 OF RENT (AGRICULTURE) ACT 1976

10. In subsection (2) the words 'or, as the case may be, subsection (4)' shall be omitted.

11. In subsection (4)–

(a)   in paragraph (b) after the words 'residing with him' there shall be inserted 'in the dwelling-house' and for the words 'period of six months' there shall be substituted 'period of 2 years': and

(b)   for the words from 'the statutory tenant' onwards there shall be substituted 'entitled to an assured tenancy of the dwelling-house by succession.'

12. In subsection (5) for the words 'subsections (1), (3) and (4)' there shall be substituted 'subsections (1) and (3)' and after that subsection there shall be inserted the following subsections–

'(5A) For the purposes of subsection (3) above, a person who was living with the original occupier as his or her wife or husband shall be treated as the spouse of the original occupier and, subject to subsection (5B) below, the references in subsection (3) above to a widow and in subsection (4) above to a surviving spouse shall be construed accordingly.

(5B) If, immediately after the death of the original occupier, there is, by virtue of subsection (5A) above, more than one person who fulfils the conditions in subsection (3) above, such one of them as may be decided by agreement or, in default of agreement by the county court, shall be the statutory tenant by virtue of that subsection.

(5C) If the original occupier died within the period of 18 months beginning on the operative date, then, for the purposes of subsection (3) above, a person who was residing in the dwelling-house with the original occupier at the time of his death and for the period which began 6 months before the operative date and ended at the time of his death shall be taken to have been residing with the original occupier for the period of 2 years immediately before his death; and in this subsection 'the operative date' means the date on which Part I of the Housing Act 1988 came into force.'

PART III
MODIFICATIONS OF SECTION 7 AND SCHEDULE 2

13.–(1) Subject to sub-paragraph (2) below, in relation to the assured tenancy to which the successor becomes entitled by succession, section 7 of this Act shall have effect as if in subsection (3) after the word 'established' there were inserted the words 'or that the circumstances are as specified in any of Cases 11, 12, 16, 17, 18 and 20 in Schedule 15 to the Rent Act 1977'.

(2) Sub-paragraph (1) above does not apply if, by virtue of section 39(8) of this Act, the assured tenancy to which the successor becomes entitled is an assured agricultural occupancy.

14. If by virtue of section 39(8) of this Act, the assured tenancy to which the successor becomes entitled is an assured agricultural occupancy, section 7 of this Act shall have effect in relation to that tenancy as if in subsection (3) after the word 'established' there were inserted the words 'or that the circumstances are as specified in Case XI or Case XII of the Rent (Agriculture) Act 1976'.

15.–(1) In relation to the assured tenancy to which the successor becomes entitled by succession, any notice given to the predecessor for the purposes of Case 13, Case 14 or Case 15 in Schedule 15 to the Rent Act 1977 shall be treated as having been given for the purposes of whichever of Grounds 3 to 5 in Schedule 2 to this Act corresponds to the Case in question.

(2) Where sub-paragraph (1) above applies, the regulated tenancy of the predecessor shall be treated, in relation to the assured tenancy of the successor, as 'the earlier tenancy' for the purposes of Part IV of Schedule 2 to this Act.

Appendix B

Relevant provisions from the Rent Act 1977 and the Rent (Agriculture)Act 1976

1977 ACT AS AMENDED BY SECTION 39(1) OF THE 1988 ACT
Statutory tenants and tenancies

2(1) Subject to this Part of this Act:
(a) After the termination of a protected tenancy of a dwelling-house the person who, immediately before that termination, was the protected tenant of the dwelling-house shall if and so long as he occupies the dwelling-house as his residence, be the statutory tenant of it; and
(b) Part I of Schedule I to this Act shall have effect for determining what person (if any) is the statutory tenant of a dwelling-house [or as the case may be, is entitled to an assured tenancy of a dwelling-house by succession] at any time after the death of a person who immediately before his death, was either a protected tenant of the dwelling-house or the statutory tenant of it by virtue of paragraph (a) above.

Part I of Schedule 1 to the 1977 Act as amended by section 39(2) and (3) of Schedule 4 to the 1988 Act

1. Paragraph 2 below shall have effect subject to Section 2(3) of this Act, for the purpose of determining who is the statutory tenant of a dwelling-house by succession after the death of the person (in this part of the Schedule referred to as 'the original tenant') who, immediately before his death, was a protected tenant of the dwelling-house or the statutory tenant of it by virtue of his previous protected tenancy.

2.(1) The surviving spouse (if any) of the original tenant, if residing in the dwelling-house immediately before the death of the original tenant, shall after the death be the statutory tenant if and so long as he or she occupies the dwelling-house as his residence.

(2) For the purposes of this paragraph, a person who was living with the original tenant as his or her wife or husband shall be treated as the spouse of the original tenant.

(3) If immediately after the death of the original tenant, there is, by virtue of sub-paragraph (2) above, more than one person who fulfils the conditions in sub-paragraph (1) above, such one of them as may be decided by agreement or, in default of agreement, by the county court shall be treated as the surviving spouse for the purposes of this paragraph.

3.(1) Where paragraph 2 above does not apply but a person who was a member of the original tenant's family was residing with him in the dwelling-house at the time of and for the period of two years immediately before his death then, after his death that person or if there is more than one such person such one of them as may be decided by agreement, or in default of agreement by the county court, shall be entitled to an assured tenancy of the dwelling-house by succession; and

(2) If the original tenant died within the period of 18 months beginning on the operative date, then, for the purposes of this paragraph, a person who was residing in the dwelling-house with the original tenant at the time of his death and for the period which began 6 months before the operative date and ended at the time of his death shall be taken to have been residing with the original tenant for the period of 2 years immediately before his death.

4. A person who becomes the statutory tenant by virtue of paragraph 2 above is in this part of this Schedule referred to as 'the first successor'.

5. If, immediately before his death, the first successor was still a statutory tenant, paragraph 6 below shall have effect for the purpose of determining who is the statutory tenant after the death of the first successor.

6. (1) Where a person who:
(a)   was a member of the original tenant's family immediately before that tenant's death, and
(b)   was a member of the first successor's family immediately before the first successor's death,

was residing in the dwelling-house with the first successor at the time of, and for the period of 2 years immediately before, the first successor's death, that person or, if there is more than one such person, such one of them as may be decided by agreement or, in default of agreement, by the county court shall be entitled to an assured tenancy of the dwelling-house by succession.

(2) If the first successor died within the period of 18 months beginning on the operative date, then, for the purposes of this paragraph, a person who was residing in the dwelling-house with the first successor at the time of his death and for the period which began 6 months before the operative date and ended at the time of his death shall be taken to have been residing with the first successor for the period of 2 years immediately before his death.

9. Paragraphs 5 and 6 above do not apply where the statutory tenancy of the original tenant arose by virtue of section 4 of the Requisition Houses and Housing (Amendment) Act 1955 or section 20 of the Rent Act 1965.

10.(1) Where after a succession the successor becomes the tenant of the dwelling-house by the grant to him of another tenancy, 'the original tenant' and 'the first successor' in this Part of this Schedule shall, in relation to that other tenancy, mean the persons who were respectively the original tenant and the first successor at the time of the succession, and accordingly:

(a) If the successor was the first successor, and, immediately before his death he was still the tenant (whether protected or statutory), paragraph 6 above shall apply on his death,

(b) if the successor was not the first successor, no person shall become a statutory tenant on his death by virtue of this Part of this Schedule.

(2) Sub-paragraph (1) above applies:

(a) even if a successor enters into more than one other tenancy of the dwelling-house, and

(b) even if both the first successor and the successor on his death enter into other tenancies of the dwelling-house.

(3) In this paragraph 'succession' means the occasion on which a person becomes the statutory tenant of the dwelling-house by virtue of this Part of this Schedule and 'successor' shall be construed accordingly.

(4) This paragraph shall apply as respects a succession which took place before 27th August 1972 if, and only if, the tenancy granted after the succession, or the first of those tenancies, was granted on or after that date, and where it does not apply as respects a succession, no account shall be taken of that succession in applying this paragraph as respects any later succession.

11.(1) Paragraphs 5 and 6 do not apply where:

(a) the tenancy of the original tenant was granted on or after the operative date within the meaning of the Rent (Agriculture) Act 1976, and

(b)   both that tenancy and the statutory tenancy of the first successor were tenancies to which section 99 of this Act applies.

(2) If the tenants under both the tenancies falling within
subparagraph (2)(b) were persons to whom paragraph 7 of
Schedule 9 to the Rent (Agriculture) Act 1976 applies, the reference
in sub-paragraph (2)(a) above to the operative date shall be taken
as a reference to the date of operation for forestry workers within
the meaning of that Act.

11A. In this part of this Schedule 'the operative date' means the
date on which Part I of the Housing Act 1988 came into force.

Section 4 of the 1976 Act as amended by section 39(4)

Statutory tenants and tenancies

'4(1) Subject to section 5 below, where a person ceases to be a
protected occupier of a dwelling-house on the termination,
whether by notice to quit or by virtue of Section 16(3) of this Act or
otherwise, of his licence or tenancy, he shall, if and so long as he
occupies the dwelling-house as his residence, be the statutory
tenant of it.

(2) Subject to section 5 below, subsection (3) below shall have
effect for determining what person (if any) is the statutory tenant of
a dwelling-house at any time after the death of a person ('the
original occupier') who was, immediately before his death, a
protected occupier or statutory tenant of the dwelling-house in his
own right.

(3) If the original occupier was a man who died leaving a widow
who was residing in the dwelling-house immediately before his
death then after his death, unless the widow is a protected occupier
of the dwelling-house by virtue of section 3(2) above, she shall be
the statutory tenant if and so long as she occupies the dwelling-
house as her residence.

(4) Where:

(a)   the original occupier was not a person who died leaving a
surviving spouse who was residing in the dwelling-house
immediately before his death, but

(b)   one or more persons who were members of his family were
residing with him in the dwelling-house at the time of and
for the period of two years immediately before his death,
then, after this death, unless that person or, as the case may
be, one of those persons is a protected occupier of the
dwelling-house by virtue of section 3(3) above, that person

or, as the case may be, such one of those persons as may be decided by agreement, or in the default of agreement by the county court, shall be entitled to an assured tenancy of the dwelling-house by succession.

(5) In subsections (1) and (3) above the phrase 'if and so long as he occupies the dwelling-house as his residence' shall be construed in accordance with section 2 (3) of the Rent Act 1977.

(5A) For the purposes of subsection (3) above, a person who was living with the original occupier as his or her wife or husband shall be treated as the spouse of the original occupier and subject to subsection (5B) below, the references in subsection (3) above to a widow and in subsection (4) above to a surviving spouse shall be construed accordingly.

(5B) If, immediately after the death of the original occupier there is by virtue of subsection (5A) above, more than one person who fulfils the conditions in subsection (3) above, such one of them as may be decided by agreement or, in default of agreement by the county court, shall be the statutory tenant by virtue of that subsection.

(5C) If the original occupier died within the period of 18 months beginning on the operative date, then, for the purposes of subsection (3) above, a person who was residing in the dwelling-house with the original occupier at the time of his death and for the period which began 6 months before the operative date and ended at the time of his death shall be taken to have been residing with the original occupier for the period of 2 years immediately before his death and in this subsection 'the operative date' means the date on which Part I of the Housing Act 1988 came into force'.

(6) A dwelling-house is, in this Act, referred to as subject to a statutory tenancy where there is a statutory tenant of it.

Appendix C

Assured and Protected Tenancies (Lettings to Students) Regulations 1998 (SI 1988 No 1967)

(As amended by SIs 1999 No 1803; 1999 No 2268 and 2000 No 2076)

Made 11th August 1998 Laid before Parliament 11th August 1998 Coming into force 1st September 1998

In exercise of the powers conferred on the Secretary of State by section 8 of the Rent Act 1977 and paragraph 8 of Schedule 1 to the Housing Act 1988, the Secretary of State for Education and Employment, as respects England, and the Secretary of State for Wales, as respects Wales, hereby make the following Regulations:

1 These Regulations may be cited as the Assured and Protected Tenancies (Lettings to Students) Regulations 1998 and shall come into force on 1st September 1998.

2 In these Regulations–

'assisted' has the same meaning as in section 579(5) and (6) of the Education Act 1996;

'further education' has the meaning assigned to it by section 2(3) and (5) of the Education Act 1996;

'higher education' means education provided by means of a course of any description mentioned in Schedule 6 to the Education Reform Act 1988;

'publicly funded' refers to an institution which is–

(a) provided or assisted by a local education authority;

(b) in receipt of grant under regulations made under section 485 of the Education Act 1996;

(c) within the higher education sector (within the meaning of section 91 (5) of the Further and Higher Education Act 1992, other than a university; or

(d) within the further education sector (within the meaning of section 91 (3) of the Further and Higher Education Act 1992), and

'the relevant enactments' means section 8 of the Rent Act 1977 and paragraph 8 of Schedule 1 to the Housing Act 1988 (lettings to students).

3 The following institutions are hereby specified as educational institutions for the purposes of the relevant enactments, that is to say–
- (a) any university or university college and any constituent college, school or hall or other institution of a university;
- (b) any other institution which provides further education or higher education or both and which is publicly funded;
- (c) the David Game Tutorial College, London.

4 The following bodies of persons (whether unincorporated or bodies corporate) are hereby specified as bodies for the purposes of the relevant enactments, that is to say–
- (a) the governing body of any educational institution specified in regulation 3 above;
- (b) the body, other than a local education authority, providing any such educational institution; and
- (c) a body listed in Schedule 1 to these Regulations.

5 The following bodies of persons (whether unincorporated or bodies corporate) are hereby specified as bodies for the purposes of paragraph 8 of Schedule 1 to the Housing Act 1988, that is to say–
- (a)   any housing association (as defined in section 1 of the Housing Associations Act 1985) which is registered by the Housing Corporation or Housing for Wales in accordance with Part 1 of the Housing Associations Act 1985 and which is not listed in Schedule 1to these Regulations; and
- (b)   a body listed in Schedule 2 to these Regulations.

SCHEDULE 1
SPECIFIED BODIES UNDER REGULATION 4(c)

International Students House
The London Goodenough Trust for Overseas Graduates

SCHEDULE 2
SPECIFIED BODIES UNDER REGULATION 5(B)

Regulation 5(b)

AFSIL Limited
[Campus Accommodation Ltd]
Derbyshire Student Residences Limited
Friendship Housing
Hull Student Welfare Association
International Lutheran Student Centre
International Students Club (Church of England) Limited

International Students' Club (Lee Abbey) Limited
International Students Housing Society
Oxford Brookes Housing Association Limited
Oxford Overseas Student Housing Association Limited
St Brigid's House Limited
St Thomas More Housing Society Limited
[SOAS Homes Limited]
The House of St Gregory and St Macrina Oxford Limited
The London Mission (West London) Circuit Meeting of the
Methodist Church
The London School of Economics Housing Association
The Royal London Hospital Special Trustees
The Universities of Brighton and Sussex Catholic Chaplaincy
Association
The Victoria League for Commonwealth Friendship
University of Leicester Students' Union
Wandsworth Students Housing Association Limited
[Willowbrook Properties Limited]
York Housing Association Limited

Amendment

Entry relating to 'Campus Accommodation Ltd' inserted by SI
1999/1803, reg 2. Date in force: 16 August 1999: see SI 1999/1803,
reg 1.

Entry 'SOAS Homes Limited' inserted by SI 2000/2706, reg 2.
Date in force: 1 November 2000: see SI 2000/2706, reg 1.

Entry 'Willowbrook Properties Ltd' inserted, in relation to
England, by SI 1999/2268, reg 2. Date in force: 1 September 1999:
see SI 1999/2268, reg 1.

SCHEDULE 3
REVOCATIONS

Regulation 6

(1) *Regulations revoked*	(2) *References*	(3) *Extent of revocation*
The Assured and Protected Tenancies (Lettings to Students) Regulations 1988	SI 1988/2236	The whole Regulations
The Assured and Protected Tenancies (Lettings to Students) (Amendment) Regulations 1989	SI 1989/1628	The whole Regulations

(1) *Regulations revoked*	(2) *References*	(3) *Extent of revocation*
The Assured and Protected Tenancies (Lettings to Students) (Amendment) Regulations 1990	SI 1990/1825	The whole Regulations
The Assured and Protected Tenancies (Lettings to Students) (Amendment) Regulations 1991	SI 1991/233	The whole Regulations
The Assured and Protected Tenancies (Lettings to Students) (Amendment) Regulations 1992	SI 1992/515	The whole Regulations
The Further and Higher Education Act 1992 (Consequential Amendments) Regulations 1993	SI 1993/559	Regulation 6
The Assured and Protected Tenancies (Lettings to Students) (Amendment) Regulations 1993	SI 1993/2390	The whole Regulations
The Assured and Protected Tenancies (Lettings to Students) (Amendment) Regulations 1996	SI 1996/458	The whole Regulations
The Assured and Protected Tenancies (Lettings to Students) (Amendment) (No 2) Regulations 1996	SI 1996/2198	The whole Regulations

EXPLANATORY NOTE
(This is not part of the Regulations)

Section 8 of the Rent Act 1977 and paragraph 8 of Schedule 1 to the Housing Act 1988 except from the definition of 'protected tenancy' and 'assured tenancy' in section 1 of the respective Acts a tenancy granted to a person who is pursuing, or intends to pursue, a course of study provided by a specified educational institution. The tenancy must be granted either by that institution or by another specified institution or body of persons. These Regulations specify the educational institutions and other bodies for the purposes of those provisions.

These Regulations consolidate the earlier Regulations specifying institutions and bodies for the purposes of the said section 8 and paragraph 8 with minor and drafting amendments to take account of the change in name of certain bodies listed therein and to delete references to certain other bodies.

Appendix D

The Assured Tenancies and Agricultural Occupancies (Forms) Regulations 1997

SI 1997 No. 194
LANDLORD AND TENANT,
ENGLAND AND WALES

The Assured Tenancies and Agricultural Occupancies (Forms)
Regulations 1997

Made   *29th January 1997*
Coming into force   *28th February 1997*

The Secretary of State for the Environment, as respects England, and the Secretary of State for Wales, as respects Wales, in exercise of the powers conferred upon them by sections 6(2) and (3), 8(3), 13(2) and (4), 22(1), 41(2) and 45(1) and (5) of, and paragraphs 7(2)(a) and 9(2)(a)(i) of Schedule 2A to, the Housing Act 1988**(a)**, and of all other powers enabling them in that behalf, hereby make the following Regulations:

Citation and commencement

1. These Regulations may be cited as the Assured Tenancies and Agricultural Occupancies (Forms) Regulations 1997 and shall come into force on 28th February 1997.

Interpretation

2. In these Regulations any reference to a section or Schedule is a reference to a section of, or Schedule to, the Housing Act 1988 and any reference to a numbered form is a reference to the form bearing that number in the Schedule to these Regulations, or to a form substantially to the same effect.

(a) 1988 c.50. In section 45(1) see the definition of 'prescribed. Section 22(1) was amended by the Housing Act 1996 (c.52), Schedule 8 paragraph 2(5). Schedule 2A was inserted by the Housing Act 1996, Schedule 7.

Prescribed forms

3. The forms prescribed for the purposes of Part I (rented accommodation) of the Housing Act 1988**(b)** are–

(a) for a notice under section 6(2) proposing terms of a statutory periodic tenancy different from the implied terms, Form No. 1;

(b) for an application under section 6(3) referring a notice under section 6(2) to a rent assessment committee, Form No. 2;

(c) for a notice under section 8 informing a tenant or licensee that the landlord intends to begin proceedings for possession of a dwelling-house let on an assured tenancy or all assured agricultural occupancy, Form No. 3;

(d) for a notice under section 13(2) proposing a new rent for an assured tenancy or an assured agricultural occupancy, Form No. 4;

(e) for an application under section 13(4) referring to a rent assessment committee a notice under section 13(2) relating to an assured tenancy or an assured agricultural occupancy, Form No. 5;

(f) for an application under section 22(1) to a rent assessment committee for a determination of rent under an assured shorthold tenancy, Form No. 6;

(g) for a notice under section 41(2) requiring a landlord or tenant to give information to a rent assessment committee, Form No. 7;

(h) for a notice under paragraph 7 of Schedule 2A, by the tenant to the landlord proposing that an assured tenancy be replaced by an assured shorthold tenancy, Form No. 8;

(i) for a notice under paragraph 9 of Schedule 2A, by the landlord to the prospective tenant, proposing an assured shorthold tenancy where the tenancy meets the conditions for an assured agricultural occupancy, Form No. 9.

Revocations and savings

4.–(1) The Assured Tenancies and Agricultural Occupancies (Forms) Regulations 1988**(a)** ('the 1988 Regulations'), the Assured Tenancies and Agricultural Occupancies (Forms) (Amendment) Regulations 1989**(b)**, the Assured Tenancies and Agricultural

---

(b) Part I is amended by Parts III and V of the Housing Act 1996.

(a) S.I. 1988/2203.

(b) S.I. 1989/146.

Occupancies (Forms) (Amendment) Regulations 1990**(c)** and the Assured Tenancies and Agricultural Occupancies (Forms) (Amendment) Regulations 1993**(d)** are hereby revoked.

(2) Nothing in paragraph (1) affects the validity of a notice served before the coming into force of these Regulations if, at the date of service of the notice, the notice was in the form then prescribed by the 1988 Regulations.

Signed by authority of the Secretary of State for the Environment

James Clappison
Parliamentary Under Secretary of State,
28th January 1997   Department of the Environment

William Hague
29th January 1997   Secretary of State for Wales

(c) S.I. 1990/1532.
(d) S.I. 1993/654.

Regulation 3
SCHEDULE
FORMS PRESCRIBED FOR THE PURPOSES OF PART I OF THE HOUSING ACT 1988

FORM No. 1

Housing Act 1988 section 6(2)

Notice proposing different terms for a Statutory Periodic Tenancy

- Please write clearly in black ink.

- Please tick boxes where appropriate and cross out text marked with an asterisk (*) that does not apply.

- This form can be used by either a landlord or a tenant to propose changes to the terms of a statutory periodic tenancy, which arises when a fixed term of an assured tenancy, an assured shorthold tenancy or an assured agricultural occupancy ends.

- This notice must be served on the landlord or tenant no later than the first anniversary of the day on which the former fixed term tenancy or occupancy ended.

- Do not use this notice if you are a landlord proposing only an increase in rent. Instead, you should use the form headed *Landlord's Notice proposing a new rent under an Assured Periodic Tenancy or Agricultural Occupancy,* which is available from a rent assessment panel or law stationers.

1. To: . . . .
. . . .

Name(s) of landlord(s)/tenant(s)

Address of premises to which the tenancy relates:
. . . .
. . . .
. . . .

2. This is to give notice that I/we* propose different terms for the statutory periodic tenancy from those of the fixed term assured tenancy which has now ended and that they should take effect from:
. . . .

. . . .
Insert date which must be at least three months after the date on which this notice is served.

3. Changes to the terms

(a) The existing provisions of the tenancy to be changed are:

. . . .
. . . .
. . . .

Please attach relevant sections of the tenancy agreement if available

(b) The proposed changes are:

. . . .
. . . .
. . . .

Continue on a separate sheet if necessary

4. Changes to the rent (if applicable). Go to section 5 if this does not apply.

• You should not propose a change to the rent on this form unless it is to take account of the proposed new terms at section 3. A change may be made if either the landlord or the tenant considers it appropriate.

(a) The existing rent is   £.......... per ....
                                                        (e.g. week, month, year)

(b) Does the rent include council tax?   Yes   ☐   No   ☐

(c) If yes, the amount that is included   £.......... per ....
     for council tax is: *(e.g. week, month, year)*

(d) Does the rent include water
     charges?   Yes   ☐   No   ☐

(e) If yes, the amount that is included   £.......... per ....
     for water charges is: *(e.g. week, month, year)*

(f) The new rent which takes into   £.......... per ....
     account the proposed changes in the   *(e.g. week, month, year)*
     terms of the tenancy will be:

(g) Will the new rent include council   Yes   ☐   No   ☐
     tax?

(h) If yes, the amount that will be   £.......... per ....
     included for council tax is: *(e.g. week, month, year)*

(i) Will the new rent include water   Yes   ☐   No   ☐
     charges?

(j) If yes, the amount that will be £.......... per ....
     included for water charges is: *(e.g. week, month, year)*

---

5. Name and address of landlord or tenant proposing the changes

To be signed and dated by the landlord or his agent (someone acting for him) or the tenant or his agent. If there are joint landlords or joint tenants each landlord/tenant or the agent must sign unless one signs on behalf of the rest with their agreement.

Signed ....   Date ....
....
....

Please specify whether: landlord ☐   landlord's agent ☐

                           tenant ☐   tenant's agent ☐

Name(s) (Block Capitals) ....
....
Address
....
....

Telephone–Daytime ....   Evening ....

What to do if this notice is served on you

- If you agree with the new terms and rent proposed, do nothing. They will become the terms of the tenancy agreement on the date specified in section 2.
- If you don't agree with the proposed terms and any adjustment of the rent (see section 4), and you are unable to reach agreement with your landlord/tenant, or you do not wish to discuss it with him, you may refer the matter directly to your local rent assessment committee, before the date specified in section 2, using the form headed *Application referring a Notice proposing different terms for a Statutory Periodic Tenancy to a Rent Assessment Committee* which you can obtain from a rent assessment panel or a law stationer.
- The rent assessment committee will decide what, if any, changes should be made to the terms of the tenancy and, if applicable, the amount of the new rent.
- If you need help or advice about this notice and what you should do about it, take it immediately to a citizens advice bureau, a housing advice centre, a law centre or a solicitor.

FORM No. 2

Housing Act 1988 section 6(3)

Application referring a Notice proposing different terms for a Statutory Periodic Tenancy to a Rent Assessment Committee

• Please write clearly in black ink.

• Please tick boxes where appropriate and cross out text marked with an asterisk (*) that does not apply.

• This form should be used by a landlord or a tenant who has been served with a notice under section 6(2) of the Housing Act 1988, varying the terms of a statutory periodic tenancy which arises when a fixed term of an assured tenancy, an assured shorthold tenancy or an assured agricultural occupancy ends.

• When you have completed the form, please send it to your local rent assessment panel with a copy of the notice served on you proposing the new terms of the statutory periodic tenancy.

1. Name(s) of tenant(s):

. . . .
. . . .

2. Address of premises to which the tenancy relates:

. . . .
. . . .

3. Name(s) of landlord(s)/agent*:

. . . .
. . . .

Address of landlord(s)/agent*:

. . . .
. . . .

4. Details of premises.

(a) What type of accommodation is rented?

Room(s)	☐	Flat	☐
Semi-Detached House	☐	Fully Detached House	☐
Terraced House	☐	Other (*Please specify*)	☐

(b) If it is a flat or room(s) what floor(s) is it on?

Ground ☐   First ☐   Second ☐   Other ☐ (*Please specify*)

(c) Give the number and type of rooms, eg living room, bathroom etc.
. . . .
. . . .

(d) Does the tenancy include any other facilities, eg garden, garage or other separate building or land?

Yes   ☐   No   ☐

(e) If yes, please give details:
. . . .
. . . .

(f) Is any of the accommodation shared with:

(i)   the landlord?   Yes ☐   No   ☐
(ii) another tenant or tenants?   Yes ☐   No   ☐

(g) If yes, please give details:
. . . .
. . . .

5. When did the statutory periodic tenancy begin?
. . . .

6. Services.
(a) Are any services provided under the tenancy (eg cleaning, lighting, heating, hot water or gardening etc.)?

Yes   ☐   No   ☐

(b) If yes, please give details:
. . . .
. . . .

(c) Is a separate charge made for services, maintenance, repairs, landlords' costs of management or any other item?

Yes   ☐   No   ☐

(d) If yes, what charge is payable?   £.......... per ....
                                                    (e.g. week, month, year)

(e) Does the charge vary according to the relevant costs?

    Yes   ☐   No   ☐

(f) If yes, please give details:

. . . .

. . . .

7.(a) Is any furniture provided under the tenancy?

    Yes   ☐   No   ☐

(b) If yes, please give details. Continue on a separate sheet if necessary or provide a copy of the inventory.

. . . .

. . . .

---

8. What repairs are the responsibility of:

(a) the landlord? Continue on a separate sheet if necessary.

. . . .

. . . .

(b) the tenant? Continue on a separate sheet if necessary.

. . . .

. . . .

---

9. Give details (if known) of the other terms of the tenancy, e.g. can you assign the tenancy (pass it on to someone else) and if so is a premium (a payment which is in addition to rent and equivalent to more than two months rent) payable on an assignment? Continue on a separate sheet if necessary.

. . . .

. . . .

. . . .

---

10. (a) Is there a written tenancy agreement? Yes   ☐   No   ☐

(b) If yes, please attach the tenancy agreement (with a note of any variations). It will be returned to you as soon as possible.

---

11. (a) I/We* attach a copy of the notice proposing changes to the statutory periodic tenancy and, if applicable, an adjustment of the amount of rent and apply for it to be considered by the rent assessment committee.

Signed . . . .   Date . . . .
. . . .
. . . .

To be signed and dated by the landlord or his agent (someone acting for him) or the tenant or his agent. If there are joint landlords or joint tenants each landlord/tenant or the agent must sign unless one signs on behalf of the rest with their agreement.

Please specify whether: landlord ☐   landlord's agent   ☐

                                 tenant   ☐   tenant's agent   ☐

(b) Name and address of landlord or tenant referring to the rent assessment committee.

Name(s) (Block Capitals) . . . .
. . . .
Address
. . . .
. . . .

Telephone–Daytime . . . .   Evening . . . .

FORM No. 3

Housing Act 1988 section 8 as amended by section 151 of the Housing Act 1996

Notice seeking possession of a property let on an Assured Tenancy or an Assured Agricultural Occupancy

•Please write clearly in black ink.

•Please tick boxes where appropriate and cross out text marked with an asterisk (*) that does not apply.

•This form should be used where possession of accommodation let under an assured tenancy, an assured agricultural occupancy or an assured shorthold tenancy is sought on one of the grounds in Schedule 2 to the Housing Act 1988.

•Do not use this form if possession is sought on the 'shorthold' ground under section 21 of the Housing Act 1988 from an assured shorthold tenant where the fixed term has come to an end or, for assured shorthold tenancies with no fixed term which started on or after 28th February 1997, after six months has elapsed. There is no prescribed form for these cases, but you must give notice in writing.

---

1. To: ....
....
Name(s) of tenant(s)/licensee(s)

---

2. Your landlord/licensor* intends to apply to the court for an order requiring you to give up possession of:
....
....
....
Address of premises

---

3. Your landlord/licensor* intends to seek possession on ground(s)
.... in Schedule 2 to the Housing Act 1988, as amended by the Housing Act 1996, which read(s):
....
....
....

Give the full text (as set out in the Housing Act 1988 as amended by the Housing Act 1996) of each ground which is being relied on. Continue on a separate sheet if necessary.

---

4. Give a full explanation of why each ground is being relied on:

. . . .
. . . .

Continue on a separate sheet if necessary.

Notes on the grounds for possession

- If the court is satisfied that any of grounds 1 to 8 is established, it must make an order (but see below in respect of fixed term tenancies).

- Before the court will grant an order on any of grounds 9 to 17, it must be satisfied that it is reasonable to require you to leave. This means that, if one of these grounds is set out in section 3, you will be able to suggest to the court that it is not reasonable that you should have to leave, even if you accept that the ground applies.

- The court will not make an order under grounds 1, 3 to 7, 9 or 16, to take effect during the fixed term of the tenancy (if there is one) and it will only make an order during the fixed term on grounds 2, 8, 10 to 15 or 17 if the terms of the tenancy make provision for it to be brought to an end on any of these grounds.

- Where the court makes an order for possession solely on ground 6 or 9, the landlord must pay your reasonable removal expenses.

5. The court proceedings will not begin until after:

. . . .

Give the earliest date on which court proceedings can be brought

- Where the landlord is seeking possession on grounds 1, 2, 5 to 7, 9 or 16, court proceedings cannot begin earlier than 2 months from the date this notice is served on you (even where one of grounds 3, 4, 8, 10 to 13, 14A, 15 or 17 is specified) and not before the date on which the tenancy (had it not been assured) could have been brought to an end by a notice to quit served at the same time as this notice.

- Where the landlord is seeking possession on grounds 3, 4, 8, 10 to 13, 14A, 15 or 17, court proceedings cannot begin earlier than 2 weeks from the date this notice is served (unless one of 1, 2, 5 to 7, 9 or 16 grounds is also specified in which case they cannot begin earlier than two months from the date this notice is served).

- Where the landlord is seeking possession on ground 14 (with or without other grounds), court proceedings cannot begin before the date this notice is served.

- Where the landlord is seeking possession on ground 14A, court proceedings cannot begin unless the landlord has served, or has taken all reasonable steps to serve, a copy of this notice on the partner who has left the property.

- After the date shown in section 5, court proceedings may be begun at once but not later than 12 months from the date on which this notice is served. After this time the notice will lapse and a new notice must be served before possession can be sought.

6. Name and address of landlord/licensor*.

To be signed and dated by the landlord or licensor or his agent (someone acting for him). If there are joint landlords each landlord or the agent must sign unless one signs on behalf of the rest with their agreement.

Signed . . . .   Date . . . .

. . . .

. . . .

Please specify whether: landlord   ☐   licensor   ☐

                          joint landlords ☐   landlord's agent   ☐

Name(s) (Block Capitals) . . . .

. . . .

Address

. . . .

. . . .

Telephone–Daytime . . . .   Evening . . . .

What to do if this notice is served on you

- This notice is the first step requiring you to give up possession of your home. You should read it very carefully.

- Your landlord cannot make you leave your home without an order for possession issued by a court. By issuing this notice your landlord is informing you that he intends to seek such an order. If you are willing to give up possession without a court order, you should tell the person who signed this notice as soon as possible and say when you are prepared to leave.

- Whichever grounds are set out in section 3 of this form, the court may allow any of the other grounds to be added at a later date. If this is done, you will be told about it so you can discuss the additional grounds at the court hearing as well as the grounds set out in section 3.

- If you need advice about this notice, and what you should do about it, take it immediately to a citizens' advice bureau, a housing advice centre, a law centre or a solicitor.

FORM No. 4

Housing Act 1988 section 13(2)

Landlord's Notice proposing a new rent under an Assured Periodic Tenancy or Agricultural Occupancy

• Please write clearly in black ink.

• Please tick boxes where appropriate.

• This form should be used to propose a new rent under an assured periodic tenancy, including an assured shorthold periodic tenancy.

• This form may also be used to propose a new rent or licence fee for an assured periodic agricultural occupancy. In such cases reference to 'landlord'/ 'tenant' can be read as references to 'licensor'/'licensee' etc.

• Do not use this form if there is a current rent fixing mechanism in the tenancy.

• Do not use this form to propose a rent adjustment for a statutory periodic tenancy solely because of a proposed change of terms under section 6(2) of the Housing Act 1988. You should instead use the form headed *Notice proposing different terms for a Statutory Periodic Tenancy* which you can obtain from a rent assessment panel or a law stationer.

---

1. To: . . . .

Name(s) of tenant(s)

---

2. Address of premises to which the tenancy relates:
   . . . .
   . . . .
   . . . .

---

3. This is to give notice that as from .... your landlord proposes to charge a new rent.

• The new rent must take effect at the beginning of a new period of the tenancy and not earlier than any of the following:

   (a) the minimum period after this notice was served,
      (The minimum period is:
      –in the case of a yearly tenancy, six months;
      –in the case of a tenancy where the period is less than a month, one month;
      –in any other case, a period equal to the period of the tenancy;)

(b) the first anniversary of the start of the first period of the tenancy except in the case of:
  −a statutory periodic tenancy, which arises when a fixed term assured tenancy ends, or;
   −an assured tenancy which arose on the death of a tenant under a regulated tenancy;

(c) if the rent under the tenancy has previously been increased by a notice under section 13 or a determination under section 14 of the Housing Act 1988, the first anniversary of the date on which the increased rent took effect.

4.(a) The existing rent is   £.......... per ....
(e.g. week, month, year)

(b) Does the rent include council tax?   Yes ☐   No ☐

(c) If yes, the amount that is included for council tax is: £.......... per ....
(e.g. week, month, year)

(d) Does the rent include water charges?   Yes ☐   No ☐

(e) If yes, the amount that is included for water charges is: £.......... per ....
(e.g. week, month, year)

---

5. (a) The proposed new rent will be: £.......... per ....
(e.g. week, month, year)

(b) Will the new rent include council tax?   Yes ☐   No ☐

(c) If yes, the amount that will be included for council tax will be: £.......... per ....
(e.g. week, month, year)

(d) Will the new rent include water charges?   Yes ☐   No ☐

(e) If yes, the amount that will be included for water charges will be: £.......... per ....
(e.g. week, month, year)

---

6. Name and address of landlord.

To be signed and dated by the landlord or his agent (someone acting for him). If there are joint landlords each landlord or the agent must sign unless one signs on behalf of the rest with their agreement.

Signed . . . .   Date . . . .
. . . .
. . . .

Please specify whether: landlord   ☐   joint landlords   ☐
                          landlord's agent   ☐

Name(s) (Block Capitals) . . . .
. . . .
Address
. . . .
. . . .

Telephone–Daytime . . . .   Evening . . . .

What to do if this notice is served on you

• You should read this notice carefully. Your landlord is proposing a new rent.

• If you agree with the new rent proposed, do nothing. If you do not agree and you are unable to reach agreement with your landlord or do not want to discuss it directly with him, you may refer this notice to your local rent assessment committee prior to the date specified in section 3, using the form headed *Application referring a Notice proposing a new rent under an Assured Periodic Tenancy or Agricultural Occupancy to a Rent Assessment Committee*. You can obtain this form from a rent assessment panel or a law stationer.

• The rent assessment committee will consider your application and will decide what the rent for the premises will be. The committee may set a rent that is higher, lower or the same as the landlord has proposed in section 5.

• If you are required to include payments for council tax and water charges in your rent, the rent the committee determines will be inclusive of council tax and water charges.

• If you need help or advice please take this notice immediately to a citizens advice bureau, a housing advice centre, a law centre or a solicitor.

FORM No. 5

Housing Act 1988 section 13(4)

Application referring a Notice proposing a new rent under an Assured Periodic Tenancy or Agricultural Occupancy to a Rent Assessment Committee

- Please write clearly in black ink.

- Please tick boxes where appropriate and cross out text marked with an asterisk (*) that does not apply.

- This form should be used when your landlord has served notice on you proposing a new rent under an assured periodic tenancy, including an assured shorthold periodic tenancy.

- This form may also be used to refer a notice proposing a new rent or licence fee for an assured periodic agricultural occupancy. In such a case references to 'landlord'/'tenant' can be read as references to 'licensor'/'licensee' etc.

- This form must be completed and sent to your local rent assessment panel – with a copy of the notice served on you proposing the new rent–before the date it is proposed that the new rent will take effect.

1. Address of premises:

. . . .
. . . .
. . . .

2. Name(s) of landlord(s)/agent*:

. . . .
. . . .

Address of landlord(s)/agent*:

. . . .
. . . .
. . . .

3. Details of premises.

(a) What type of accommodation do you rent?

Room(s) ☐　　Flat ☐
Terraced House ☐　　Semi-Detached House ☐
Fully Detached House ☐　　Other (*Please specify*) ☐

(b) If it is a flat or room(s) what floor(s) is it on?

Ground ☐   First ☐   Second ☐   Other ☐ (*Please specify*)

(c) Give the number and type of rooms, eg living room, bathroom etc.
. . . .
. . . .

(d) Does the tenancy include any other facilities, eg garden, garage or other separate building or land?

Yes   ☐   No   ☐

(e) If yes, please give details:
. . . .
. . . .

(f) Do you share any accommodation with

    (i)   the landlord?   Yes ☐   No ☐
    (ii) another tenant or tenants? Yes ☐   No ☐

(g) If yes to either of the above, please give details:
. . . .
. . . .

4. When did the present tenancy begin?
. . . .

5. (a) Did you pay a premium?

Yes   ☐   No   ☐

• a premium is a payment which is additional to rent and is equivalent to more than two months rent. It may give you the right to assign the tenancy (pass it on to someone else) unless the tenancy agreement states or implies otherwise.

(b) If yes, please give details:
. . . .
. . . .

6. Services

(a) Are any services provided under the tenancy (eg cleaning, lighting, heating, hot water or gardening)?

Yes ☐   No ☐

(b) If yes, please give details:

. . . .
. . . .

(c) If yes, is a separate charge made for services, maintenance, repairs, landlord's costs of management or any other item?

Yes ☐   No ☐

(d) What charge is payable?   £. . . . .   per . . . .
                                                          (e.g. week, month, year)

(e) Does the charge vary according to the relevant costs?

Yes ☐   No ☐

(f) If yes, please give details:

. . . .
. . . .
. . . .

7. (a) Is any furniture provided under the tenancy?

Yes ☐   No ☐

(b) If yes, please give details. Continue on a separate sheet if necessary or attach a copy of the inventory:

. . . .
. . . .

8. Improvements
(a) Have you, or any former tenant(s) carried out improvements or replaced fixtures, fittings or furniture for which you or they were not responsible under the terms of the tenancy?

Yes ☐   No ☐

(b) If yes, please give details. Continue on a separate sheet if necessary:

. . . .
. . . .

9. What repairs are the responsibility of:

(a) the landlord?

....
....

(b) the tenant?

....
....

10. (a) Is there a written tenancy agreement? Yes   ☐   No   ☐

(b) If yes, please attach the tenancy agreement (with a note of any variations). It will be returned to you as soon as possible.

....
....

11. Do you have an assured agricultural occupancy?

    Yes   ☐   No   ☐

12. (a) I/we* attach a copy of the notice proposing a new rent under the assured periodic tenancy and I/we* apply for it to be considered by the rent assessment committee.

Signed ....   Date ....
....
....

To be signed and dated by the tenant or his agent. If there are joint tenants each tenant or the agent must sign unless one signs on behalf of the rest with their agreement.

Please specify whether: tenant   ☐   joint tenants   ☐
                          tenant's agent   ☐

(b) Name and address of tenant(s) referring to the rent assessment committee.

Name(s) (Block Capitals) ....
....
Address
....
....

Telephone–Daytime ....   Evening ....

FORM No. 6

Housing Act 1988 section 22(1) as amended by section 100 of the Housing Act 1996

Application to a Rent Assessment Committee for a determination of a rent under an Assured Shorthold Tenancy

• Please write clearly in black ink.

• Please tick boxes where appropriate and cross out text marked with an asterisk (*) that does not apply.

• This form should be used by a tenant with an assured shorthold tenancy which began (or for which a contract had been made) before 28th February 1997, to apply to the local rent assessment committee, during the fixed term of the original tenancy, to have the rent reduced.

• This form should also be used by a tenant with an assured shorthold tenancy which began on or after 28th February 1997 (unless a contract had been made before that date), to apply to the rent assessment committee within six months of the beginning of the original tenancy, to have the rent reduced.

• This form cannot be used in the cases specified at the end of this form.

• When you have completed the form please send it to your local rent assessment panel.

1. Address of premises:

. . . .
. . . .

2. Name(s) of landlord(s)/agent*

. . . .

Address of landlord(s)/agent*

. . . .
. . . .

3. Details of premises.

(a)   What type of accommodation do you rent?

Room(s)	☐	Flat	☐
Terraced House	☐	Semi-Detached House	☐
Fully Detached House	☐	Other (*Please specify*)	☐

(b) If it is a flat or room(s) what floor(s) is it on?

Ground ☐   First ☐   Second ☐   Other ☐ (*Please specify*)

(c) Give the number and type of rooms, eg living room, bathroom etc.
. . . .

(d) Does the tenancy include any other facilities, eg garden, garage or other separate building or land?

Yes   ☐   No   ☐

(e) If yes, please give details:
. . . .
. . . .
. . . .

(f) Do you share any accommodation with:

(i)   the landlord?   Yes ☐   No ☐
(ii) another tenant or tenants?   Yes ☐   No ☐

(g) If yes to either of the above, please give details:
. . . .
. . . .
. . . .

4. (a) What is the current rent?   £. . . . .   per . . . .
                                                                (*e.g. week, month, year*)

(b) Does the rent include council tax?   Yes ☐   No ☐

(c) If yes, the amount that is included
for council tax is: £. . . . .   per . . . .
                                                                (*e.g. week, month, year*)

(d) Does the rent include water charges?   Yes ☐   No ☐

(e) If yes, the amount that is included for water
charges is: £. . . . .   per . . . .
                                                                (*e.g. week, month, year*)

5. (a) When did the present tenancy begin?
. . . .

(b) When does the present tenancy end?

. . . .

(c) Does the tenancy replace an original
      tenancy?   Yes   ☐   No   ☐

If yes, when did the original tenancy begin . . . .

6. (a) If the tenancy began before 28th February 1997, please confirm by
ticking the box that you received a notice saying that the tenancy was to be
an assured shorthold tenancy before the agreement was entered into.

(b) Attach a copy of the notice, if available. It will be returned to you as
      soon as possible.

7. (a) Did you pay a premium?

      Yes   ☐   No   ☐

• a premium is a payment which is additional to rent and is equivalent to
  more than two months rent. It may give you the right to assign the
  tenancy (pass it on to someone else) unless the tenancy agreement states
  or implies otherwise.

(b) If yes, please give details:

. . . .
. . . .
. . . .

8. Services.

(a) Are any services provided under the tenancy (eg cleaning, lighting,
      heating, hot water or gardening)?

      Yes   ☐   No   ☐

(b) If yes, please give details:

. . . .
. . . .

(c) Is a separate charge made for services, maintenance, repairs,
      landlord's costs of management or any other item?

      Yes   ☐   No   ☐

(d) If yes, what charge is payable?   £. . . . .   per . . . .
                                                               (e.g. week, month, year)

(e) Does the charge vary according to the relevant costs?

Yes   ☐   No   ☐

(f) If yes, please give details:

. . . .
. . . .
. . . .

9. (a) Is any furniture provided under the tenancy?

Yes   ☐   No   ☐

(b) If yes, please give details. Continue on a separate sheet if necessary or
     provide a copy of the inventory.

. . . .
. . . .
. . . .

10. What repairs are the responsibility of:
(a) the landlord. Continue on a separate sheet if necessary:

. . . .
. . . .
. . . .

(b) the tenant. Continue on a separate sheet if necessary:

. . . .
. . . .
. . . .

11. (a) Give details (if known) of the other terms of the tenancy, eg whether
the tenancy is assignable and whether a premium may be charged on an
assignment. (Continue on a separate sheet if necessary).

. . . .
. . . .

(b) Is there a written tenancy agreement?   Yes   ☐   No   ☐

(c) If yes, please attach the tenancy agreement (with a note of any
     variations). It will be returned to you as soon as possible.

12. (a) I/We* apply to the rent assessment committee to determine a rent
for the above mentioned premises.

Signed . . . .   *Date* . . . .
        . . . .
        . . . .

To be signed and dated by the tenant or his agent. If there are joint tenants each tenant or the agent must sign unless one signs on behalf of the rest with their agreement.

Please specify whether: tenant   ☐   joint tenants   ☐
                          tenant's agent   ☐

(b) Name and address of tenant(s) referring to the rent assessment committee.

Name(s) (Block Capitals) ....

....

Address

....

....

....

Telephone–Daytime ....

Cases where this form should not be used

- An application cannot be made if–

  (a) the rent payable under the tenancy is a rent previously determined by a rent assessment committee; or

  (b) the tenancy is a replacement tenancy and more than six months have elapsed since the beginning of the original tenancy. A replacement tenancy is an assured shorthold tenancy that came into being on the ending of a tenancy which had been an assured shorthold of the same, or substantially the same, property and the landlord and tenant under each tenancy were the same at that time.

- The rent assessment committee cannot make a determination unless it considers–

  (a) that there is a sufficient number of similar properties in the locality let on assured tenancies (whether shorthold or not) for comparison; and

  (b) that the rent payable under the shorthold tenancy in question is significantly higher than the rent which the landlord might reasonably be expected to get in comparison with other rents for similar properties let on assured tenancies (whether shorthold or not) in the locality.

FORM No.7

Housing Act 1988 section 41(2)

Notice by Rent Assessment Committee requiring further information

1. To: ....

☐   landlord(s)   ☐   tenant(s)

of:

....
....
....
Address of premises

2. An application has been made to the rent assessment committee for consideration of:

☐   the terms of a statutory periodic assured tenancy
☐   an increase in rent under an assured periodic tenancy
☐   the rent under an assured shorthold tenancy
☐   an increase in rent under an assured agricultural occupancy

of the above property. The committee needs more information from you to consider the application.

3. The information needed is:

....
....
....

4. Please send it to:

....
....
....
....
no later than ....

5. If you fail to comply with this notice without reasonable cause you will be committing a criminal offence and may be liable to a fine.

6. Signed on behalf of the rent assessment committee.

Signed .... *Date* ....

Name(s) (Block Capitals) ....
....
Address
....
....
....

Telephone ....

FORM No. 8

Housing Act 1988 Schedule 2A, paragraph 7(2) as inserted by Schedule 7 to the Housing Act 1996

Tenant's notice proposing that an Assured Tenancy be replaced by an Assured Shorthold Tenancy

• Please write clearly in black ink.

• Please cross out text marked with an asterisk (*) that does not apply.

• This notice should only be used by an assured tenant. You should only use this notice to notify your landlord that you wish your assured tenancy to be replaced by an assured shorthold tenancy.

• This notice must be served by a tenant on a landlord before an assured tenancy can be replaced by an assured shorthold tenancy.

• **You should be aware that by serving this notice, you will be giving up your right to stay in the property after the first six months of the assured shorthold** tenancy or, if you agree a fixed term with your landlord, after the end of the fixed term.

• **You do not have to complete this form even if your landlord has asked you to do so. Your existing security of tenure as an assured tenant will be unaffected if you do not complete it.**

• **If you are in any doubt about whether to complete this form, take it immediately to a citizens' advice bureau, housing advice centre, a law centre or a solicitor.**

• Once you are clear that you wish to issue this notice, complete the form and send it to your landlord.

---

1. To: ....

Name(s) of landlord(s)

---

2. I/We*, the tenant(s) of:
....
....
....

Address of premises

give notice that I/we* propose that the assured tenancy to which this notice relates should be replaced by a shorthold tenancy.

---

3. I/We* propose that the new shorthold tenancy should commence on:
............/............/...........
day   month   year

•The new shorthold tenancy cannot commence until after the date this notice is served on the landlord.

---

4. (a) I/We* understand that under my/our* existing tenancy, I/we* can only be required to give up possession in accordance with the grounds set out in Schedule 2 to the Housing Act 1988, whereas under the new shorthold tenancy, the landlord(s) will be able to recover possession of the premises without being required to prove a ground for possession, after the first six months of the assured shorthold tenancy, or, if there is a fixed term for longer than 6 months, at the end of that fixed term, subject to two months' notice.

Signed .... *Date* ....
....
....

To be signed and dated by the tenant. If there are joint tenants each tenant must sign.

(b) Name and address of tenant.

Name(s) (Block Capitals) ....
....
Address
....
....
....

Telephone– Daytime ....   Evening ....

FORM No. 9

Housing Act 1988 Schedule 2A, paragraph 9, as inserted by Schedule 7 to
the Housing Act 1996

**Landlord's notice proposing an Assured Shorthold Tenancy where the
tenancy meets the conditions for an Assured Agricultural Occupancy**

• Please write clearly in black ink.

•Please tick boxes where
appropriate.

•If the agricultural worker
condition in Schedule 3 to the
Housing Act 1988 is met with
respect to the property to which
the proposed assured tenancy
relates, and the landlord wishes
that tenancy to be an assured
shorthold tenancy, he must serve

this notice on the tenant before the
tenancy is entered into.

•This notice cannot be used where
the landlord has already granted
to the prospective tenant (or, in
the case of joint tenants, to at least
one of them) a tenancy or licence
under section 24 of the Housing
Act 1988 (an assured agricultural
occupancy).

•This notice does not commit the
tenant to taking the tenancy.

1. To: ....
....
....

*Name of the proposed tenant. If a joint tenancy is being offered, enter the names of
the joint tenants.*

2. You are proposing to take a tenancy at the following address:
....
....
....

commencing on   ..../.........../..........
                       day   month   year

3. This notice is to tell you that your tenancy is to be an assured shorthold
tenancy.

•Provided you keep to the terms of the tenancy, you are entitled to remain
in the property for at least six months after the start of the tenancy.
Depending on the terms of the tenancy, once the first six months have
elapsed, the landlord may have the right to seek possession at any time,
subject to two months' notice.

• As an assured shorthold tenant, you have the right to apply to a rent assessment committee for the determination of a reasonable rent for the tenancy. An application to your local rent assessment committee must be made on the form headed *Application to a Rent Assessment Committee for a determination of a rent under an Assured Shorthold Tenancy* within six months of the beginning of the tenancy. You can obtain the form from a rent assessment panel or a law stationer.

• If you need help or advice about this notice, and what you should do about it, take it immediately to a citizens' advice bureau, a housing advice centre, a law centre or a solicitor.

4. Name and address of landlord.

To be signed and dated by the landlord or his agent (someone acting for him). If there are joint landlords each landlord or the agent must sign unless one signs on behalf of the rest with their agreement.

Signed . . . .   Date . . . .
. . . .
. . . .

Please specify whether: landlord   ☐   joint landlords   ☐
                          landlord's agent   ☐

Name(s) (Block Capitals) . . . .
. . . .
Address
. . . .
. . . .
. . . .

Telephone–Daytime . . . .   Evening . . . .

EXPLANATORY NOTE

(This note is not part of the Regulations)

These Regulations revoke and replace the Assured Tenancies and Agricultural Occupancies (Forms) Regulations 1988 ('the 1988 Regulations'). They prescribe forms for the purposes of various provisions of Part I of the Housing Act 1988 relating to assured tenancies and assured agricultural occupancies. The use for those purposes of forms substantially to the same effect as the prescribed forms is authorised by regulation 2.

Forms 3 and 4 prescribed by the 1988 Regulations have been amalgamated as new Form 3 with minor drafting amendments and with other amendments consequential on the Housing Act 1996. Forms 6A, 6B and 7 prescribed by the 1988 Regulations (Forms 6A and 6B were inserted by the Assured Tenancies and Agricultural Occupancies (Forms (Amendment) Regulations 1993) have not been reproduced. Other forms prescribed by the 1988 Regulations have been reproduced with minor drafting amendments and with other amendments consequential on the Housing Act 1996. New Forms 8 and 9, which relate to the replacement of assured tenancies and assured agricultural occupancies by assured shorthold tenancies, are prescribed in consequence of amendments made to the Housing Act 1988 by the Housing Act 1996.

Regulation 4 revokes the 1988 Regulations, the Assured Tenancies and Agricultural Occupancies (Forms) (Amendment) Regulations 1989, the Assured Tenancies and Agricultural Occupancies (Forms) (Amendment) Regulations 1990 and the Assured Tenancies and Agricultural Occupancies (Forms) (Amendment) Regulations 1993.

Civil Procedure Rules

PART 55 – POSSESSION CLAIMS

Contents of this part

Interpretation

55.1 In this Part–

(a) 'a possession claim' means a claim for the recovery of possession of land (including buildings or parts of buildings);

(b) 'a possession claim against trespassers' means a claim for the recovery of land which the claimant alleges is occupied only by a person or persons who entered or remained on the land without the consent of a person entitled to possession of that land but does not include a claim against a tenant or sub-tenant whether his tenancy has been terminated or not;

(c) 'mortgage' includes a legal or equitable mortgage and a legal or equitable charge and 'mortgagee' is to be interpreted accordingly; and

(d) 'the 1988 Act' means the Housing Act 1988

I GENERAL RULES

Scope

55.2 (1) The procedure set out in this Section of this Part must be used where the claim includes–

(a) a possession claim brought by a–
(i) landlord (or former landlord);
(ii) mortgagee; or
(iii) licensor (or former licensor);

(b) a possession claim against trespassers; or

(c) a claim by a tenant seeking relief from forfeiture.

(2) This Section of this Part

(a) is subject to any enactment or practice direction which sets out special provisions with regard to any particular category of claim; and

(b) does not apply where the claimant uses the procedure set out in Section II of this Part.

(CCR Order 24, rule 10(1) provides that where an application for an interim possession order is made, unless otherwise provided, Part 55 does not apply)

Starting the claim

55.3(1) The claim must be started in the county court for the district in which the land is situated unless paragraph (2) applies or an enactment provides otherwise.

(2) The claim may be started in the High Court if the claimant files with his claim form a certificate stating the reasons for bringing the claim in that court verified by a statement of truth in accordance with rule 22.1(1).

(3) The practice direction refers to circumstances which may justify starting the claim in the High Court.

(4) Where, in a possession claim against trespassers, the claimant does not know the name of a person in occupation or possession of the land, the claim must be brought against 'persons unknown' in addition to any named defendants.

(5) The claim form and form of defence sent with it must be in the forms set out in the relevant practice direction.

Particulars of claim

55.4 The particulars of claim must be filed and served with the claim form.

(The relevant practice direction and Part 16 provide details about the contents of the particulars of claim)

Hearing date

55.5(1) The court will fix a date for the hearing when it issues the claim form.

(2) In a possession claim against trespassers the defendant must be served with the claim form, particulars of claim and any witness statements–

- (a) in the case of residential property, not less than 5 days; and
- (b) in the case of other land, not less than 2 days,

before the hearing date.

(3) In all other possession claims–

- (a) the hearing date will be not less than 28 days from the date of issue of the claim form;
- (b) the standard period between the issue of the claim form and the hearing will be not more than 8 weeks; and
- (c) the defendant must be served with the claim form and particulars of claim not less than 21 days before the hearing date.

(Rule 3.1(2)(a) provides that the court may extend or shorten the time for compliance with any rule)

Service of claims against trespassers

55.6 Where, in a possession claim against trespassers, the claim has been issued against 'persons unknown', the claim form, particulars of claim and any witness statements must be served on those persons by–

(a) (i)   attaching copies of the claim form, particulars of claim and any witness statements to the main door or some other part of the land so that they are clearly visible; and

   (ii) if practicable, inserting copies of those documents in a sealed transparent envelope addressed to 'the occupiers' through the letter box; or

(b)   placing stakes in the land in places where they are clearly visible and attaching to each stake copies of the claim form, particulars of claim and any witness statements in a sealed transparent envelope addressed to 'the occupiers'.

Defendant's response

55.7(1) An acknowledgment of service is not required and Part 10 does not apply.

(2) In a possession claim against trespassers rule 15.2 does not apply and the defendant need not file a defence.

(3) Where, in any other possession claim, the defendant does not file a defence within the time specified in rule 15.4, he may take part in any hearing but the court may take his failure to do so into account when deciding what order to make about costs.

(4) Part 12 (default judgment) does not apply in a claim to which this Part applies.

The hearing

55.8(1) At the hearing fixed in accordance with rule 55.5(1) or at any adjournment of that hearing, the court may–

   (a)   decide the claim; or

   (b)   give case management directions.

(2) Where the claim is genuinely disputed on grounds which appear to be substantial, case management directions given under paragraph (1)(b) will include the allocation of the claim to a track or directions to enable it to be allocated.

(3) Except where–

   (a)   the claim is allocated to the fast track or the multi-track; or

(b)   the court orders otherwise;

any fact that needs to be proved by the evidence of witnesses at a hearing referred to in paragraph (1) may be proved by evidence in writing.

(Rule 32.2(1) sets out the general rule about evidence. Rule 32.2(2) provides that rule 32.2(1) is subject to any provision to the contrary)

(4) Subject to paragraph (5), all witness statements must be filed and served at least 2 days before the hearing.

(5) In a possession claim against trespassers all witness statements on which the claimant intends to rely must be filed and served with the claim form.

(6) Where the claimant serves the claim form and particulars of claim, he must produce at the hearing a certificate of service of those documents and rule 6.14(2)(a) does not apply.

Allocation

55.9(1) When the court decides the track for a possession claim, the matters to which it shall have regard include–

(a)   the matters set out in rule 26.8 as modified by the relevant practice direction;

(b)   the amount of any arrears of rent or mortgage instalments;

(c)   the importance to the defendant of retaining possession of the land; and

(d)   the importance of vacant possession to the claimant.

(2) The court will only allocate possession claims to the small claims track if all the parties agree.

(3) Where a possession claim has been allocated to the small claims track the claim shall be treated, for the purposes of costs, as if it were proceeding on the fast track except that trial costs shall be in the discretion of the court and shall not exceed the amount that would be recoverable under rule 46.2 (amount of fast track costs) if the value of the claim were up to £3,000.

(4) Where all the parties agree the court may, when it allocates the claim, order that rule 27.14 (costs on the small claims track) applies and, where it does so, paragraph (3) does not apply.

Possession claims relating to mortgaged residential property

55.10(1) This rule applies where a mortgagee seeks possession of land which consists of or includes residential property.

(2) Not less than 14 days before the hearing the claimant must send a notice to the property addressed to 'the occupiers'.

(3) The notice referred to in paragraph (2) must–

(a)   state that a possession claim for the property has started;

(b)   show the name and address of the claimant, the defendant and the court which issued the claim form; and

(c)   give details of the hearing.

(4) The claimant must produce at the hearing–

(a)   a copy of the notice; and

(b)   evidence that he has served it.

II ACCELERATED POSSESSION CLAIMS OF PROPERTY LET ON AN ASSURED SHORTHOLD TENANCY

When this section may be used

55.11(1) The claimant may bring a possession claim under this Section of this Part where –

(a)   the claim is brought under section 21 of the 1988 Act to recover possession of residential property let under an assured shorthold tenancy; and

(b)   all the conditions listed in rule 55.12 are satisfied.

(2) The claim must be started in the county court for the district in which the property is situated.

Conditions

55.12 The conditions referred to in rule 55.11(1)(b) are that–

(a)   the tenancy and any agreement for the tenancy were entered into on or after 15 January 1989;

(b)   the only purpose of the claim is to recover possession of the property and no other claim is made;

(c)   the tenancy did not immediately follow an assured tenancy which was not an assured shorthold tenancy;

(d)   the tenancy fulfilled the conditions provided by section 19A or 20(1)(a) to (c) of the 1988 Act;

(e)   the tenancy–

   (i)   was the subject of a written agreement;

   (ii)   arises by virtue of section 5 of the 1988 Act but follows a tenancy that was the subject of a written agreement; or

   (iii) relates to the same or substantially the same property let to the same tenant and on the same terms (though

not necessarily as to rent or duration) as a tenancy which was the subject of a written agreement; and
(f)   a notice in accordance with sections 21(1) or 21(4) of the 1988 Act was given to the tenant in writing.

Claim form

55.13(1) The claim form must –
(a)   be in the form set out in the relevant practice direction; and
(b)   (i)   contain such information; and
       (ii) be accompanied by such documents, as are required by that form.
(2) All relevant sections of the form must be completed.
(3) The court will serve the claim form by first class post.

Defence

55.14(1) A defendant who wishes to–
(a)   oppose the claim; or
(b)   seek a postponement of possession in accordance with rule 55.18, must file his defence within 14 days after service of the claim form.
(2) The defence should be in the form set out in the relevant practice direction.

Claim referred to judge

55.15(1) On receipt of the defence the court will–
(a)   send a copy to the claimant; and
(b)   refer the claim and defence to a judge.
(2) Where the period set out in rule 55.14 has expired without the defendant filing a defence–
(a)   the claimant may file a written request for an order for possession; and
(b)   the court will refer that request to a judge.
(3) Where the defence is received after the period set out in rule 55.14 has expired but before a request is filed in accordance with paragraph (2), paragraph (1) will still apply.
(4) Where–
(a)   the period set out in rule 55.14 has expired without the defendant filing a defence; and
(b)   the claimant has not made a request for an order for

possession under paragraph (2) within 3 months after the expiry of the period set out in rule 55.14,

the claim will be stayed.

Consideration of the claim

55.16(1) After considering the claim and any defence, the judge will–
   (a)   make an order for possession under rule 55.17;
   (b)   where he is not satisfied as to any of the matters set out in paragraph (2)–
         (i)   direct that a date be fixed for a hearing; and
         (ii)   give any appropriate case management directions; or
   (c)   strike out the claim if the claim form discloses no reasonable grounds for bringing the claim.
   (2) The matters referred to in paragraph (1)(b) are that–
   (a)   the claim form was served; and
   (b)   the claimant has established that he is entitled to recover possession under section 21 of the 1988 Act against the defendant.
   (3) The court will give all parties not less than 14 days' notice of a hearing fixed under paragraph (1)(b)(i).
   (4) Where a claim is struck out under paragraph (1)(c)–
   (a)   the court will serve its reasons for striking out the claim with the order; and
   (b)   the claimant may apply to restore the claim within 28 days after the date the order was served on him

Possession order

55.17 Except where rules 55.16(1)(b) or (c) apply, the judge will make an order for possession without requiring the attendance of the parties.

Postponement of possession

55.18(1) Where the defendant seeks postponement of possession on the ground of exceptional hardship under section 89 of the Housing Act 1980, the judge may direct a hearing of that issue.
   (2) Where the judge directs a hearing under paragraph (1)–
   (a)   the hearing must be held before the date on which possession is to be given up; and

(b) the judge will direct how many days' notice the parties must be given of that hearing.

(3) Where the judge is satisfied, on a hearing directed under paragraph (1), that exceptional hardship would be caused by requiring possession to be given up by the date in the order of possession, he may vary the date on which possession must be given up.

Application to set aside or vary

55.19 The court may
  (a) on application by a party within 14 days of service of the order; or
  (b) of its own initiative,
set aside or vary any order made under rule 55.17.

PRACTICE DIRECTION – POSSESSION CLAIMS
This Practice Direction supplements Part 55

SECTION 1 – GENERAL RULES

55.3 – STARTING THE CLAIM

1.1 Except where the county court does not have jurisdiction, possession claims should normally be brought in the county court. Only exceptional circumstances justify starting a claim in the High Court.

1.2 If a claimant starts a claim in the High Court and the court decides that it should have been started in the county court, the court will normally either strike the claim out or transfer it to the county court on its own initiative. This is likely to result in delay and the court will normally disallow the costs of starting the claim in the High Court and of any transfer.

1.3 Circumstances which may, in an appropriate case, justify starting a claim in the High Court are if–
  (1) there are complicated disputes of fact;
  (2) there are points of law of general importance; or
  (3) the claim is against trespassers and there is a substantial risk of public disturbance or of serious harm to persons or property which properly require immediate determination.

1.4 The value of the property and the amount of any financial claim may be relevant circumstances, but these factors alone will not normally justify starting the claim in the High Court.

1.5   The claimant must use the appropriate claim form and particulars of claim form set out in Table 1 to Part 4 Practice Direction. The defence must be in form **N11**, **N11B**, **N11M** or **N11R**, as appropriate.

1.6   High Court claims for the possession of land subject to a mortgage will be assigned to the Chancery Division.

55.4 – PARTICULARS OF CLAIM

2.1   In a possession claim the particulars of claim must:
   (1)   identify the land to which the claim relates;
   (2)   state whether the claim relates to residential property;
   (3)   state the ground on which possession is claimed;
   (4)   give full details about any mortgage or tenancy agreement; and
   (5)   give details of every person who, to the best of the claimant's knowledge, is in possession of the property.

Residential property let on a tenancy

2.2   Paragraphs 2.3 and 2.4 apply if the claim relates to residential property let on a tenancy.

2.3   If the claim includes a claim for non-payment of rent the particulars of claim must set out:
   (1)   the amount due at the start of the proceedings;
   (2)   in schedule form, the dates when the arrears of rent arose, all amounts of rent due, the dates and amounts of all payments made and a running total of the arrears;
   (3)   the daily rate of any rent and interest;
   (4)   any previous steps taken to recover the arrears of rent with full details of any court proceedings; and
   (5)   any relevant information about the defendant's circumstances, in particular:
      (a)   whether the defendant is in receipt of social security benefits; and
      (b)   whether any payments are made on his behalf directly to the claimant under the Social Security Contributions and Benefits Act 1992.

2.4   If the claimant knows of any person (including a mortgagee) entitled to claim relief against forfeiture as underlessee under section 146(4) of the Law of Property Act 1925 (or in accordance with section 38 of the Supreme Court Act 1981, or section 138(9C) of the County Courts Act 1984):

(1) the particulars of claim must state the name and address of that person; and

(2) the claimant must file a copy of the particulars of claim for service on him.

Land subject to a mortgage

2.5 If the claim is a possession claim by a mortgagee, the particulars of claim must also set out:

(1) if the claim relates to residential property whether:

(a) a land charge of Class F has been registered under section 2(7) of the Matrimonial Homes Act 1967;

(b) a notice registered under section 2(8) or 8(3) of the Matrimonial Homes Act 1983 has been entered and on whose behalf; or

(c) a notice under section 31(10) of the Family Law Act 1996 has been registered and on whose behalf; and

if so, that the claimant will serve notice of the claim on the persons on whose behalf the land charge is registered or the notice or caution entered.

(2) the state of the mortgage account by including:

(a) the amount of:

(i) the advance;

(ii) any periodic repayment; and

(iii) any payment of interest required to be made;

(b) the amount which would have to be paid (after taking into account any adjustment for early settlement) in order to redeem the mortgage at a stated date not more than 14 days after the claim started specifying the amount of solicitor's costs and administration charges which would be payable;

(c) if the loan which is secured by the mortgage is a regulated consumer credit agreement, the total amount outstanding under the terms of the mortgage; and

(d) the rate of interest payable:

(i) at the commencement of the mortgage;

(ii) immediately before any arrears referred to in paragraph (3) accrued;

(iii) at the commencement of the proceedings.

(3) if the claim is brought because of failure to pay the periodic payments when due:

(a) in schedule form, the dates when the arrears arose,

all amounts due, the dates and amounts of all payments made and a running total of the arrears;

(b) give details of:

    (i)   any other payments required to be made as a term of the mortgage (such as for insurance premiums, legal costs, default interest, penalties, administrative or other charges);

    (ii) any other sums claimed and stating the nature and amount of each such charge; and

    (iii) whether any of these payments is in arrears and whether or not it is included in the amount of any periodic payment.

(4) whether or not the loan which is secured by the mortgage is a regulated consumer credit agreement and, if so, specify the date on which any notice required by sections 76 or 87 of the Consumer Credit Act 1974 was given;

(5) if appropriate details that show the property is not one to which section 141 of the Consumer Credit Act 1974 applies;

(6) any relevant information about the defendant's circumstances, in particular:

(a) whether the defendant is in receipt of social security benefits; and

(b) whether any payments are made on his behalf directly to the claimant under the Social Security Contributions and Benefits Act 1992;

(7) give details of any tenancy entered into between the mortgagor and mortgagee (including any notices served); and

(8) state any previous steps which the claimant has taken to recover the money secured by the mortgage or the mortgaged property and, in the case of court proceedings, state:

(a) the dates when the claim started and concluded; and

(b) the dates and terms of any orders made.

Possession claim against trespassers

2.6 If the claim is a possession claim against trespassers, the particulars of claim must state the claimant's interest in the land or the basis of his right to claim possession and the circumstances in which it has been occupied without licence or consent.

55.5 – HEARING DATE

3.1   The court may exercise its powers under rules 3.1(2)(a) and (b) to shorten the time periods set out in rules 55.5(2) and (3).

3.2   Particular consideration should be given to the exercise of this power if:
  (1)   the defendant, or a person for whom the defendant is responsible, has assaulted or threatened to assault:
    (a)   the claimant;
    (b)   a member of the claimant's staff; or
    (c)   another resident in the locality;
  (2)   there are reasonable grounds for fearing such an assault; or
  (3)   the defendant, or a person for whom the defendant is responsible, has caused serious damage or threatened to cause serious damage to the property or to the home or property of another resident in the locality.

3.3   Where paragraph 3.2 applies but the case cannot be determined at the first hearing fixed under rule 55.5, the court will consider what steps are needed to finally determine the case as quickly as reasonably practicable.

55.6 – SERVICE IN CLAIMS AGAINST TRESPASSERS

4.1   If the claim form is to be served by the court and in accordance with rule 55.6(b) the claimant must provide sufficient stakes and transparent envelopes.

55.8 – THE HEARING

5.1   Attention is drawn to rule 55.8(3). Each party should wherever possible include all the evidence he wishes to present in his statement of case, verified by a statement of truth.

5.2   If relevant the claimant's evidence should include the amount of any rent or mortgage arrears and interest on those arrears. These amounts should, if possible, be up to date to the date of the hearing (if necessary by specifying a daily rate of arrears and interest). However, rule 55.8(4) does not prevent such evidence being brought up to date orally or in writing on the day of the hearing if necessary.

5.3   If relevant the defendant should give evidence of:
  (1)   the amount of any outstanding social security or housing

benefit payments relevant to rent or mortgage arrears; and

(2) the status of:

   (a) any claims for social security or housing benefit about which a decision has not yet been made; and

   (b) any applications to appeal or review a social security or housing benefit decision where that appeal or review has not yet concluded.

5.4 If:

   (1) the maker of a witness statement does not attend a hearing; and

   (2) the other party disputes material evidence contained in his statement,

the court will normally adjourn the bearing so that oral evidence can be given.

Evidence in mortgage possession claim

5.5 Attention is drawn to section 113 of the Land Registration Act 1925 which provides that office copies of the register and of documents filed in the Land Registry, including original charges, are admissible in evidence to the same extent as the originals.

55.9 – ALLOCATION

6.1 The financial value of the property will not necessarily be the most important factor in deciding the track for a possession claim and the court may direct a possession claim to be allocated to the fast track even though the value of the property is in excess of ˙15,000.

CONSUMER CREDIT ACT CLAIMS RELATING TO THE RECOVERY OF LAND

7.1 Any application by the defendant for a time order under section 129 of the Consumer Credit Act 1974 may be made:

   (1) in his defence; or

   (2) by application notice in the proceedings.

SECTION II – ACCELERATED POSSESSION CLAIMS OF PROPERTY LET ON AN ASSURED SHORTHOLD TENANCY

55.18 – POSTPONEMENT OF POSSESSION

8.1   If the judge is satisfied as to the matters set out in rule 55.16(2), he will make an order for possession in accordance with rule 55.17, whether or not the defendant seeks a postponement of possession on the ground of exceptional hardship under section 89 of the Housing Act 1980.

8.2   In a claim in which the judge is satisfied that the defendant has shown exceptional hardship, he will only postpone possession without directing a hearing under rule 55.18(1) if–

(1)   he considers that possession should be given up 6 weeks after the date of the order or, if the defendant has requested postponement to an earlier date, on that date; and

(2)   the claimant indicated on his claim form that he would be content for the court to make such an order without a hearing.

8.3   In all other cases if the defendant seeks a postponement of possession under section 89 of the Housing Act 1980, the judge will direct a hearing under rule 55.18(1).

8.4   If, at that bearing, the judge is satisfied that exceptional hardship would be caused by requiring possession to be given up by the date in the order of possession, he may vary that order under rule 55.18(3) so that possession is to be given up at a later date. That later date may be no later than 6 weeks after the making of the order for possession on the papers (see section 89 of the Housing Act 1980).

Index

A

T

TRANSFER
- Mark 1 Assured Tenancies to new regime 17–18
- of existing tenancies for public to private sector 18–19